Bruce C. Johnson

Invite Yourself To The Party!

How Being Assertive And Standing Out From The Crowd Will Get You Invited To The Party ... Every Time!

Michael Patrick Shiels

Invite Yourself to the Party by Michael Patrick Shiels

Published by
National Writers Press, Inc.

Cover and Book Design: NZ Graphics, www.nzgraphics.com

Printed in the United States of America
First Edition

Library of Congress Cataloging-in-Publication Data:

Shiels, Michael Patrick
Invite Yourself to the Party/ by Michael Patrick Shiels

International Standard Book Number 13: 978-0-88100-150-1
International Standard Book Number 10: 0-88100-150-3

Library of Congress Number: 2010931119

1. Biography/Autobiography   2. Literary Collections/General
3. Social Science/Essays   4. Self-Help
I. Title   2010931119

To Janet, Paula, Theresa, Renee, Meshelle, Maria, Paula, Kristen, Amy, Marla, Lona, Sandi, Paula, Amy, Karen, Nancy, Renee, Sue, Jill, Nadia, Kelly, Patricia, Mandy, Colleen, Isabel, Shanda, Annie, Joleen, Andrea, Renee, Maria, Gingy, Amy, Jennifer, Marsha, Holly, Tonia, Susan, Amy, Karla, Lori, Patti, Teresa, Paula, Carol, Michelle, Donna, Gina, Mary, Lynn, Terri, Lisa, Ann Marie…and Vera, Rose and Christine.

For Harrison Ambrose Shiels

CONTENTS

1: A SEAT AT THE TABLE 9

INVITE YOURSELF TO THE PARTY 11

PARTY CRASHER TO THE STARS 20

TRICK OR TREATING TO RICHES 24

DOING THE IMPOSSIBLE 30

DRIPS ARE WINNERS 33

ICEBREAKER 34

WALKING AROUND MONEY 38

SIMPLE LESSONS FROM A MULTI-MILLIONAIRE 41

DINNER PARTY PARITY 45

ALL THE BEST, GEORGE BUSH 46

YOUR SECRET SUPER POWER 57

2: INVITE YOURSELF TO A CAREER 61

OUTTA SIGHT 63

KICKED OUT OF SCHOOL AND INTO
    DICK PURTAN'S PARTY 73

GREAT MEN AND THEIR SILLY SALARIES 88

SMILE THOUGH YOUR FACE IS BREAKING 94

BEING COMPARED TO GIANTS
    IN YOUR INDUSTRY 97

COACH BO SCHEMBECHLER'S THRONE 107

LLOYD CARR TO THE RESCUE! THE POWER
    OF THANK YOU NOTES 109

DUMMY OR IDIOT? 117

STRANDED WITH THE ROCKET
   ROGER CLEMENS 119

SNUGGLING WITH MORGAN FAIRCHILD 127

MASTERS MOM 132

KEN VENTURI'S COMPLIMENT 137

ON THE AIR…INVITING MYSELF
   TO OTHER SHOWS 145

OUTSMART A CAR DEALER WITH
   TIGER WOODS IN YOUR TANK 158

THERE ARE, IN FACT, BAD QUESTIONS 163

3: INVITE YOURSELF TO THE ROAD –
TRAVEL TATTLES! 181

ROMANCE ON THE ROAD 183

FEAR AND PARENTING IN LAS VEGAS 188

THE TOO-FRIENDLY SKIES 191

MAY THE IRISH ROAD RISE TO MEET YOU 193

WE'LL ALWAYS HAVE PARIS 195

DANCE FEVER AND ISLAND FEVER
   ON MACKINAC 210

INSIDE THE GATES OF EXCLUSIVE BEL-AIR 211

ISTANBUL NOT CONSTANTINOPLE…
   TURKISH DELIGHT! 213

LURKING IN KEY BISCAYNE 215

LAUNDERING FRENCH MONEY IN NAPA VALLEY ... 217

KOREAN CAR BOMB 219

INSTANTLY ELDERLY 222

SNAKES ON AN ICE BREAKER 225

THAI ME UP WITH YOUR TIE, TY? 230

BEING INVITED TO INVITE YOURSELF
    TO THE PARTY...IN HAWAII 241

4: INVITE YOURSELF TO ROMANCE 247

HONEYMOON WITH JIM NANTZ 249

PAUL ANKA PROPOSAL...AND DR. PHIL DIVORCE .. 253

THE COMPLEX LIVES OF THE SIMPLE IRISH 273

**5: INVITE YOURSELF TO DO IT
    "YOUR WAY"** 301

WRITE YOUR OWN EULOGY 303

I SHOT AN ARROW....AIMING HIGH 308

1

A Seat At The Table

INVITE YOURSELF TO THE PARTY

Can you imagine what it would be like to see your life story recounted in a book? Would it be flattering…or embarrassing? (Or both!) Or worst of all, would it be boring?

It's time for the tell-all.

On the off-chance some yellow journalist would decide to write the proverbial expose, tell-all-style book about me, Michael Patrick Shiels, I decided it was time for me to, as they say in the public relations business, "get out in front of the story." Consider this book a preemptive strike in order to avoid the eventual damage control I would have to spin! I am writing my own "tell all," in which I promise to recount the page-turning moments comprising my lifetime of everything from brushes with celebrity to run-ins with the law!

Am I a Walter Mitty-type?

I think most everyone who knows me, or thinks they know me, would have to conclude that I am. What is a "Walter Mitty type?" Expedia.com describes Walter Mitty, played by Danny Kaye in the film *The Secret Life of Walter Mitty*, based on James Thurber's short story in the *New Yorker*, as a "meek, mild man with a vivid fantasy life." *The American Heritage Dictionary* defines a "Walter Mitty-type" as "an ordinary, often ineffectual person who indulges in fantastic daydreams of personal triumphs."

Am I, like Mitty, the archetype for the dreamy and hapless? I am afraid so, because even in Mitty's heroic daydreams he does not triumph. And neither did I, much of the time. I insisted on tilting at windmills. Much like Don Quixote in the novel by Cervantes, I fought unwinnable, futile battles…and took courses of action based on misguided heroic, romantic justifications. Do you remember the story of Quixote, who fought windmills he imagined to be giants coming over the hill? "Take care, sir," his trusty sidekick Sancho advised. "Those are not giants but windmills."

Maybe I should have listened to the various "Sanchos" who tried to advise me along the way, but the resulting timid, colorless course of action may have resulted in an awfully dull journey.

So there were plenty of missteps.

Large scale mistakes of the foot-in-mouth variety!

World class miscalculations!

Judgment calls missing any discernable judgment!

Foolish notions.

Fuzzy math.

Begging forgiveness instead of asking permission.

Foul balls; whiffs, air balls and misfires.

Rushing in where angels feared to tread.

Leaping before looking.

You name it – I've done it…or failed to do it…or forgotten to do it!

You get the idea. I am a very regular person…who just happens to be living a very extraordinary life.

You can, too!

That's why I've written this book.

That's why I am sharing these stories with you.

You, too, can live an extraordinary life.

I'd like to meet you there.

Emma Goldman, a popular anarchist, once wrote, *"I'd rather have roses on my table than diamonds on my neck."*

What does that mean?

Are you spending your life working in order to collect things? Or to pay for the things you've already collected? Big house? Fancy luxury car? Designer shoes? Diamonds on your neck? If so, are you literally "'spending' your life?"

Or are you spending your life working in order to collect experiences? Are you investing a part of each day towards enriching your life?

Are you enhancing your own personality?

Are you enjoying the family and friends you love?

Are you saying, at least once each day, "Wow, this is fun! Life is amazing?"

Are you often filled with appreciation and wonderment?

Are you dining with roses on your table?

I grew up in an industrial, small, working class town south of Detroit. My father sold and delivered beer and wine for a living and my mother worked as a bank teller. We drove our family car to a rented vacation cottage for one week each summer, where we rowed boats out into the lake to fish or swam off the dock. I graduated from a tiny Catholic high school and cobbled together my education by bouncing through three colleges.

I've endured two bankruptcies too, been married three times, and engaged four times.

Yet by the age of forty three, twenty-two years after leaving college a few elective credits short of a double major, I've traveled to more than 35 countries, met Presidents, world leaders, captains of industry and celebrities. I've dined with celebrated chefs in top-rated restaurants, lived out fantasies I'd only dreamed of or seen in movies, and stayed in some of the most intriguing hotels and resorts on earth.

And yet I own virtually no "things."

I have no diamonds on my neck.

But I've had countless roses on my table.

I've had so many moments in my life when I literally stopped, looked around, took a breath and said, "Wow...Am I really here?! Is this really happening to me?!"

It really happened.

And I'd sure like to do some of it again!

Try not to let your golden moments slip by. They're happening to you every day.

Sitting on a golf cart in Tarpon Springs, Florida, I was puzzling over what to use for the title of this book. My friend Ken Dallafior was sitting on the seat next to me as we played golf while dodging rainstorms on Innisbrook Resort's famed Copperhead course. Dallafior played in the National Football League for the Pittsburgh Steelers, San Diego Chargers, and his hometown Detroit Lions. Since his playing days, Dallafior, or "Diesel," as he was called by some, remade himself into a very successful business executive and is Senior Vice-President of Sales and Marketing for Blue Cross Blue Shield of Michigan. We became reacquainted twenty-three years after first meeting and are now both at very different stations in life. I met Dallafior when I was seventeen years-old and he was playing for the United States Football League Champion Michigan Panthers team, which competed in the Spring months. He was an offensive lineman;

I was the team's sideline and locker room gopher, though I preferred the title "Equipment Assistant."

Though I was only a junior in high school in Wyandotte, Michigan, I took two weeks off during the school year to work with the Michigan Panthers – for no pay, mind you – at their winter preseason training camp in Tempe, Arizona. Two weeks with a professional football team will help any teenager grow up quickly. The trip was the first time I'd been on an airplane and the first time I'd drank beer in a bar. Though I was underage, I swigged Coors Light with the team's support staff in the hotel lounge…with the rookie result you can imagine the next morning.

I handed out towels, picked up the locker room, set up the dusty Arizona practice field for practice, retrieved all of the footballs and tackling dummies afterward, and sometimes got to catch passes from the quarterbacks when they warmed up.

Sitting on the golf cart all those years later, Dallafior recalled how I secured the priceless experience of working with the Michigan Panthers.

"I remember, do you?" he asked me.

"Yeah. I wrote a letter the Al Taubman, the owner of the team. He was a billionaire. Can you imagine what he thought about getting a letter from a high school kid who wanted to be the ball boy? That was so far below his level of concern," I answered.

"But did you end up hearing from him?"

"Yes."

"How'd you do that?"

"Well, he sent me back a letter saying they'd let me know if anything opened up."

"And what did you do then?" Ken queried.

"I wrote letters to the general manager, coach and equipment manager mentioning the note I got from Taubman. I dropped his name. Then I followed up with phone calls."

"They gave you a job to do, didn't they?"

"Yeah. I ended up on the sideline for every home game in the first season…the season they won the championship," I said. "I was in the locker room covered with champagne after the title game!"

"Right where the action was…you got yourself right into the action," said Ken. "You invited yourself to the party!"

And right there in that golf cart I realized he'd given me the title for this book!

Invite Yourself to the Party.

In recounting the episodes and incidents in this book, it became apparent to me that not only was "Invite Yourself to the Party" a title for this memoir, but it was also a major theme in my life.

…And maybe a lesson for all of us.

In order to truly grasp life, you've got to get yourself to the party! Sit around and wait to be invited? Nonsense! Throw yourself into the action. Find a way to be near the people you want to know and the places you want to go. I'm not suggesting you be a gate crasher or a pest. I am saying, however, that you can spin gold with your golden moments… and most of the time all it takes is to show up.

If you're not sure whether to go out tonight because you might not know someone at the cocktail party or charity event, GO anyway, and arrive early. What have you got to lose?

Always wanted to be a part of a political campaign or a local service group? GO. They will be more than happy to welcome you and help you channel your energies.

Want to meet someone you admire or who is well known? Send them a letter. You'd be surprised how flattered people are when you show them attention or even better yet – ask them for advice. Everyone loves to give advice.

When I began working in media, I found myself in rooms with well-known business executives, celebrities, sports stars, politicians, and journalists. I would freeze up, though. I was too shy, and too nervous to approach them and talk to them let alone try and make a connection. So I would fret and try to work up the courage to talk to them, and before I could do it, they would end up leaving the room. The resulting extreme disappointment in myself and frustration at that moment far outweighed any fear I felt in approaching them, or any embarrassment or rejection I imagined I might get as a result of simply introducing myself. I knew not meeting the person was a shameful missed opportunity. After this happened a few times I simply couldn't bear the thought of feeling that disappointment and frustration again. So I vowed never to let it happen again.

You know what?

Never once did I regret approaching someone.

Not once.

It's not to say every introduction was fruitful or even useful. And as you might expect, some people were more sincere and engaging than others. But each occasion was interesting.

I always followed up by mailing a handwritten note (not an E-mail) to the individual. I very often got a note back. And almost always, the next time I ran into that person, they mentioned how much they appreciated my note. (I have included some of the specific stories of these meetings – good and bad – in this these pages.)

I then extrapolated my newfound "approach theory" to other aspects of life. I applied for jobs I had no business asking for. I attended special events…or flittered around the outskirts of them. I got myself into the action – invited to the party – as often as I could, and in the most imaginative ways. I was never offensive. I was sometimes persistent. And sometimes I was crafty. I remember, for instance, knowing that it would be good for my career to attend the North American International Auto Show's Charity Preview Gala. It was a black-tie fundraiser held on the show floor among the cars at Detroit's Cobo Exhibition Hall. Thousands of captains of industry, business leaders, elected politicians, celebrities, and journalists from around the world would be in attendance. The ticket price, however, was $500 per person: far beyond my young professional's budget. But I could rent a tuxedo, which I did, and headed to downtown Detroit. Why? Certainly a number of the attendees would frequent the bars and hotel lounges surrounding Cobo Hall before and after the event. I also knew that the massive lobby and coat check area at Cobo Hall did not require a ticket, so I hung around the lobby chatting up attendees, shaking hands, and meeting people going in and out. I met far more people in that position than I would have actually inside the event. After all, everyone goes to the coat check, or the taxi and limo stand out front, or even the restroom. Since I was in a tuxedo, everyone assumed that I was attending the event. I observed the crowd and made contacts.

Showing up turned into "making my own luck" on one occasion when I made my way to the restroom along the desolate, outside hallway of the show floor. As I walked back toward the main lobby and front entrance, I noticed a side entrance to the show being guarded by a teenaged security guard in a crooked hat sitting on a metal folding chair. I stopped and peered through the door to try to catch a glimpse of the cars inside.

"Nice cars, it looks like," I said to him.

"Yeah," he mumbled.

"Did you pick yours out yet?"

"No man," he said. Then he looked at me. "You have a ticket?"

"No man," I answered.

"You want to go in?" he asked, looking away from me in a nonchalant fashion.

"Okay, how much?"

"Five bucks and the rest of the champagne in your glass," he said quietly.

"Deal."

I slipped him the fiver, he slurped the champagne, and suddenly my pumpkin had turned into a coach! I was in the big dance!

The moral? Show up! You never know what can happen! Following this philosophy has resulted in my enjoying what Shakespeare dubbed "Life's Rich Pageant."

If you don't believe me, ask God himself. There is even Biblical precedent: *"Ask, and it will be given to you; search, and you will find; knock, and the door will be opened for you. For everyone who asks receives, and everyone who searches finds, and for everyone who knocks, the door will be opened." - Luke 11:1-13*

Invite yourself to the party.

PARTY CRASHER TO THE STARS

When a Washington couple – would be socialites – allegedly snuck into President Barak Obama's first official State Dinner at the White House without an invitation, the world took notice! The couple crashed the glitzy, elegant affair at which they met President Obama and even instantly uploaded photos of themselves taken with vice president Joe Biden and other dignitaries and celebrities to their Facebook page.

While United States Secret Service officials say the President was never in any danger, security officials were embarrassed and tried to press charges against the couple. While trespassing is illegal, they were, after all, essentially admitted to the party, so it is unclear whether "party crashing" is technically breaking the law.

As a travel writer and journalist, I have crossed a couple of lines in my day. I was provoked to do so mainly by harmless professional curiosity more than mischief. I have found that the best way to slip into a private party, special event, VIP gathering, restricted area, or even a first class seat on an airline, is simply pretend you belong there. Nod and say "hello" confidently when confronted with barriers, but do so in a hurried, slightly impatient manner. Sometimes maneuvering behind the velvet rope requires overdressing appropriately and perhaps carrying a clipboard or some other official-looking prop, such as a camera.

On a London evening in March of 2002, I was out on the town and very well dressed in a camelhair blazer, tan slacks and light blue tie. After drinks and an early dinner with some British journalists at the Wig and Pen Club in Covent Garden, the group broke up for the night. I decided I wasn't quite finished with the evening, and, feeling adventurous, I instructed the London cabbie to drive me to Annabel's, a famous, but very private nightclub I'd heard about on Berkeley Square in Mayfair. Princess Diana, Prince Charles, Aristotle Onassis, Frank Sinatra, and even Her Majesty the Queen of England had been members of the tiny, but posh, elegant establishment. I wanted to be the next…so I invited myself to the party!

The cabbie, who reminded me, or rather, warned me, that Annabel's was an exclusive, private club, dropped me off at the doorstep. Without a hint of hesitation, I marched directly to the stairway leading from the street down to the small door, and drafted into Annabel's behind an apparently wealthy, cosmopolitan couple. It was very quiet inside, so in the manner of a human divining rod, I went straight to a seat at the bar and ordered a Scotch whisky – neat. While taking a sip from the two fingers of Glenlivet in the rocks glass, I took a deep breath and thought to myself: "So this is what it is like to be inside Annabel's."

As might a secret agent, I took mental note of the details around me, kept my eyes peeled and my ears open for celebrities, and rather enjoyed my suddenly elite status. I hadn't yet thought about how I would pay for my drinks, since I noticed the very few other patrons using only member numbers – not cash – to settle up. "Devil may care, for now," I figured. "After all, I was in Annabel's. Who knew what the night would bring me!

An heiress? A starlet? A smashing business relationship? A secret scandal?"

Then came my nearly fatal error. I needed to go to the loo (or water closet, or toilet, if you prefer) which was back up front near the curtained entrance to the club. The ladies room is on one side of the lobby – gentlemen's on the opposite side, behind velvet curtains. My slight hesitation – in whether to turn right or left – caught the eye of the very tall, French maitre'd. He approached me immediately.

"Sir, of course you know the men's room is over here," he said politely, and gesturing while looking down at me.

"Thank you, of course," I replied, turning to move on my way. But before I could slip away he asked me a question I dreaded hearing.

"Sir, you are a member of Annabel's, correct?"

This was my moment of truth. I knew that my only hope was to look him straight in the eye, with all the confidence in the world, and answer his question directly.

"Naturally," I said.

He stared at me over his glasses.

"Then as a member of Annabel's, sir, you surely must be aware of not only where the men's loo is, but also of our dress code. Gentlemen are to wear suits with matching trousers and jacket. Not, as you are wearing, trousers with a matching blazer."

It was my move in this potentially embarrassing chess game, but I didn't flinch.

"Since when?" I countered, in a secretly desperate reach.

He cracked.

"Well, sir, you're right. It is true that during the holiday period the club had relaxed the restrictions a bit. But we found that some of the members were becoming too casual. For instance, some people arrived in denim."

"Jeans!" I scoffed, shaking my head with indignity. "That's bloody unimaginable!"

"Indeed, sir. So you see why we've restored the dress code. I am terribly sorry you were not properly informed. Please, though, continue with your evening. I apologize for interrupting you."

I withheld a grin, but knew I'd dodged a bullet, so I seized the opportunity to retreat unscathed.

"Out of respect for the rules of my club," I told the maitre'd, "I shall depart for the evening. I wouldn't wish to set a bad example for the other members, or trouble you with the burden of making an exception to the dress code for me."

"You needn't do that, but I understand, sir."

I nodded.

"It's what's best," I said, reaching for the exit and tugging the door handle before I turned back around to admonish him. "But you will make a better effort to properly inform me of these capricious policy changes next time, won't you?"

"I will, sir. Have a good evening."

Did I outsmart him or did he know I was fibbing? Maybe he allowed me to save face with my charade and was just happy to see me go under any terms. I will never know…until the next time I sneak in!

TRICK OR TREATING TO RICHES

What do you remember about Halloween? Can you recall your youthful days of trick-or-treating throughout your neighborhood in a creative costume, collecting candy?

Like most kids, my Halloween experiences are memories of excitement, adventure and surprise.

I remember carefully crafting my costume each year... Darth Vader; a gorilla in a top hat and tie; a ghost with white hair; a vampire; Arthur "the Fonz" Fonzerelli; Spiderman; and others. I remember, too, that my mother, when I was very young, dressed me up as "Raggedy Andy." (I wonder if any of those photos still exist?)

Perhaps, as I did, you toted a pillowcase to carry all of the Blow-Pops, Milk Duds, Jolly Rangers, Dots, licorice, chocolate bars, and penny candy I could gather climbing up and down on porch after porch of house after house.

Harrison Street was four blocks long. Our house was near the end, so my brother and sister and I, at the first hint of darkness, would set out going all the way down one side, turning around, and completing the loop by coming back up the other side. If there was time, we would then empty our pillowcases at home, go one block over, and trick or treat at a few dozen homes on Cloverlawn Street.

Like mowing a lawn in careful rows, we covered as much ground as we could.

But, from a management standpoint was our trick-or-treating strategy sound?

I think it is safe to say that most of us long for the simpler days of our youth and the joy that came from a carefree event like trick-or-treating. But now our schedules are crammed with responsibilities. There are bills and taxes to pay. We've got mouths to feed. We're struggling to hit our sales targets and please our bosses. We've got paperwork to catch up on, and countless calls to return. There are appointments to keep. In some cases, we have exams to try to pass or grades to achieve. We're expected to contribute to the company for which we work and be an asset to the community in which we live. We're trying to be professionals. We're attempting to be parents. We're striving to be loving spouses and good friends. We're struggling to advance – and trying not to fall behind!

How in the world can we manage to do all of this?

Simple – let's go trick-or-treating!

What?!

Sure, trick-or-treating in the face of all that responsibility sounds like a nice escape from reality. But the answers you seek may actually lie in trick-or-treating.

Consider the concept of Ken Dallafior, the former NFL player who is now senior vice-president of marketing and group sales for Blue Cross Blue Shield of Michigan.

"I meet with my sales team and account reps often, and, they, like many these days, struggle to find ways to manage all of their responsibilities and service their accounts and opportunities," Ken told me over lunch during a rainy Saturday golf delay.

"There are so many demands of our time and so many things and people who need to be taken care of. Every time I open an E-mail it requires some action," I agreed. "I feel like I am just trying to keep my head above the water level in a tide of never ending things to do."

Dallafior then gave me a parable he says he has given to members of his staff on a number of occasions:

"When most kids go trick-or-treating, they go up and down the streets as long and as late as they can to collect candy, right?" he asked.

"That's how I did it, yes. And I went as fast as I could, too," I answered.

"Just like a paper route. That was very industrious of you," Dallafior said. "But let me tell you how I approached trick-or-treating as a kid. While going up and down the streets like you did, I decided to keep track of which houses gave the best candy. And I asked my friends and classmates where some of the best houses were. I kept all of the addresses on a spreadsheet. The next year, and every year after that, instead of going house-to-house, I spent my time trick-or-treating at the houses that gave the good candy first. Then, only after I'd gone to all of the houses on my list and collected a nice, valuable bag, did I take my chances enterprising new blocks of houses. Only when I had ensured a great collection of candy from known sources did I add to it by exploring and expand my list for the next year."

I took Ken's point to heart.

His advice to me was essentially the same counsel he gave his sales staff: when tackling our day-to-day projects, we should trick-or-treat first at the houses that give the best candy. We should take a look at our manner of doing things and ask ourselves if we're spending the time we have properly.

What are your priorities?

Are they properly stacked?

Are you getting the good candy for your efforts before you spend time on goose chases?

We can look at Ken Dallafior's Trick-Or-Treat parable many different ways:

At home, if your family is contented and happy, and your children are properly parented, you have the most important candy of all. A solid home life will allow you to enterprise at work without worries of children getting into trouble or stress from a bad relationship. Don't forget to trick-or-treat at home, first.

If you're a salesperson, are you spending enough time taking care of and servicing the clients you have – you know, the ones who have given you good candy – before you're out selling the next deal? It's always easier to keep a customer than to try to win them back or find a new one.

Solid, large-scale prospects deserve large-scale effort and attention.

It's not always easy to meet all of your responsibilities and the demands placed upon you, but, you're only one person. Triage your activities. Insert some priorities.

I once interviewed Lou Holtz, best known as a successful football coach at Notre Dame, over lunch at a golf tournament in South Carolina. I've also seen him give fantastic motivational speeches on a number of occasions. In those speeches, the friendly little fellow talks about his WIN strategy. Do you want to win? If so, Holtz says, you should understand that win is spelled: W-I-N.

What's
Important
Now?

What's important now? If winning is important, you will do whatever it takes to win, and your efforts should be first and foremost focused at that goal. Ask yourself what you have to do to accomplish what you want? And that will tell you the action you have to take.

And, by the way, what's important now is likely to change often. But ask yourself "What's important now?"

Are you focused on doing the things geared toward whatever your WIN is?

What's important now?
Is something or someone - or even just bad planning - standing in your way?

Again, you have to prioritize. Trick-or-treat at the houses that help you WIN.

When you prioritize, you surely will have to say "no" from time to time. If you're having trouble saying "no," Dr. Joe Arrends, the health and wellness doctor from Troy, Michigan who made so many radio appearances on the *J.P. McCarthy Show* and other programs, gave me what he calls:

Basic Assertive Principles

- You have the right to offer no reasons or excuses for justifying your behavior.
- You have the right to judge if you are responsible for finding solutions to other people's problems.

- You have the right to change your mind.
- You have the right to make mistakes.
- You have the right to say "I don't know."
- You have the right to be illogical in making decisions.
- You have the right to say "I don't understand."
- You have the right to say "I don't care."
- You have the right to say "no" without feeling guilty.
- You have the right to say that you don't have time.

DOING THE IMPOSSIBLE

In addition to his "W-I-N: what's important now?" strategy, another of the tenants of football coach Lou Holtz's motivational speeches, for which he is paid huge sums of money, is the importance of making a list of lifetime goals, which may be better described as "intentions." One hundred of them, in fact.

Holtz tells the story of how he, as a young man, after being fired, made a list of 107 things he wanted to accomplish in his lifetime. Some of the intentions involved traveling, such as wanting to attend the annual "Running of the Bulls" in Pamplona, Spain. He wanted to learn a foreign language and become a scratch golfer.

While Holtz admits some of the goals were a little crazy, more than 100 of the 107 he wrote down, despite the odds against them, happened. Holtz appeared on *The Tonight Show with Johnny Carson*. He had dinner at the White House. He became head coach at Notre Dame. He won a national championship. He was invited to join Augusta National Golf Club. He became a father.

Lou Holtz, because of his list of goals, was a participant in life, not just a spectator. He invited himself to the party.

There is undeniable magic that comes with the act of physically writing down goals and intentions and reviewing them from time to time. By actually putting the goals on paper, you are also etching them in your subconscious mind. Given this direction the subconscious mind can go to work on its own…and help make the goals happen. Your desires and plans are better registered by the act of committing to them, so put them in writing. I am very grateful that I happened upon this philosophy from Holtz at a young age! I can remember the day that, as a twenty year-old, I cranked a powder blue piece of stationary into a manual typewriter and, with two fingers, tapped out my list.

I can honestly confirm that many of those goals I typed came true – and, amazingly, many of them happened without even conscious effort! Here are a few of those intentions which came true in the twenty three subsequent years:

I wanted to meet the President of the United States. Not only did I meet George Herbert Walker Bush, I worked for him on advance teams during two Presidential campaigns and almost wrote a book with him! Just last year I sat in the front pew with the former President and First Lady Barbara at Sunday services in Kennebunkport.

- I wanted to visit Paris, which I have three times now.
- I wanted to play golf at the Old Course at St. Andrews, which I have three times now.
- I wanted to be married, which I have three times now.
- I wanted to be a father, which I have.
- I wanted to see NBC TV's *Tonight Show with Johnny Carson* in person. (Bill Murray and Shelley Winters were Carson's guests the night I was in the audience, to add icing to the cake!)
- I wanted to travel to see America. I've been to almost every state, and over 35 countries.
- I wanted to work for the Walt Disney Company. I did,

when Disney bought ABC-WJR, and I hosted radio shows live from inside Walt Disney World!

- I wanted to go to the Kentucky Derby. Didn't pick the winner, but sipped mint juleps along the turn just beyond the finish line.
- I wanted to write a book. I've authored almost ten.
- I wanted to go to the Rose Bowl. I did, and saw the Michigan Wolverines complete an undefeated season and win the national championship!
- I wanted to see *The Price is Right* in person. I not only got to the CBS studio, I got to watch my friend Jeff Elliott compete on *Cardsharks*.
- I wanted to win $10,000 in a casino. (Okay, I won $2,500, but it felt like a million! This goal remains open, but I make regular attempts at Firekeepers Casino, in Battle Creek, Michigan.)
- I wanted to earn $100,000 in one year. (My cable tv job at the time I wrote the list in 1987 paid me $13,500 yearly, so, at the time, it was a big leap!)
- I wanted to host a morning radio show. My morning talk show program is now syndicated on twelve radio stations and on television, too.

These goals, and more, happened…and they are still happening!

You can get in on the action, too, no matter your age. Write your list with no limits. I have often heard the phrase "what would you do if you knew you could not fail?"

Make your list today.

Invite yourself to the party!

DRIPS ARE WINNERS

I've hosted a roundtable format small business radio hour in Lansing called the "Mid Michigan Business Rap," created and produced by the very professional and creative Suzanne Huard, who partners with Todd Pride. Their company is called Spotlight Media. The program features the opinions and expertise of a select panel of small business owners plus special guests.

One particular week the special guest was James Coe, Dean of Business at Spring Arbor College.

"I can always tell the entrepreneurs who are going to make it when they start a business," he said. "They're all 'drips!'"

We were startled. Whatever did he mean by that? Were the small business owners in the room to be offended? Professor Coe noticed the expressions on our faces.

"Drips; they're all drips. That's what they all have in common," he insisted. Then he explained. "D-R-I-P: they each have *determination, resources, intentionality and persistence*. Drips."

Determination

Resources

Intentionality

Persistence

Are you a "drip?" Have you invited yourself to the party?

ICEBREAKER

Need something to break the ice at the beginning of a meeting, social gathering, or even a date?

You might be surprised what a great ice-breaker it is if you show up with a Powerball Mega Millions Jackpot Lottery ticket as a gift. It costs you only one-dollar, but it represents the possibility of essentially giving the recipient millions of dollars.

Handing someone a ticket to the twice-weekly drawing usually catches them off guard, but almost always brings a smile. I believe, too, that it subliminally sends a message that you are an optimist. You're a believer!

If you want to make the ticket gift extra special, select numbers on the ticket meaningful to the recipient. A birthday, address, lucky number, jersey number they wore in sports, anniversary dates, etc.

If the recipient is lucky, they will win.

If you're lucky, the recipient will cut you in on the winnings!

You can, of course, tailor a gift to be a good icebreaker. I find the most effective gifts, though, are not luxurious or valuable because that seems showy and smacks of bribery. It is far better to select an inexpensive, thoughtful, or funny, token.

For instance, when I was producer for radio star J.P. McCarthy, the Walt Disney Company bought ABC. Since we were one of the most significant news-talk shows among the ABC/Disney owned-and-operated radio affiliates, I thought it would be a good idea to book a radio interview via telephone with our new boss, Disney CEO Michael Eisner. Working through the Disney media relations department, I secured a time in Mr. Eisner's schedule when he would be available for a five-minute phone call.

"Phone him at eight a.m. next Thursday morning. He will be in his room at the Yacht Club Hotel at Walt Disney World," I was instructed. As always, I would be placing that call, and once the guest, in this case, Mr. Eisner, was on the line, I would patch him through to the host, J.P., to be live on the radio show. I knew I'd have one chance to make an impression with Eisner, so I invited myself to the party. Here's how…

At that time, in the early 1990's, there was a new voice-activated gag gift freshly available called "The Yes Man." It was a 12-inch tall plastic statue of a man in a suit with a smile on his face. He was called "The Yes Man" because, if you asked him a question, sickly supportive suck-up answers would emanate in return from the statue: "Oh yes, that's a great idea!" Or "I will take care of that right away!" Or "You know you're absolutely brilliant!"

I secured one of these "Yes Man" toys, wrapped it up, and sent it via overnight Fedex delivery to Michael Eisner, Hotel Guest, c/o Disney's Yacht Club Hotel. I also called the hotel to make sure they'd place the item in Eisner's hotel suite before he arrived.

Included with the "Yes Man" was a note from me, which read: "*If you want a 'Yes Man' working for you at Disney, he's inside this box. But if you prefer a creative, dedicated man, I am ready to meet with you any time. I look forward to talking when I phone you for the radio interview Thursday.*"

When I phoned Eisner for the interview, I introduced myself. "You sent the 'Yes Man,' right?" he asked immediately. *"Oh yes sir, Mr. Eisner, that was me alright. You're so right. Brilliant deduction,"* I joked in the "yes man" voice. He laughed. Then he said, "That was a very creative way to get my attention. Someone will be in touch with you."

I thanked him and patched him though for the interview.

Within a week I was contacted for an interview for a media relations position with Disneyland in Anaheim, California... with a recommendation from no less than the company CEO Michael Eisner!

One of the most creative gifts Dr. Christine Tenaglia and I received at our wedding was from our friends Ken and Karen Dallafior. Knowing that we enjoyed wine, they presented us with two bottles. The first was the acclaimed Opus One – a premier wine from Oakville, CA which retails for almost $200 per bottle. The second bottle was an aquamarine blue bottle of Boone's Farm Blue Hawaiian apple wine, which sells for less than $3 per bottle! The accompanying note read: *Remember, there will be good times and bad, but celebrate every moment."*

The further significance was we got engaged in Napa...and planned to honeymoon in Hawaii.

Dallafior, having played in the NFL and working for a health insurance company, is a fitness freak. So in return, on his 50th birthday, I presented him with a glass jar labeled *"Stress Reducer. In Case of Emergency, Break Glass."* Plainly visible inside the glass jar was a pack of cigarettes and matches, a mini bottle of Jack Daniels bourbon, and a Twinkie!

A sense of humor, when carefully used, can give everyone a good laugh. Dan Loepp is President and CEO of Blue Cross-Blue

Shield of Michigan, and a very good friend of mine. In his role leading the insurance company and its' 9,000 employees through a time of national health care reform, Dan was very busy and rarely had time to let his hair down. When I heard he was partnering with Pat Prichard, a Blue Cross manager and close common friend, in the Country Club of Lansing Invitational Tournament, I couldn't resist driving over there to surprise Dan and Pat with a little heckling. When I arrived at the club, I spotted Dan on the practice green and approached him immediately.

"Dan, I heard you were in an urgent situation here before the tournament. Here, this may help," I said, handing him a copy of a book I wrote titled, *Golf's Short Game For Dummies*.

Dan got a big kick out of the irreverent but playful insult, and I am told, destroyed his opponents Pat Gillespie and Steve Wickens on the back nine with superb chipping and putting!

In the ultimate gift-giving disaster, much was made, and many people chuckled, when the new U.S. President Barack Obama welcomed British Prime Minister Gordon Brown to the White House early in Obama's presidency. Prime Minister Brown presented his host, Obama, America's first black President, with a pen holder made from the wood of a warship what helped stamp out the slave trade – a sister ship of the vessel from which timbers were taken to build Obama's Oval Office desk. Exceedingly thoughtful, right? What did President Obama give Prime Minister Brown in return? A box of Hollywood films on DVD. Not only did the gift seem cheap and insignificant, but because of technical formatting issues, U.S.-made DVD's will not work in United Kingdom or European DVD players!

Know your audience. Put some time and thought into gift giving!

WALKING AROUND MONEY

In the classic 1957 film *The Bridge on the River Kwai*, starring Alec Guinness and William Holden, British soldiers are held prisoner by the Japanese in a work camp in western Thailand. The British Colonel, played by Guinness, orders his men to cooperate in the building of a bridge along the Burma railway, despite its military value to their captors, for the sake of his men's morale.

The Japanese camp commandant, Colonel Saito, would often address his assembled prisoners by shouting out, "*Are you happy in your work?*"

Are you happy in your work?

Or are you, too, a prisoner?

I considered Dave Diles a confidant, advisor and friend. He shared with me his theory about "being happy in your work." I was a young producer at WJR Radio. Who was Diles?

Diles had been the sportscaster for the radio station's morning star J.P. McCarthy for a short spell, but his career beyond that earned him honors and Hall of Fame inductions. He was seventy eight years-old when he passed away in late 2009, after a lifetime authoring books and being named the AP's "Sportswriter of the Year" three times. Diles was also the long-time host of ABC' TVs *Prudential College Football Scoreboard Show*. In two decades with ABC Sports, Diles covered the

Olympics, the Indy 500 and hosted "Wide World of Sports." He also served as the play-by-play voice of the Los Angeles Clippers, Detroit Lions and Pistons and Ohio State University basketball.

He ran around with the likes of Bo Schembechler, Howard Cosell, Bear Bryant, Mickey Mantle, Frank Gifford, Al Michaels, Dick Vitale, Roone Arledge, and other luminaries of sports and network television.

I admired Diles because he was a Midwesterner who refused to be intimidated by the New York network big shots. He was a far more literate, intelligent, and thoughtful than anyone he interviewed or covered, but he was professional and not openly condescending. God knows Diles must have had to bite his tongue (something he didn't always succeed in doing) with some of the ego maniacs he dealt with, but he was a spiritual man, as well, so he always seemed grounded.

Diles captivated my friend Tim McGuire and me with his big time network tv stories, but he also gave me personal counsel...and professional direction.

His most memorable professional advice came when I asked him about how he managed to succeed so long with ABC and the other media companies for which he worked.

"How did you maintain balance in your life between the demands of work and your personal life?" I asked him, "Dave, how did you handle it when they tried to take advantage of you? How did you advance without playing petty politics? How did you survive and not compromise your integrity?"

I expected a typically erudite answer from the acerbic Diles.

"If you really want to know the truth about how I did all that, and how you can do it, too, I will tell you," he leaned forward and said. "If you want to control your employment situation, you've got to have *'fuck you money.'*

You've got to have *'fuck you money.'*"

Diles, of course, meant that if you'd saved enough money to not worry about being fired – at least enough cash to stay afloat while you look for a new job – you will portray confidence in simple, daily negotiations. You won't be scared to stand up for yourself when you're being unfairly pushed around or mistreated. If you have so-called "fuck you money" you can insist on proper, equitable, appropriate treatment.

So start your savings now!

SIMPLE LESSONS FROM A MULTI-MILLIONAIRE

I walked around the showroom of the Star Lincoln Mercury dealership in Southfield at the corner of Telegraph and 12 Mile Roads.

An older man in a fawn-colored cashmere sweater, silk pants and Gucci loafers approached me. He pushed up his glasses with his finger before extending his hand.

"I'm Hoot McInerney," he said. "I own the place."

He had a broad and strong grip.

"Michael Patrick Shiels," I said. "Thank you for seeing me."

He led me across the showroom and through the back hallway. I was surprised by the simple, spartan nature of the office in which I soon found myself seated across his cluttered desk from the mighty McInerney.

McInerney is a legend in the car business. The son of Irish Catholic immigrants, McInerney grew up in Detroit, was educated by nuns, and found work as a porter at a car dealership in the city. He had the very humble duty of scrubbing and cleaning out new and traded-in vehicles and driving them wherever they needed to go. He started, literally, on the ground floor of the car business and, by developing savvy personal relationships through unbridled moxie and community involvement, ended up owning 13 dealerships and grossing over $100-million per year in sales.

McInerney gained celebrity status in the car business and in Detroit. He hopped on his personal jet to fly down to Lakeland, Florida to catch Detroit Tiger Spring Training games. He played golf in the Bob Hope Chrysler Classic in Palm Springs. He had personal relationships with Presidents of the United States. He donated a $250,000 organ to St. Hugo in the Hills Church in Bloomfield Hills. He built a home on the eighth hole of the Bloomfield Hills Country Club which stretched nearly the entire length of the par-5 hole, complete with fountains and televisions in each of the seventeen bedrooms which rose out of the floor at the touch of a button. The Big-Three chairmen and CEO's, and Toyota officials, each paid their respects to "Hoot" because he sold virtually every type of car manufactured – and lots of them – at his various dealerships.

I had called McInerney to ask his advice, just as I had a handful of other business leaders and executives when I was twenty seven years-old. I was considering which direction to take my career and seeking ways to leverage my position as a member of the media, which gave me incidental access to movers, shakers and experts in every field and, presumably, valuable information and networking power.

I asked for appointments with some of these people, which each of them granted, presumably because I was the producer for their friend J.P. McCarthy – Detroit's morning radio legend. Each of the business leaders who socialized with McCarthy were frequently interviewed by J.P. on his powerful morning news-talk show.

Crain Communications Chairman Keith Crain; Heinz Prechter, the CEO of the American Sunroof Company; public relations guru Anthony Franco; Bill Kast, a German industrialist and political fundraiser; and Michigan Governor John Engler were among the potential mentors I visited and queried.

I'd asked each of them the same question: If you were my age, in my position, what would you be thinking? What should I be thinking?"

It was McInerney who gave me the most colorful and demonstrative advice. It was a parable, of sorts.

"You want to be successful?" Hoot asked me. "Invent something that people need to buy, use, throw away and buy again. Something people need to use over and over again."

Simple enough.

Then he slid a piece of scrap paper across the desk and tossed a plastic ink pen toward me. "Do me a favor. Write down your answers to the questions I ask you. Don't tell me what you write."

I grabbed the pen, poised it on the paper, and listened.

"Write down a number between 1 and 10."

I thought of a number and wrote it down, concealing the paper with my left hand.

"Okay, write down a flower."

I did so.

"A piece of furniture."

I scribbled a word.

"Pick a color."

Again, I wrote my answer.

"Okay, said McInerney, looking at me through his thick glasses. "Your answers are: 7…rose…chair…and…blue."

I pushed my paper to the middle of the desk. On it were written the words "7, rose, chair, blue."

McInerney nodded but did not smile. To him it wasn't a trick – it was a fact:

"People think alike. We all think alike. Remember that," McInerney told me. "We all think alike."

Hoot McInerney was more than double my age and earned over 3,000 times my yearly salary. And yet we thought alike!

The next time you feel intimidated about a job interview or business meeting, you might wish to remember Hoot's lesson.

DINNER PARTY PARITY

I once heard a story that one of the ways conservative talk radio host Rush Limbaugh increased his influence with political power brokers was by holding dinner parties with very selective guest lists. For instance, if Limbaugh had struck up a friendship with, let's say, Donald Trump after meeting him at a golf event, and Trump accepted an invitation to a dinner party, Limbaugh could then contact someone else he didn't know too well, and invite them to join him and Donald Trump at a dinner party. While the second invitee may not know Rush that well, he certainly knows Trump and will probably draw the conclusion that if Trump is attending, it must be a party worth going to.

The party thrower, in this case Rush, can build on that to invite a few more well known, high-powered people.

It wasn't long before buzz got around that Limbaugh threw very well-attended parties and that exciting people seemed to congregate at them. An invitation to Limbaugh's house became a desired and welcomed item.

It is also interesting to see how certain people will mix together socially? Know someone who is trying to do business with Company X? Know someone at Company X? Perhaps they both get invited to the dinner party, and some mutually beneficial business occurs. That'd feel good, wouldn't it?

Choose your guests wisely and, I say, always add someone new – a wild card – to the party, to expand your sphere of friends and influence.

ALL THE BEST, GEORGE BUSH

A simple thank you note can alter your life. I was given some exceedingly valuable advice early in life by Jerry St. James, a morning radio star in San Diego who has produced stage plays and is a friend of the great comic actor Jerry Lewis.

"Whenever you meet anyone, anyone at all, you should send a note to them in the mail," he advised. "A simple note telling them you enjoyed meeting them. If they want to get back to you, they will. If they don't, you can be sure they will at least remember you down the road should the day come when you cross paths with them again."

Maybe that person will be someone who can help you. Maybe that person will be someone who needs your help. But in either case, you will have made an impression…and a connection.

In the days of modern E-mail and texting, sending a handwritten, signed note through the U.S. Mail is still the most effective manner to contact someone in this scenario. E-mail simply will not suffice – it will not make the same impression. People receive hundreds of E-mails every day, and most of them are a nuisance or require some action on the part of the recipient. Do you want your note lumped in with the other digital insignificancies on a computer screen, easily deleted?

There is always anticipation in tearing open an envelope and seeing that someone took the time to write a note, or choose a card, even a postcard, and paid to send it. If you want to insure it is looked at, spend a little extra on postage and send it in a Priority Mail envelope. I can't tell you how many times I've run into someone and the first thing they say to me is, "Hey thanks for the note."

I can assure you this is, without question, the very best advice I have ever been given. It has paid off ten-fold in my networking efforts and friendship making.

In fact, each St. Patrick's Day, I send out over 600 whimsical custom St. Patrick's Day cards. I put a photo of myself in some silly situation in Ireland on the front, for example, me standing in front of a betting shop, or wearing a kilt. The photo is a great ice-breaker and conversation starter as people will often mention the photo or ask me where it took place? Everyone sends Christmas cards, I figured. But how many St. Patrick's Day cards do you get? It catches people off guard, cuts through the clutter, and elicits a response. After nine years of sending the cards, people look forward to receiving them. It's a nice tradition. Find your niche. Facebook makes it easy to learn the birthdays of your friends and associates. But many will send "Happy Birthday" messages through Facebook or E-mail with the simple click of a mouse. How many will send cards? I even received, if you can believe it, birthday greetings in a telegram, in 2010! The old-school gesture was from my friends Gary and Julia Hutnik, and it had me smiling all day. I didn't even know you could still send a telegram!

The thank you notes and greeting cards I've sent have sometimes yielded interesting responses. Steve Forbes, publisher of *Forbes Magazine* and one-time Presidential candidate, sent me a tie emblazoned with the words "Capitalist Tool" all over it. I've received personal notes from Jack Nicklaus, Gary Player, Vice-President Dan Quayle, Sparky Anderson, Lou Holtz, Pete Dye, Ernie Harwell, Cardinal Adam Maida, Michael Eisner – the CEO of Disney, Governor John Engler, Governor Jennifer Granholm, Governor Haley Barbour, Harold Poling – Chairman of the Ford Motor Company at the time, Michigan State University basketball coach Tom Izzo, and Dan Burke – the CEO of ABC.

Two of my prized possessions are personal letters I received from former U.S. President George Herbert Walker Bush. He gets my St. Patrick's Day cards sent to his Houston, Texas office each year. There is a code name for people who have a credible connection to the 41st President to put on the envelope, and I was given it, so I use it.

I was an advance team volunteer for President Bush's two campaigns in 1988 and 1992 and met him a few times. In 1980, when Bush ran a presidential primary campaign against Ronald Reagan, I was 13 years old. I'd seen a campaign infomercial on television called "Ask George Bush." Even though I was in seventh grade, I was impressed with Bush's genuine manner in delivering his message and his credentials: Yale graduate; World War II Naval Aviator; successful businessman; U.S. Congressman; U.S. Envoy to China, U.S. Ambassador to the United Nations; Republican Party Chair; and CIA Director. The man had experience!

Ronald Reagan, of course, won the nomination, and named Bush his running mate. Their winning ticket made George Bush vice-president, and in 1987, the vice-president came to my little hometown of Wyandotte, Michigan to march in the Independence Day Parade. I stood near the end of the parade route down

Biddle Avenue hoping to catch a glimpse of "the Veep." Sure enough, as a marching band played the Spencer Davis Group's song *Gimme Some Lovin' (So Glad You Made It)*, Bush swept by along the rope line in a light blue short-sleeve dress shirt, shook our hands, jumped up above the red, white and blue bunting on the grandstand, and gave a brief, energetic "Happy Fourth of July" greeting to the crowd. As the crowd waved little American flags, he climbed down from the grandstand, waving all the time, and ducked into a black limousine waiting behind the grandstand to whisk him away.

I was hooked. It was all so precisely managed and yet so enthusiastic.

So I invited myself to the party.

I volunteered as a campaign advance worker, so that the next time George Bush came to Michigan to campaign for the presidency, I could be closer to the action. Believe it or not, after a security check, I was given a hard-pin credential and included in Bush's next visit, which was an overnight stay at the Hilton Hotel near Detroit Metro Airport and a morning rally. We met at the hotel, where the staff was awaiting the arrival of the vice-president, and were briefed about our duties by a fellow everyone referred to as "Uncle Rich." Hotel rooms had been emptied out and the furniture replaced with photo copiers, telephones and tables to serve as offices, and an entire floor of the small hotel had been commandeered by the campaign and secret service. I got to see the machinery in action.

"He's almost here," I heard advance team workers whispering with excitement and importance. The VP's arrival, by limo though a side door, was quiet and carefully managed. Bush did stick his head into the campaign office door to quickly say thanks before heading to bed, which energized everyone who would be working through the night painting signs and finishing up details for the morning campaign event.

The Vice-Presidential and Presidential events I provided advance work for were very often, in format, identical. My role was to drive campaign staff and VIP's in a van in the motorcade. We would line vehicles up on the tarmac at the airport: first the Vice President's limousine, then the "spare limousine," followed by a black SUV with dark windows, presumably loaded with Secret Service agents and firepower. Behind that was a station wagon with photographers, including one who sat up and out the back tailgate videotaping every moment of the drive. Then came my van and others. We would watch Air Force II land, taxi over to us, and then see Vice-President Bush emerge, climb down the stairs, shake hands, and head to his limo. Staffers who piled into my van included the likes of James Baker III and Lee Atwater, who directed the presidential campaign. Can you imagine being twenty-one years-old and being able to listen to these two political giants talk strategy during a 30-minute drive? It was fascinating, and all the while police motorcycles buzzed up and down the sides of the motorcade.

All because I invited myself to the party.

I came very close to writing a book with him about his family's impressive legacy in golf. Bush's father Prescott Bush served a term as president of the USGA. His maternal grandfather, Herbert Walker, donated the Walker Cup Trophy, which is given now in the prestigious amateur version of the Ryder Cup. The Bush family has long enjoyed the quaint, semi-private Cape Arundel Golf Club, in Kennebunkport, Maine, which has, due to Bush, seen a steady stream of PGA Tour

stars and other presidents, namely George W. Bush and Bill
Clinton, pass through its' screen door clubhouse. Cape Arundel's
longtime golf professional, Ken Raynor, keeps the clubhouse taste-
fully decorated with photos of the President, family golf heirlooms,
and logoed golf balls emblazoned with "DC – ME." President Bush
has been involved in the PGA Tour's President's Cup Matches, and
is the honorary chairman of the PGA Tour's "First Tee" program,
which makes golf accessible to young people in urban and rural
areas. I proposed the book concept to Joe Louis Barrow, the son of
the great boxer Joe Louis, who was executive director of the First
Tee initiative. Barrow liked the idea, so he personally presented my
book proposal and my writing credentials to the former President,
whom he referred to as "#41" because he was America's 41st
President. The book President Bush and I would have written
would have included examples of the Bush family golf legacy, and
"life lessons" for the First Tee students to show them how golf can
help them advance and network in the professional world...
maybe even all the way up to the Presidency, as was the case for
George Bush. Our book would have also talked about the life
lessons golf teaches: honesty, integrity, and politeness.

Former President Bush initially agreed to collaborate with
me on the book, which was the thrill of a lifetime. But then,
when his son George W. got serious about making a run at the
Presidency, George senior was reticent to commit to the time it
might take to write the book. I was disappointed, but I understood, and certainly respected his decision. After all, history was
being made!

Bush's best book, written before I approached him, is a thick
tome titled *All the Best, George Bush*. It is a compilation of thank
you letters and notes Bush had sent to people throughout his

political and personal life. Bush was known as a dedicated letter writer, which is, in part, how he built such a consensus that he could maneuver his way to the Presidency. It was quite a climb, and the thank you notes published in the book document every step of his journey.

One of my letters from President Bush reads like this,

George Bush
November 6, 1999
Dear Michael,

Thanks so much for sending me your book "Good Bounces and Bad Lies." I know I will love reading it.

Barbara and I have a collection of signed books. I am wondering if you and Ben Wright could sign these two bookplates for our copy?

I do remember your book about my late friend J.P. McCarthy, a great guy.

Sincerely,
George Bush

In July of 2010, I spent a weekend in Kennebunkport at the Captain Lord Mansion, a thoroughly charming bed-and-breakfast in the quaint seaport. I decided to attend Sunday morning services, so I pedaled my bike over to the church along the Atlantic. Services that morning, for the very small congregation, were held outside, in a setting along a stone wall with the sea as a backdrop behind the altar. Arriving only moments before the service was to begin, there were only seats open in the front row. So, even though I was a newcomer to the parish, I invited myself to the party. I quietly sat in the open pew in the front row. It hadn't occurred to me that those front-pew seats may have been saved for someone. Moments later, the former

First Lady Barbara Bush walked in and sat down in the pew, followed by former President Bush, with some other members of their family, including children Doro and Neil, and grandchildren in tow! Mrs. Bush wore paisley cloth loafers and the President sported a vibrant blue blazer, open collar, and multi-colored socks.

Once they were settled in, Reverend Martin Luther Agnew, walked over to me, out of the blue, in front of the entire congregation, and asked, "Did you enjoy your game of golf yesterday at Cape Arundel?"

Somehow he must have been at the tiny golf club and, for some reason, recognized me.

"I enjoyed it very much, Reverend, but how did you know I was there?"

"I only look for reformed sinners," he joked.

Meanwhile, former President Bush was leaned over, peering at me, watching this exchange, and likely trying to figure out who I was sitting here in the front pew!

Another of my prized letters, which hangs framed in my radio and television studio, came from Ruth Moran, who promotes my beloved Emerald Isle with Tourism Ireland, which is the Irish Tourist Board, or Board Failte, in the Irish language.

"*Michael Patrick, you continue to be an amazing ambassador for Ireland,*" she wrote.

It's funny that Ruth should use the word "ambassador." During his run at the Republican nomination for President, I interviewed former Massachusetts governor Mitt Romney via telephone.

"It's great to be on your show," Romney told me in his greeting. "Dick Purtan, J.P. McCarthy…you've worked with the best of them!"

Obviously he'd been thoroughly and impressively briefed on my credentials.

"Governor Romney," I asked, "if you get elected President, what shot have I got at being named U.S. Ambassador to Ireland?"

Romney laughed and said, "Well, with a name like Michael Patrick I'd say you have a pretty good shot!"

I came across Romney in person once, on Mackinac Island, of all places. His father George was Governor of Michigan, so Mitt spent part of his younger days on the island because there is an official summer residence that sitting governors get to enjoy.

Dignitaries, including U.S. Presidents, have been guests in the historic, stately residence, but actually staying in the home is a rare and priceless occurrence. From the porch, residents enjoy sweeping views of Grand Hotel to the far right, and, in the distance, the Mackinac Bridge dividing Lake Huron from Lake Michigan. It is easy to spend the day mesmerized by the scene, gazing at the ferryboats taking tourists back and forth from the harbor below across the strait to Mackinaw City or St. Ignace. You can, in fact, catch a whiff of the fudge from the shops below when the wind is just right. And when the wind is strong, the wooden-framed windows throughout the delicate, old home sound a startling cacophony of rattling and banging.

The various bedrooms, connected with narrow, dark hallways and sometimes creaky staircases, are individual and quaint in their décor – and it is fun to ask in which bedrooms various notables chose to bunk. Similar to what I imagine a White House stay to be like, the house's staff of two, a caretaker and a chef hand-picked by Michigan's first family, will prepare any meal desired.

I was lucky enough to be staying in the residence for a couple of days by invitation of Michigan's First Gentleman Dan Mulhern, the husband of Democratic Governor Jennifer Granholm. My wife Christine and I were the only occupants that weekend, while the Republican Leadership Conference was taking place over at Grand Hotel, which is why Romney was on the island.

During his speech at the conference, Romney spoke fondly of the number of youthful summers in what he called, "that big, white home on the hill."

"I would love to have take a nostalgic walk through the old house – if only its' current occupant were a Republican," he bemoaned.

Later that day, I was on a bicycle down in town, when I saw Mitt Romney climb out of a horse-drawn carriage in front of the Ann Cottage. While he was having his photo taken with the horses, I thought about inviting myself to the party. I wanted to pedal over, introduce myself, and invite him up to the Governor's Residence for a look around. The Governor was not there, and we were the only inhabitants that day, so I figured it would be fine. But then I thought about the possibility that members of the media might follow him, since it would be a brilliant photo opportunity. If that happened, what if Governor Granholm saw footage of me walking a Republican, who'd been vocally very critical of her, through the residence while I was Granholm's guest? Probably not cricket. Still, I wish I had done it. It's a party I regret not inviting myself to.

During that campaign, I also enjoyed a chat with Mayor Rudy Giuliani. He was calling into the show from Savannah, and he laughed heartily when I asked him, with all the barnstorm campaigning he was doing, if he ever woke up in a hotel room in the morning not knowing where he was?

"Yes, for a minute or two! I've traveled a lot in the last five-and-a-half years; all over America and to 35 countries. One of the things I have learned to do before I go to bed at night is to remind myself of where I am. And I make sure I clear a path to the bathroom."

Jimmy Buffett sang the lyrics, "Some of it's magic, and some of it's tragic, but I had a good life, just the same." Let me assure you, not all of the letters I have saved are good ones. I also saved my rejection letters – a big stack of rejection letters from companies that said, "Thanks, but no thanks," to the prospect of hiring me. They are interesting to read and provoke memories and motivation.

Now, can you remember where to find the good old fashioned Post Office?

YOUR SECRET SUPER POWER

Whether you know it or not, you are a very powerful person. You can, in the course of your day, provoke a very meaningful ripple. You can create kings, bestow knighthood, and change the future.

Don't worry, this is not some scheme to encourage you to vote. You don't need to elect a leader when you, alone, have the secret power you have.

So what do I mean?

United States President George Herbert Walker Bush used to play a game he called "Light 'em Up!" The 41st President's limousine drove him from Air Force One to various appearances and campaign events. Allegedly, the President liked to sit in the seat facing backward so that, as the limo drove slowly along rope lines and crowds of people gathered to watch and wave, he could look out the window and point very directly at one specific person he picked out of the crowd. When that person saw the President pointing and looking directly into their eyes, they tended to "light up" with surprise and delight. President Bush did this repeatedly down the road, "lighting them up!" VIP's who rode in the limo with Bush allege that he seemed more delighted than the people at whom he'd pointed!

President Bush founded the "Thousand Points of Light" foundation based on a phrase he used during his convention nomination speech in 1988: "For we're a nation of community…a brilliant diversity, spread like stars, like a thousand points of light in a broad and peaceful sky."

You have countless opportunities to light someone up, too.

Think about how many times in the course of a day you conduct a simple, robotic transaction with another human being. You buy gas; stop to get a coffee or a bagel or the newspaper; order lunch; pass someone in the hallway at work; pay for something while shopping at the mall; take countless phone calls and send E-mails; pick your kids up from school, etc. Whether you are the shopper or the clerk you can manage, if you choose, to get through each of those experiences without any meaningful human communication. You might be told or tell the price, hand over or collect money and make change, and maybe even get a perfunctory mumble or grunt.

But one of these days, just for fun, try engaging everyone you meet in the course of your day with a human, meaningful, positive communication. Just try it and see what happens.

Watch what happens when you tell the shop clerk how nice her hair looks. Or when you tell the airline gate agent, as you board your flight, how much you appreciate how friendly she's been. Mention how you like a co-worker's tie. When you notice someone wearing a name tag, say something like, "Prudence is a pretty name," or "my mother was named Gladys, too."

You will light people up. You'll be shaking them out of their routine.

You will be inviting them to the party.

You'll never know just how down that person might have been when you approached them or how much you might have helped them feel better. You will never really know the ripple effect you might cause when that person you encountered is nicer to someone else they subsequently encounter. In the extreme, you might inadvertently save someone's life. At minimum, you'll get a smile out of someone.

Doris Buffett, the millionaire sister of billionaire Warren Buffett told me, "We take our work seriously, but we don't take ourselves seriously." You're not too important to be friendly.

If you're shy, start by filling out the "comment cards" certain businesses, hotels, health clubs, restaurants and various companies make available. Most everyone tips the waitress, but hardly anyone takes the time to fill out a comment card – unless it's to complain about something. Try writing something nice about someone, and use their name, so they will get some recognition from their boss, supervisor or co-workers. You can never underestimate the power of appreciation, recognition, or a simple pat on the back.

Try it…for one day.

It costs you nothing.

You'll become addicted to it.

Light 'em up!

2

Invite Yourself
To A Career
(How I Did It)

OUTTA SIGHT

Jeff Elliott and Jerry St. James are a duo of very popular morning radio funnymen. Jerry came from Baltimore; Jeff from Wooster, Ohio.

I met "Jeff and Jer," as their "'Show'gram" is known, when they were partnered on WMJC "Magic 95" FM in Detroit.

Once again, I invited myself to the party.

Heading into my senior year of high school at Our Lady of Mount Carmel, in Wyandotte, Michigan, I had the idea that I wanted to be a radio host. I was intrigued hearing the noonday news broadcasts of Paul Harvey during the summertime when my grandfather Frank would listen daily on our family vacation. *"Stand by for news! Good day!"* I was also hooked by all of those hours under the covers at night falling asleep to the peaceful play-by-play drawl of Ernie Harwell calling Detroit Tiger baseball games over the transistor radio on WJR; followed by Jay Roberts' *Night Flight* overnight program. *Night Flight* was enchanting. The show was total theater of the mind. It would open with the sound of airliner engines whining to a start, followed by the tone of a seatbelt sign alert. With a soothing, bouncy and light instrumental underneath, the host would open the microphone and introduce himself as "Captain Jay Roberts." His monologue would go something like…"*This is Captain Jay Roberts. Welcome to Night Flight, bound tonight for*

San Diego, California. We are preparing for takeoff now here on the flight deck, so I'd ask you to settle back into your seat, buckle your safety belt, and relax. We appreciate you flying with us. After take off, we will climb to 35,000 feet, and set a course west-by-southwest. We will be passing over the southern shore of Lake Michigan, so those of you on the right side of the aircraft might just catch a glimpse of Chicago turning out their lights for the night…."

Roberts would then list the cities over which the "night flight" would pass, and the sound effects would take over as the plane powered up. The show would feature easy listening, classical and jazz music of all varieties, with "Captain Roberts" interrupting occasionally with announcements from the cockpit. The flight would eventually end by landing at its destination in the pre-dawn hours.

When WJR fired Roberts, he used the final moments of his last show to crash the plane. Classic.

Sometimes I'd listen to Larry King's unpredictable and eccentric overnight syndicated radio talk show, which he would close each night by playing a song called *Duke's Place*. King, at the time, was a much more wild man than when he went to CNN. His late night interviews were often off topic and unique, and his open line segments with callers bordered at times, on bizarre. Middle of the night listeners, drunk or sober, ringing in under the moonlight with conspiracy theories, rants, or far out questions. King would then, as he does now, bark out the names of the cities from which the phone calls came when he greeted listeners on the air:…"Jacksonville, Florida, hello!"…. "La Jolla, California, hello!"….

I had also listened closely to the friendly country music deejay Deano Day on Detroit's WCXI, and the romantic, deep-voiced host of WNIC's *Pillow Talk*, Alan Almond, which was essentially a show of bedroom – or at my age, backseat – music every evening. Almond would close the show at midnight over a bed of music with the sign-off: "*Sweet dreams, Angel.*"

Sometimes I would nervously phone in to radio shows, as I remember doing once with *Harper and Gannon*, a morning comedy team in Detroit, and tape record my brief appearance on the show so I could hear what I sounded like and have it as a souvenir. I also remember putting on headphones and spinning Beatle records on the basement turntable of my childhood home, trying to talk up the intro's like a deejay, "hit the post," and time the song selections to end the hour on time.

The question I had, though, was could I really make a living in radio? There were only so many jobs available, and I presumed it was highly competitive. So…was it even possible for a kid from a small town to make it in radio? I was practical enough to know I needed an answer to that question before I could plan my collegiate studies and future direction. How would I get that question answered?

By inviting myself to the party.

An article in the *Detroit Free Press* gave the details of a radio study conducted by an outside consulting firm. Three national judges had come in to the Motor City and secretly listened to all of the Detroit morning radio shows. The consultants then judged the morning shows not by Arbitron ratings, but rather, by quality. Dick Purtan and J.P. McCarthy- future Hall of Famers – were ranked in the top three, but it was the comedy morning team of Jeff Elliott and Jerry St. James who ranked #1.

The article's critique read:

"*Great dynamics in voices, good sense of humor, fast wit.*

Sound enthusiastic. They're obviously having fun and it comes across that way. Genuine humor. Very entertaining program."

After reading that, I decided that "Jeff and Jer" must have the answer I was looking for. So I got the phone number to their radio station, skipped high school one morning by pretending I had a stomachache, and listened to their entire show. From my basement bedroom, I synchronized and timed the dialing of my rotary phone so the request line into their WMJC studio would ring the very second Jeff and Jer signed off the air. After what seemed like five minutes of ringing, they answered on what sounded like a speaker phone!

I am sure my voice was shaking with nervousness, but I managed to explain to Jeff and Jer that I was a high school student wondering about working in radio.

"Would you have time to answer just a few quick questions?" I asked.

"Yes, we'd have time," one of them answered, "but only if you agree to come here to the station and watch an hour of the show in the studio, then ask us all of your questions in person afterward."

What a break! I was thrilled! I agreed immediately. It would be the first time I was ever even inside a radio station.

I often think about where I would be today if Jeff and Jer had not been so nice to me on the phone. What if they'd blown me off or decided they didn't have time to answer my questions? What if they hadn't invited me into their studio? What if they had not encouraged me to pursue broadcasting? What if the phone line had been busy? And, ultimately, *what if I had not invited myself to the party?*

The studio visit went great with Jeff and Jer. I remember

they made me relax by insisting I remove the tie I was wearing. That fateful meeting gave me two mentors for life. In addition to providing me with advice many times throughout my career, we became good friends. We worked together on a few projects and I almost became their producer.

When Jeff and Jer left Detroit to take a job at WFYR 103.5 FM in Chicago, I went to visit them on a number of occasions. The WFYR studios were downtown in the Prudential Building. I stayed with Jeff in his big home in Barrington. They were in their thirties, suddenly rich, and bright, friendly professionals.

After a contract dispute in which Jeff and Jer decided to stage an on-air strike by "not being funny," (which almost brought them back to Detroit), they moved on to KKYY "Y95" FM in San Diego, I went out to see Jeff and Jer a number of times there, too. I was twenty years-old, and the radio business seemed more exciting than ever, but the first time I went to Southern California to see them, they were new to San Diego, and still getting settled. Jeff, instead of staying in a big suburban home, this time was living in a tiny studio apartment in the G Street Hotel near downtown San Diego's Gaslamp Quarter. It was going to be close quarters that first night. In fact, the apartment was so small that Jeff had a red burn mark on his thigh because he'd tried to iron a pair of shorts…while he was wearing them!

We'd have to sleep in that same room – Jeff on his bed and me on the floor. After a night out drinking at Croce's, I was settling under my covers on the floor when Jeff asked me a question.

"When you were young did you ever stay overnight at a friend's house?"

"Yeah, sure," I said.

"Well, this is kind of like that here, isn't it?"

I laughed.

"But during those sleepovers when you were younger," he continued, "did you ever see anything like this?"

Jeff then reached on top of his head and very quickly tugged the toupee he was wearing straight up and off! He then flicked off the light and jumped straight into his bed. I was too flabbergasted to say anything, really, so we both just went to sleep. Jeff was a young guy with what I thought was full head of wavy hair. In the morning, as we got ready to go to the radio station, I watched him blow dry the toupee on a mannequin head, and it was now no big deal. But I thought how about how embarrassed Jeff must have been. He knew there would be no way around it since we were staying in the same room and that he would have to reveal the toupee that night. He must have fretted about how to tell me, and that was the best he could come up with. He later told me he appreciated how I didn't react with shock.

Ironically, later in life, I was producer for the radio giant J.P. McCarthy, and he, too, wore a toupee, though I only saw him without it once. Late in his career, he decided to try to freewheel it, and so he appeared, without warning, at Tiger Stadium for our annual Opening Day pre-game focus show with no rug. I saw him there standing at home plate with a wireless microphone, ready to start the show. My immediate reaction was, "Oh my God, did his toupee blow off and he doesn't know it?!"

Jeff and Jer and I had a lot of fun as they rose to prominence and dominance in San Diego, where they have enjoyed a long run. One night we took a trip across the border into Tijuana for a Mexican dinner and merriment. As you may have heard, an evening in Tijuana is a less than sublime experience…but it was intriguing! Wild nightclubs and show bars with naked dancers squatting on beer bottles – and opening them – promoted out of control drinking. We saw it all, including bars with barber chairs for "Tequila Poppers." Patrons would sit in the barber chair, which would then be tilted back so a waitress or bartender could, while blowing a loud referee's whistle, pour straight tequila from two separate bottles directly into the mouth of the customer. The bartender would stop pouring the booze once the customer's mouth was full and then spin the barber chair madly around in a dizzying fashion!

Probably the most outrageous thing I saw in Tijuana was a chimpanzee in a tuxedo, sitting at a bar, smoking a cigarette. This was no pink elephant. Honestly, I really saw that chimp.

Seeing a mouse, on another occasion with Jeff and Jer, was maybe even more shocking. The mouse, you see, was none other than Mickey Mouse. We'd gone up to Anaheim to shoot some promotional television commercials and were "backstage" at Disneyland. Sitting in an air-conditioned motor home functioning as a makeup trailer, we were sipping bottles of Coors Light when I looked out the window into the staging area and could not believe my eyes! There he was – Mickey Mouse – or, at least the life-sized character of Mickey Mouse getting dressed to head out into the theme park to delight the children and take photos with them. The Mickey Mouse character was half dressed and about to put the "Mickey head" on when I noticed that the person in the costume was a woman!

"Mickey Mouse is a woman?" I asked the Disneyland public relations person.

She then informed me that the parks use women to play Mickey because they are shorter, smaller, more graceful, and gentler with children. So the next time you see "Mickey" at a

Disney theme park, remember that the gender-confused super-star rodent is likely a "Minnie" underneath!

After the promotional shoot at Disney was finished, we drove over to Burbank to attend NBC's *Tonight Show* starring Johnny Carson. It had always been a dream of mine to see Johnny Carson and the *Tonight Show* in person. I had even gone so far as to put it on my "bucket list" of 100 goals I wanted to accomplish when I drew up the list two years earlier at age eighteen. Now, because I had invited myself to the party, one of my goals was about to happen!

Due to Jeff and Jer's media status, we had a little bit of help getting seated for the show and were able to avoid the long line of tourists out front. We settled into our seats in the frigid studio, excited that we were about to see the legendary Carson in person and at work. Anyone who attends the taping of a television show has the same impression I did – the studio and stage appear smaller than they look on TV. And while the *Tonight Show* appears to be live when it airs, it is actually taped at 5:30 p.m. Pacific Time.

Out came Carson's sidekick Ed McMahon to warm up the audience before the show. He pointed out where the applause signs were, told a few jokes, and then, as show time neared, he got down to business. McMahon told the audience that the actress Shelley Winters and comic actor Bill Murray would be appearing on the show. We figured we hit the jackpot! Two outstanding guests! Then McMahon continued. "Hosting tonight's show, we'd like you to give a warm welcome to a bright, up-and-coming comedian who is hoping to catch on and really make it big someday…"

You could just about hear the entire audience, especially me, groan and sigh at that moment. We didn't come all this way to see a substitute guest host! But McMahon went on…"So please welcome this young man, show him your support and make him feel welcome. Tonight's host is… comedian Johnny Carson!"

The audience erupted in relief and excitement. Ed had played a little misdirection trick on us! Johnny came out and said a few pre-show words, and seemed to be a very nice, warm, Midwestern fellow. Who could ever have guessed that years later I would interview actress Morgan Fairchild, who dated Johnny Carson, on my own radio show:

"Johnny was an absolutely wonderful, wonderful man," the blonde actress told me. "He was so smart. He had a great love of astronomy and an eclectic group of interests. We were very entertaining to each other in that way."

"Did it end well," I asked her. "I mean, how do you break up with Johnny Carson?"

"I may be the only woman in his adult life who ever broke up with Johnny Carson," she answered with a laugh.

As nice as Johnny seemed, later in my radio career, I interviewed singer/songwriter Paul Anka, who wrote the very recognizable theme music for the *Tonight Show*.

"Johnny had a lot of demons. He was really great at what he did. No one's ever been better. But he was a big drinker and had a dark side," Anka told me.

I asked Anka if he was suggesting Carson was a mean drunk?

"Yeah, he was mean. I didn't know him well because I just couldn't be around people that get physical and abusive when they drink. He got very mean and was a bad drunk, unfortunately. He had a lot of dark side."

Jeff and Jer didn't have a dark side. We always had lots of

fun. One year we hopped a flight from San Diego for an overnight trip to the Maxim Hotel in Las Vegas. On the flight over, I taught Jerry how to play Craps. We both did very well that night throwing the bones at the Flamingo and The Dunes.

We did so well shooting craps that we took a taxi for a little late night excursion to the Palomino Club to celebrate with some gentleman's entertainment. Jerry had the line of the night. One of the stunning female entertainers had shimmied over to dance near a man who was seated at the side of the stage. We watched as he reached over and put a five-dollar bill in the side of her stringy undergarment. In return, the dancer, a buxom blonde, smiled at him while gyrating to the music, tossed her hair, and teased him by reaching down, running her fingernails through his hair, and removing his eyeglasses. As the music thumped through the club, she folded up the eyeglasses and provocatively slid them down into the front of her panties.

Jerry, seeing this, stood up and shouted…"I've got contact lenses!"

KICKED OUT OF SCHOOL
AND INTO DICK PURTAN'S PARTY

B efore I became host of my own radio show in 2006, I was a producer for a number of radio personalities in Detroit. I'd worked with WWJ 950 AM's morning news anchor Roberta Jasina; with the comedy team of Jeff Elliott and Jerry St. James (their morning show went by the title 'Jeff and Jer,' on WMJC 94.7 FM, which is now WCSX); with 60's era heartthrob disc jockey Tom Shannon, who earned his fame on Windsor's CKLW 800 AM; and with WJR AM 760's Frank Beckmann, Bob Hynes, Jimmy Barrett, Jimmy Launce, Kevin Joyce, and Joel Alexander.

Most notably, though, I was first a production assistant for morning funnyman Dick Purtan on WCZY 95.5 FM; and then finally morning news-talk ratings king J.P. McCarthy on WJR, "The Great Voice of the Great Lakes."

So how did I manage to get the opportunity to work for radio legend Dick Purtan at the age of eighteen?

I invited myself to the party.

I was home for Christmas break during my first year of college. I got the idea that I'd like to work for Purtan or at least secure an internship working on his radio show *Purtan's People*. I also presumed, rightly or wrongly, that many young people had the same idea. Purtan's office, I guessed, had a stack of inquiries, letters and resumes... so I knew I'd need to set myself apart from the average internship-seeker. I decided to show up in person at the radio station and drop in on Purtan while he was on the air during his radio show. Sure I would be dressed professionally in a jacket and tie, but I had the sense that I needed something more. I could not just show up empty-handed asking for something – that might be seen as rude and maybe even presumptuous. But what could a start-up college student offer the mighty Dick Purtan? With his salary, surely he was a man who had everything. On my budget, any gift would be insignificant to a radio star, I figured.

I finally had an idea. I would bring a gag gift for the funny-man! I would bring him "breakfast"...with a twist.

I implemented my plan on the way to the radio station. It was the first working day after New Year's Day, and the January temperature in Michigan was below ten degrees. It was a freezing cold, scrape the ice off of your car window-type of morning. I stopped at the local grocery store and bought some white paper plates, plastic cutlery, and a white paper bag. Then I bought a frozen microwave breakfast, opened the package, and put the frozen scrambled eggs, rock hard sausages, and frosty hash brown potatoes onto one of the paper plates and slid it sideways into the white paper bag. The little package appeared as if it was a hot breakfast from a carry out restaurant. I attached a note to the top of the bag which read: *"Dear Mr. Purtan, I brought you breakfast.* **I hope it did not get too cold** *on the drive over. I'd love to have an internship with your show."* –Michael Shiels

Once at the radio station, WCZY, or "Z 95.5," as they called it on the air, I took a deep breath to calm my nerves and gave the breakfast plate to the receptionist.

"I have a food delivery for Mr. Dick Purtan," I told her. "Can you please get this to him?"

"Oh, of course," she said. "I will take care of that right away. Do I need to sign for anything or is there a bill?"

"It's all taken care of," I assured her.

She then took the delivery to Mr. Purtan in his studio, which was just off the lobby. The show was visible from where I stood through a big soundproof glass window. So I watched with a clear view when, during a commercial, she hustled the plate into the studio and gave it to him. Purtan seemed surprised, and I watched as he read the note and opened the bag to reveal the icy, frozen breakfast. Though I couldn't hear him, I saw him toss his head back and laugh from behind his trademark bushy, black mustache. He seemed genuinely delighted by the gag! He then asked the receptionist something; she pointed at me through the window in the lobby. Purtan squinted from behind he glasses to see me, and waved and nodded with a smile. I waved back and shrugged. He gestured to me to stay in the lobby and signaled that he would come out to see me after the show. I had apparently amused him!

I waited in that lobby for more than an hour. Dick Purtan came out after the show and sat with me for a few minutes to find out what I was all about.

He then hired me on the spot.

He summoned his producer, the very talented writer and character voice Gene Taylor, to meet with me and work out the details of my internship, which would begin as soon as the winter semester was over! Success! I made the Hall of Fame funnyman laugh!

This was an important lesson in thinking outside the box... and one that I have used variations of throughout my career.

The gig with Dick Purtan, though, almost never happened.

After securing the internship during the holiday break, I returned to Central Michigan University, three hours from Detroit in Mount Pleasant, to continue my freshman year. I was hosting my own little comedy morning show three mornings a week on WMHW 91 Rock FM, the university's 500-watt radio station. How did I get that gig as a freshman?

I invited myself to the party. I applied for the job before I even started my freshman year at CMU. Very few of the other applicants wanted to get up so early in the morning to host a 6 a.m. radio show, but I knew that mornings were "prime time" in radio: the most listened to daypart! I was given three mornings a week to do my show and, after one term, ended up with a small broadcasting scholarship…all because I invited myself to the party!

On that WHMW morning show, in an attempt to emulate Purtan, who was known for his funny comedy bits and dry wit, I added some of the same to my morning show. We played mainly album rock, but my partner and I, John Lazarski, created comedy sketches and performed them live on the air. Sometimes we recorded "Put on Calls:" gag calls which were a hallmark of Purtan's show. Purtan would phone an unsuspecting person on the air with a seemingly reasonable – but then increasingly ridiculous – premise. The rube would usually fall for it hook, line and sinker right on the radio, with hilarious results…until they were let off of the hook, Candid Camera-style, by Purtan. One on occasion, for instance, Purtan phoned a woman who, for her long-awaited vacation, had planned a Caribbean cruise for herself and some of her family members and friends. Purtan, sounding very official and matter-of-fact, claimed to be a representative from the airline.

"Madam," he said, "I am sorry to say your flight has been oversold and we have to bump you from your scheduled flight."

Furious, the woman became almost hysterical as she complained.

"Calm down, please, madam," Purtan reassured her. "We have a solution for you, of course."

"And what is your solution?" she demanded almost breathlessly. Purtan's answer almost caused her to hyperventilate.

"Instead of going to Detroit Metro Airport," he instructed, "if you and your friends can simply go to Selfridge Air National Guard Base in nearby Mount Clemens, we think we can get you onto a military cargo transport plane. You'll have to make half a dozen stops or so on your way to Puerto Rico, but we can get you there."

"A CARGO PLANE!?" she shrieked!

Purtan once called my high school girlfriend Amy's mother, Judee Montry, because we tipped him off that she had just taken the Civil Servant's test and was nervous about getting the results. Purtan, in his most official voice, claimed to be from the testing agency.

"Judee, we have a little follow up to do with you on the 'typing proficiency' section of the test," Purtan told her. "I need you to lay the telephone next to your keyboard there. We will listen and time you while you type the following sentence: *The quick brown fox jumped over the lazy civil service worker.*"

Poor Judee actually put the phone next to the keyboard and typed the sentence three times for Purtan, each time waiting to hear the result.

"The 'totalizator' indicates that took you nine seconds Judee. Can you go a little faster this time?"

He also told her that getting coffee is an important part of every civil service worker's responsibilities. "Could you please pour a cup of coffee next to the phone?" Hearing the sound of the coffee actually spilling into a mug was too much for everyone. Purtan and his producers broke down in laughter.

Purtan's Put on Calls were always taped ahead of time, as were the ones we attempted to do on the CMU campus station. One of my favorites was when we called the local hardware store near the Christmas holiday asking for advice. Without a hint of humor in my voice, I claimed to be the public relations manager of the Mount Pleasant movie theater.

"We're planning a special event – a premier – of the motion picture "Santa Claus – The Movie," I explained to the hardware store owner as the tape rolled. I played it totally deadpan straight. "We'd really like to promote the movie and draw some attention to it."

"Okay, well, how can I help?" he asked.

"Do you carry ceiling fans?"

"We do, yes."

"Are they very powerful?"

"I guess they are. I mean, they all have varying speeds, fast medium and slow."

"Good. What we'd like to do, sir, is to get four ceiling fans. We have a sleigh. One of our ushers is willing to dress up as Santa Claus and be in the sleigh. But to get more attention, we'd like to buy those four ceiling fans and mount them upside down on the corners of the sleigh, turn them on, and have the fans lift Santa's sleigh up into the air."

"Well…"

"You know, sir, we'd like to use the ceiling fans to create a helicopter effect. The question is, would the ceiling fans be powerful enough to create the lift?"

The hardware store owner actually began to consider the question and wondered how we planned to get power to the fans?

"The extension cord we will use to get power to the ceiling fans onboard the sleigh will also serve as a tether so that the sleigh doesn't fly too high in the sky or fly away altogether," I told him.

He then actually asked how big the sleigh was and started to factor in the circumference of the four fans!

"We'd need room for the Santa character in the sleigh to wave down to the people who attend the premier," I reminded him.

When he began to describe various fans and displacement and power I took the gag to the next level.

"If the weight of the sleigh is a problem I could see about maybe getting a midget to play Santa Claus. And instead of deer for the reindeer, maybe we could use a team of Chihuahua dogs, since they would also be smaller and lighter."

But another one of our Put on Calls at CMU went too far. Only a month or so before the end of the semester, four weeks before I was supposed to begin my prized internship with Dick Purtan, Lazarski and I sat in the recording studio, started the tape, and phoned Thomas Martin, who was the Mount Pleasant City Manager. As we recorded the call, we told Martin, again in humorless, straight-arrow fashion, that we were from the Mount Pleasant Historical Society.

"Our research has revealed a very famous, historically significant person was born in Mount Pleasant. People are going to be just thrilled by this news. I will really put Mount Pleasant on the map," I told Martin. He seemed very intrigued. We went on to ask him about the process for honoring the person, from fundraising to petitioning the city to designate a location for and commissioning a statue to commemorate the person. He answered the questions politely and thoroughly. We told him we wanted him to play a major role in the celebration.

"I realize that you'll want to make a major announcement," Martin said, "but may I ask you, in complete confidence, just between us, to reveal to me who the famous, historically significant person is?"

We relented. "Yes, Mr. Martin, if you promise to be careful with this sensitive, confidential information. You seem to be helpful and eager to move forward with creating the statue," I said. "So we can reveal to you that the important person you are helping us commemorate and honor…is…Cyndi Lauper."

"What?"

"You know, sir, the recording star of popular music, the fine performer Cyndi Lauper."

Then Lazarski and I took turns rapidly peppering Martin: "The creator of the song *Girls Just Want to Have Fun*."

"'*She Bop*,'" I said. "Surely you've tapped your toes to that one, Mr. Martin? '*True Colors*?' '*Time After Time*?'"

Finally he broke in to interrupt us.

"Listen, I'm busy here. Tell you what, why don't you put something in writing and get it to me and we'll have another look at it."

"Mr. Martin, Cyndi Lauper is a daughter of Mount Pleasant. Do you realize the significance?"

Martin said, "Well listen, it sounds like you're pulling my

leg…it sounds like a good laugh. I appreciate it, but I don't have time for it."

"And on behalf of the Mount Pleasant Historical Society we are requesting the proper honor be paid by having the city commission a life-sized statue of her."

Martin then became agitated.

"I'm hanging up now…," Martin warned.

"Could it be a nude statue?" I quickly asked.

"Now I am hanging up," he insisted.

And Tom Martin, City Manager of Mount Pleasant, hung up on us. The sound of the phone slamming down was clearly audible. It was the first time one of our put on calls had ended that way…without us letting them in on the joke, telling them who we were, and everyone having a good laugh. Martin knew he'd been had. What he didn't know is that he'd been had by two college radio deejays who had recorded the entire thing. Once we stopped laughing, I looked over at my radio cohort.

"You know according to the FCC we're supposed to call him back, tell him who we are, right?" Lazarski asked me.

"Yeah, I know. And then we're supposed to get his permission to air it, too."

Lazarski looked at me. We both sat there for a moment.

"If we call him back he will never give us permission to air that," I said.

Lazarski nodded.

The decision was made.

We aired the tape of the put on call three times the next morning – once an hour between 6am and 9am. It was, after all, funny.

Ninety minutes later I was in my Broadcasting Department

MICHAEL PATRICK SHIELS

Mass Media class when the professor, Dwight Wilhelm, had his lecture interrupted by a knock at the door. I didn't know this could happen in college – I thought it was only a high school thing – but Professor Wilhelm announced that Lazarski and I were to report to the office of Dean Robert Craig, Chairman of CMU's Broadcasting Department, immediately.

Upon arrival, Craig was at us almost before we could sit down.

"I don't know what you two did on the air this morning, but Mr. Tom Martin's office has received a number of phone calls from people who had heard him being made fun of on the radio."

I confess to feeling a small surge of pride that we obviously had listeners, but I knew the other shoe was about to drop.

"Martin is the City Manager, in case you didn't know. He is now threatening to sue us, the radio station, and the university." We were immediately suspended from on-air work.

"I strongly advise you two to make an appointment to go to Mr. Martin's office and apologize for embarrassing him."

Within a day, the student newspaper, *Central Michigan Life*, began investigating the situation and trying to get the CMU Broadcasting Department to go public with the information. Since Martin, Craig, University Counsel Eileen Jennings, and WMHW student advisor Jerome Henderson had refused to comment to the reporters, the stories printed in the papers were largely speculative. This left me to spin the story any way I wished. After all, I wanted my morning radio show back. The experience gave me a quick lesson in damage control and public relations.

I was the only one quoted in the paper: "If your rumor was

true, it would have happened Thursday," I told the reporter, which was exactly how he printed it. I thought that was a pretty crafty way of confirming what had happened without being too brazen. I figured the more light I could get on this situation, the more accountable CMU's broadcasting professors would have to be in their treatment of us.

The resulting headlines over the next few days read:

WMHW VIOLATES REGULATION

DISC JOCKEYS TO APPEAL FIRING

DJ DISMISSALS PROMPT CHANGE IN STATION POLICY

STUDENT MISTAKES ARE IMPORTANT TO LEARNING

The newspapers called for the department to reinstate our radio show.

This was a great lesson for me in the power of managing the media…and mismanaging it.

"The people in charge are not giving their side of the story," the final editorial read. "The fact remains students deserve the right to learn and should have the opportunity to gain practical experience."

So we won the media war. But the Broadcasting Department struck back a week later. Professor Craig called me back to his office.

"I see you're scheduled to have an internship in Detroit this summer," he said. "Internships are typically only available to Juniors and Seniors, you know. We granted an exception for you."

"Yes, I appreciate that. You'll recall that I secured that internship on my own, and not through the University." I said.

"Still," he said, "you're going to be getting college credit for the internship. Therefore, you're going to be representing the university. In light of the put on call and FCC violation, I am not certain we're comfortable endorsing this internship."

"But it's a rare opportunity with a radio superstar in a major market. And I secured it on my own," I protested.

"It will be, indeed, a very valuable experience," Craig admitted. "Perhaps, then we should do this. I will phone Mr. Purtan and disclose to him what's happened here. If he then still wants you as his intern, we can proceed. Do you want to go forward with this?"

I had no way of predicting how Purtan would react to such an alarming, official call.

"Can you give me some time to think about this, professor? This is a big decision which could affect my professional reputation in Detroit," I said.

"Very well. You let me know. It's your decision."

I walked back across campus to my dorm room in Barnes Hall thinking as fast as I could. Grabbing the phone, I called the University of Detroit, asked for the head of the Communications Department, and was connected to the Dean, Chuck Dause.

"Internship with Dick Purtan?" Dause said after I asked if U of D allowed underclassmen to have internships. "Of course we'd grant that. That's fantastic. Congratulations! C'mon over."

I then called Professor Craig.

"Dr. Craig," I said, "There will be no need for you to phone Mr. Purtan."

"Really?" he asked.

"Yes. I have decided not to pursue the internship as a sophomore at CMU after all."

"Are you sure?" That's a big decision," he asked. He seemed

startled. After all, I had "shot his hostage," as the expression goes.

"Yes, I am certain, sir. Thank you for your guidance in this matter."

I then transferred to the University of Detroit that very day.

After I'd stopped working for Purtan, I climbed up the production hierarchy at WJR, starting with weekend overnights, until, at age twenty five, I became only the third producer in the long history of the *J.P. McCarthy Show.*

"I have socks older than you," J.P would joke to me.

Though he was a wildly successful legend, McCarthy was very pleasant to work for, just as Purtan had been. I called him "Mr. McCarthy" on my first day on the job.

"Call me 'Joe,'" he immediately insisted.

A few minutes after my very first broadcast as producer, at about 10:15 in the morning, I was in my new office when McCarthy knocked at the door, came in, and sat down. I couldn't believe it. To my mind, protocol would have dictated he have his secretary summon me to his office if he wanted to talk to me about something. But no, there was J.P. McCarthy, sitting in a chair in front of my desk.

"You'll remember to call me 'Joe,' right?"

"Oh, right. Yes, sir. Thank you very much."

"And I just want you to know that things can get a little harried up there in the studio during the show. But whatever happens in the studio during the show, whatever is said, stays up there. We forget about it when it's over. We come down here and have some fun. Okay?"

"That's nice of you to say. Thank you. I'll remember that, too," I said.

With that he was gone: headed down the Fisher Building elevator and on his way home.

I worked hard that first day trying to get organized and schedule good guests for the following morning. My office phone rang at 3 p.m.

"It's Joe," said the voice at the other end.

"Oh, yes sir. What can I do for you?"

"What are you still doing there?" McCarthy asked.

"Just working to prepare tomorrow morning's show," I told him.

"Well get out of there. You're going to burn yourself out. Don't worry about it. We'll take care of it tomorrow."

These were very kind gestures from a superstar radio host to a green rookie on his first day.

I was careful to emulate my boss, J.P., as much as I could. I studied his approach to people and things. And by checking his schedule, I knew where all of the important gatherings and events were. So what did I do?

I invited myself to the party. In fact, many, many parties. And at those parties, events, charity fundraisers, and media announcements, I met plenty of important people in the business world. People I also observed, learned from, networked with and befriended. I built a massive network of successful colleagues and mentors in almost every field of endeavor. To this day, I continue to benefit from those relationships.

It was at one of these functions, about two months after my start with J.P., that I met his wife Judy. She pulled me aside.

"I have been waiting to meet you," she said. "I just wanted to thank you."

"That's nice of you to say, but 'thank you' for what?" I asked.

"Joe comes home so much happier now since you've started working for him," Judy told me. "He tells me about how much more fun it is to work with someone who is smiling, pleasant and happy. He likes seeing you there on the other side of that glass. You've made him a much happier man…so I am happier, too!"

That's the day I learned that if you're going to invite yourself to the party…smile and be happy when you get there! Proficiency is fine. But being a happy, pleasant person is a very valuable, noticeable quality.

Later in life, I collaborated on a book with CNN talk show host Larry King. It was called *Lessons I Learned from My Father*. I interviewed many celebrities for Mr. King's book, asking each of them what their fathers had taught them.

Sparky Anderson, the Major League Baseball Hall of Fame manager, who had appeared many, many times on J.P.'s show as Detroit Tigers manager while I was producer, gave me, in his gravelly voice, a very simple answer: "Be nice to people. It doesn't cost you anything to…be nice to people."

Take it from Hall of Famers Dick Purtan, J.P. McCarthy and Sparky Anderson: "Be nice to people."

GREAT MEN AND THEIR SILLY SALARIES

J.P. had been rated #1 for over thirty years, won radio's Marconi Award, and was inducted into the National Radio Hall of Fame. He was vital to the region with an untouchable share of the audience and daily newsmaker interviews.

Purtan's longevity matched McCarthy's, but his niche was morning comedy and music. Purtan's humor and ensemble cast also eventually won him the Marconi Award and a place in the Radio Hall of Fame.

In the 1990's, these two men, each plying their specific brand of morning radio – McCarthy on AM radio and Purtan on FM. J.P. commanded a 14.0 ratings share while Dick Purtan pulled an 8.0 share. No other morning show was close to the two of them. And to think I'd been lucky enough to work with Purtan...and then J.P.

After about a month on the job with J.P., Walt Disney World Resort, in Orlando, was celebrating its 20th Anniversary and had invited McCarthy down to the Magic Kingdom for a weekend of media celebrations. That was not really J.P.'s kind of thing, but he allowed me to go, which I appreciated.

The parties, which rotated each night between the Magic Kingdom, Epcot, and the Disney Hollywood Studios theme parks, were lots of fun because they'd actually closed the parks to everyone but media members and VIP's. Radio and television personalities and celebrities from across America sipped champagne, enjoyed live, top-name entertainment, and rode any of the attractions without having to wait in line.

I was walking along "Sunset Boulevard" at Disney's Hollywood Studios when I noticed Dick Purtan sitting alone on a park bench. I hadn't seen him since I'd stopped working for him, so I casually sat down on the bench next to him.

"Long time no see," I joked. "Had to come all the way to Florida to catch up with you."

Purtan grinned. "So," he said, "you're working for Joe now, eh?"

"Yeah," I said, shrugging and feeling a little sheepish.

"No, no," said Purtan, "that's a very good job for you. Very good."

"Thank you," I said. "And thank you for the time you let me spend working with you."

He nodded and shrugged.

"You know, Michael, there's one thing you should know."

"Oh?"

"Yes. It's about Joe. He's a very jealous man."

I listened…he continued.

"Joe is very jealous of me because I make a lot more money than he does."

I wasn't certain how to respond, so I just sort of chuckled and changed the subject before saying goodnight and moving along. It was nice to see him.

Monday morning, back in WJR's Studio D, I bid McCarthy good morning during the news break and he inquired about the Disney weekend.

"It was fun," I said. "There were lots of well-known people there. And, oh, I ran into Dick Purtan. He was sitting on a bench at one of the parties."

McCarthy nodded just enough to make his Irish-style cap bob up and down.

"Funny thing about Purtan," he then said, "is that he's always been jealous of me because I make more money than he does." I just nodded and grinned.

Imagine these two men…both at the top of their game; each at the height of their powers. And each certain the other was envious!

Ironcially, after J.P. McCarthy passed away of a rare blood disorder in 1995, WJR considered who to name as his successor. A few days after his passing, while announcer Jimmy Barrett hosted the morning show on an interim basis, program director Skip Essick called me to ask me who I thought should replace McCarthy.

"Simple," I said. "Dick Purtan. He's the only other morning legend in town."

Essick was non-committal and thanked me for my thoughts on the matter. I was then kept mainly in the dark about the process of who they would offer the job to while I continued as morning show producer. This didn't bother me too much since I assume negotiations with any air talent were sensitive in nature. But as the weeks became months, I began to wonder about my own future options. Would a new host bring his own producer? Would the new host be the type of person I would want to work with? Selfishly, McCarthy's stardom and gentlemanly, easygoing nature, in addition to the creative freedom he gave me, after all, would be a tough act to follow. But WJR's management offered me little to no information about my future role or who the host would be.

Then...I got the irresistible opportunity to invite myself to the party:

I was attending a media showing of *Phantom of the Opera* at the Masonic Temple Theater in Detroit and happened to be seated in front of Marc "Doc" Andrews, who was Purtan's sportscaster. Doc and I had a nice chat about life and the business. I didn't ask him if he'd heard any rumors about who McCarthy's replacement would be, and he didn't ask me. Doc did, though, express his condolences about the passing of McCarthy. Then he asked me the perfect question.

"So, Michael, are you going to stay at WJR?"

I was hoping he'd ask, because it allowed me to throw out the bait.

"No way," I answered. "I'm leaving within the next few weeks. I am going to go back to Florida and work for the PGA Tour again."

Andrews played it cool. The house lights dimmed, we sat down in our seats, and "Phantom" began.

The next morning Essick phoned.

"Gotta ask you something," he said. "You don't have to tell me, but, you're not thinking of leaving are you? Are you going anywhere?"

Andrews must have done exactly what I thought he'd do. He took the misinformation I gave him straight to Purtan...and Purtan must have called whomever he was negotiating with at WJR. The fact that the buzz got to Essick so quickly confirmed to me that WJR was indeed negotiating with Dick Purtan to succeed J.P. McCarthy.

"Why do you ask, Skip?"

"Can you come back into the radio station so we can talk?" Later that day I met with Essick and WJR general manager Mike Fezzey, who "brought me in from the cold" and filled me in on the negotiations and future plans for the morning show. Purtan was, indeed, the top choice to host the show. I would be elevated to executive producer, managing Purtan's entire crew – the same fellows I was an intern for in college. The moment I knew I had leverage, and was instrumental in the negotiating process, was when Fezzey told me, "Dick Purtan is considering the offer, and he'd expressed comfort with the fact he's worked with you in the past. He's insisting that you be here to continue as producer if he were to make the leap and follow in J.P.'s top-rated chair."

This resulted in, after negotiations of my own, a $25,000 raise – all because I, in a clandestine manner that night at *Phantom of the Opera*, invited myself to the party.

We then had extensive meetings about how the new WJR morning show, starring Dick Purtan, would sound. How would we go about executing it? During my planning consultations with Purtan I learned that his main concern, since he was used to playing songs between comedy bits, was how he would adjust to hosting a talk radio show without the songs. I tried to ease his mind about the process and tell him that he'd have his normal cast surrounding him as well as my production direction and briefing information. Andrews, Gene Taylor, and John "Ankles" Stewart, plus his character voice actors, were all familiar to me and friendly.

The concept of Dick Purtan succeeding J.P. McCarthy was a thrilling one. We imagined being able to blend the two giant audiences together. J.P. McCarthy had a 14 share; Dick Purtan had an 8 share. While it wasn't realistic to imagine that every listener would stay with WJR or that every Purtan listener would come over, it seemed reasonable to think that a good percentage of both audiences would enjoy Purtan on WJR. More importantly, Purtan's advertisers would follow him any-where, and J.P.'s advertisers would be introduced to Purtan and comforted by the fact that WJR made such a strong move to stabilize the audience and ratings.

What would the new show have sounded like?

It would have been a news show-turned funnier and a funnyman-turned newsier. New York's Don Imus was a perfect example of the hybrid we imagined. Purtan's humorous spin on the news with the WJR machine behind him would have given him a David Letterman-like relevance. There is no doubt he would have dominated the Detroit morning radio airwaves by enjoying the decades of WJR and J.P. McCarthy momentum combined with his reputation and star power.

In the end, though, when WJR presented Purtan, and his agent Henry Baskin, with a contract, Purtan decided not to make the jump, instead shifting from WCZY to WOMC FM, where he could retain his music format with oldies and work at the same station as his former partner Tom Ryan.

As a result, Detroit's radio listeners splintered across the dial spreading the ratings out across many morning shows. During the fifteen years since McCarthy passed away, no morning radio host, not even Purtan, held the #1 spot and dominated the attention of listeners like J.P. did. Dick Purtan chose to retire in March of 2010, leaving the airwaves by playing the Sinatra song *Softly As I Leave You.*

SMILE THOUGH YOUR FACE IS BREAKING

In the days following J.P. McCarthy's passing, WJR radio went through a number of management changes and on-air adjustments. Program Director Skip Essick was the ultimate "player coach" when it came to working with and understanding air talent.

Essick had replaced the much-taller Phil Boyce, who went on to New York to work for ABC Radio, where he dealt with the likes of Rush Limbaugh and Sean Hannity. During my employment review after my first year producing McCarthy's morning show at WJR, Boyce, from behind his goatee and his desk, actually told me, "Well, you've done a better job than the previous producer Bill Plague, but then again, a monkey could have done a better job than him." This was not exactly what I would call an inspiring endorsement. But it was my first lesson in how corporate America finds ways to not pay you what you're worth when it comes time for a raise.

Needless to say, Essick was a breath of fresh air. He was an old school kind of guy who smoked and liked to have a beer to settle disputes. He didn't care at all for drama and had little tolerance for co-workers who "threw each other under the bus." In short, he detested and ignored bitching.

Unfortunately, Essick decided to hit the road and take a

general manager position in Grand Rapids. Before Essick left, he had the opportunity to introduce his replacement, Al Mayers, to everyone at the radio station.

Mayers came to Detroit from Boston. He was a round fellow with a receding black hairline. Mayers was wearing a white dress shirt and tie when Essick walked him around the radio station to give him a tour and to introduce him everyone along the way. I knew I was in trouble the very moment I met Mayers.

How did I know?

When Esseck introduced me to him, Mayers extended his hand but *did not smile*. Not even the hint of a crack of a smile. It seems to me that when people are introduced to each other, it's almost an involuntary reaction to smile or at least make some kind of recognized, friendly gesture. Mayers didn't even give a nod of his head. He also didn't verbally connect by saying "nice to meet you" or any of the other normal pleasantries. He was expressionless – his eyes like those of a great white shark: chilling.

It became quickly apparent that Mayers' idea of management was to come in and play hard guy, a philosophy he presumably felt he needed to telegraph from the very first moment of his arrival. That first impression, though, didn't inspire a welcoming feeling, or even respect. Instead, it was intimidating and made people defensive. And, it turned out, with good reason.

On one occasion Mayers, without any sense of irony, said to me, "You know what's wrong with you people here in the Midwest? *No one here likes to give anybody bad news.*"

"Gosh," I thought to myself, "what kind of person likes to give someone bad news? It must be an east coast kind of thing!"

Since we carried the Detroit Tiger baseball games on WJR,

there was plenty of baseball paraphernalia around the radio station. Mayers had a habit of walking around with a baseball bat in his hand. He reminded me of Robert DeNiro playing Al Capone in *The Untouchables* movie. Mayers, on one particular occasion, raised his voice in an argument with me over something simple. With his jaw clenched and the bat in hand, he made for a menacing figure.

"Are you going to hit me with that bat?" I asked him.

He stared at me, turned, and went into his office.

I watched him close the door to his office, turned, and went immediately to phone my lawyer Roger Young to relate the story to him.

"Did he hit you with the bat?" Young asked me.

"No."

"Too bad," Young said. "If only he'd hit you with the bat we'd have a much better case! Maybe next time."

I laughed.

"If it ever happens, can I at least duck?" I asked Young.

"Hmmm…let me get back to you on that," he answered.

BEING COMPARED TO GIANTS IN YOUR INDUSTRY

What do you like to be known as professionally? Executive? Manager? Business Leader? Consultant? Practitioner? Doctor? Professor? Banker? I realize many of people have multiple titles. Mother and Father aren't bad titles, either.

It is known for instance, that the great singer Frank Sinatra had pillows in his home embroidered with the letters "F-T-A." What did the letters F-T-A stand for? "Frank the Artist." Sinatra preferred to consider himself an "artist." Ol' Blue Eyes did a little painting, but you can be sure he was more than just a singer or crooner. His work on stage, in recordings and his acting on film and television meant Sinatra did so much more than just warble out songs. "Artist" seems like a very appropriate title for such a multi-talented iconic performer.

So what are you? What is your brand?

Personally, I am a radio talk show host, a television personality, a travel writer, a public speaker, and an author. I like to play golf, but my lack of skill is such that I can't really be classified as a "golfer." I think "writer" will be perfectly fine with me. Just plain "writer." Being able to call myself a writer is really what I am most proud of. For all of those radio and television segments that fly off live into the ethos, seeing my name in print, whether it is on the spine of the books I've authored or the byline of a newspaper or magazine article, has always given me a special kick. My mother always thought I should be a writer; my father always wanted to be one.

I remember, after my very first book was published, I walked into 220 Merrill, a snazzy bar and eatery in downtown Birmingham, Michigan. As the young blonde waitress led my small group to the table, I realized she was seating us at a table next to Elmore "Dutch" Leonard, the world famous crime novelist, who lived nearby. Dutch had many of his successful books turned into movies, including *Get Shorty*, starring John Travolta and *Out of Sight* with George Clooney and Jennifer Lopez. When the waitress spotted Mr. Leonard sitting there, she loudly and proudly looked at both of us and announced, "Oh my gosh! Isn't this something? I've got the two authors sitting in my section!"

I quickly stopped her.

"Now, now," I said. "Let's not get carried away here. It's hardly 'two authors.' I've authored one book. I'm still a writer. Mr. Leonard has written more than forty bestsellers. He's an author. A real author! I'm sorry, Mr. Leonard. There is no comparison!"

Dutch just smiled and insisted it was all good and that we were both authors. In fact, he'd actually given an interview for and an endorsement of my first book, *J.P. McCarthy...Just Don't Tell 'em Where I Am*.

I sent a drink over to Mr. Leonard's table.

As a writer and author I have had to opportunity to collaborate with some famous people and assist them in the writing of their autobiographies. I have contributed to titles authored by financial giant Donald Trump and television talk show host

Larry King. I also worked with golf course architect Arthur Hills on his coffee table autobiography *The Works of Art*, and interviewed hundreds of golf course designers for my book *Secrets of the Great Golf Course Architects.*

But how does one become an "author?" By inviting yourself to the party.

Hall of Fame morning radio host J.P. McCarthy, my late boss and mentor, had passed away in August of 1995. The following year, I was still producing the morning show with his successor when Brian Lewis, the owner of a Chelsea, Michigan-based publishing company called Sleeping Bear Press, had phoned to be interviewed to promote one of his company's books.

I chatted with Lewis during the commercial break while he waited for his turn to be punched through and put on the radio. "We sure miss J.P.," said Lewis.

"Thanks for saying so," I said. "Have you ever considering publishing a book about J.P.?"

"I will meet you this afternoon. What time can you be here?"

"Hold on a minute," I laughed. "Tomorrow will be fine…if you're really interested in the idea."

"Two-o'clock tomorrow then at my office, okay? Can you come?"

My question to Lewis about a J.P. book was really nothing more than shoot-the-breeze, rhetorical small talk, but I could tell by his immediate enthusiasm that he was very serious.

I drove to the Sleeping Bear Press offices the next day and sat across from Lewis in his upstairs office. We talked about the incredible demand there would be for a book about the influential, beloved J.P. McCarthy, who had passed away all too young and rather suddenly at the height of his powers. We also brainstormed about the topics and events the book would cover and the many famous people who might be interviewed for the biography. We talked about including transcripts and excerpts of some of J.P.'s most interesting interviews. There was no shortage of ideas.

Lewis then stopped the conversation. He was dead set on publishing a book about J.P.

"But…who should we get to write it?" he asked.

There was total silence in the room. It's funny, but the question took me by surprise. Time, for me, seemed to stop. Maybe Lewis, in his mind, was rattling through a list of potential author candidates from the staff of the *Detroit Free Press*? And maybe my mind was reflexively thinking of candidates, too.

But my subconscious would have none of it.

My subconscious was screaming at me.

I heard, "Invite yourself to the party! Invite yourself to the party, dammit!" in my head.

So, I swallowed hard, and spoke up.

"Well, I would like to write it," I said, with as much confidence in my voice as I could muster. "Yeah, I think I'd like to write it myself."

Lewis looked a little surprised by my answer.

"Have you ever authored a book?" he asked.

"No," I answered.

Lewis stared at me again, but only for a beat or two.

"Okay, he said, "fine."

I thought I had misheard him, but he was serious.

"Just write an outline and a sample chapter for me," he said. "Then we'll take it from there."

We shook hands.

The next day I faxed Brian Lewis a one-page introduction to the proposed J.P. McCarthy book and a simple outline of prospective chapters. Within a week he presented me with my first publishing contract. Before I'd written any significant newspaper stories, magazine articles or anything, really, of any significance, I had a book deal!

There are countless print journalists all over the world who dream of, but never achieve, obtaining a publishing deal to author a book. I suddenly had one because....I invited myself to the party. I often think about what might have happened if I didn't muster up the courage to suggest I write the book. It would have been easy to suggest someone else author the book – someone with book writing experience; a recognizable, marketable name with a proven track record in writing biographies. Sometimes I still can't believe I shook off my fear and stepped up that day: "I'd like to write it. Yes, I think I'd like to write it myself."

I will never know what would have happened if I didn't invite myself to the party...but I know what exactly what happened because I did.

I appeared at over forty well-attended book signings that year all across Michigan. The book launch party was a $30,000 reception sponsored by Jacobson's department store and attended by celebrities like Ernie Harwell and business leaders such as Ford Motor Company Chairman Red Poling. Poling was among the luminaries who actually wrote dust-jacket endorsements for my book which appeared on the cover.

"I'm delighted that a book is being written about 'The Great Voice of the Great Lakes' by someone who was a business associate and friend," Poling wrote.

Endorsements by Frank Sinatra Jr., Larry King, Detroit Mayor Coleman Young, former Governors Jim Blanchard and John Engler, and Detroit Red Wings and Tigers owner Mike Ilitch graced the cover.

I was able to meet and connect with the more than fifty business leaders, celebrities and important people and family members of J.P. I interviewed for the book.

The book, my first book, *J.P. McCarthy…Just Don't Tell 'em Where I Am,* became a regional bestseller and sat in the #1 spot ahead of *Midnight in the Garden of Good and Evil,* by John Berendt and Mitch Albom's *Tuesdays With Morrie.*

$25,000 of the book's earnings were donated to fight the blood disorder which took J.P.'s life.

And I had rebranded myself as a #1 best-selling author and writer.

I have seen the world, stayed at its greatest resorts, and met the most fascinating people while writing countless travel articles for magazine such as *Sports Illustrated, The Bermuda Royal Gazette, Golf Magazine, Travel + Leisure, Northwest World Traveler, Automotive News,* the *Los Angeles Times,* the *Honolulu Star Bulletin,* and *CBS Sports.*

Naturally, I also owe a debt of gratitude to Brian Lewis for having the initial faith in me, an untested writer, to author that book.

Lewis and Sleeping Bear Press also published my second book, which came about in a similar fashion.

I had come to know Ben Wright, the Emmy Award-winning CBS Sports golf commentator, from a distance. I would phone the Englishman, again to get him on the line for radio interviews with J.P., when he was broadcasting from the Masters or reporting from other major golf events. I was a big fan of Ben and his so-phisticated delivery and wry commentary, so we would often chat on the phone during the commercial breaks while he was waiting to be connected through to J.P. for his radio interviews. During those quick chats, Ben would relay an interesting   anecdote about his decades covering the likes of Arnold Palmer, Jack Nick-laus, Greg Norman, and other famous golfers. He always had a compelling take on events in the golf world.

One day I mustered up some courage, phoned Ben, and invited myself to the party.

"Mr. Wright," I said after telling him who I was, "I hope you don't mind but I am not calling to arrange a radio interview."

"Then what can I do for you, my dear boy?"

"You tell me the most interesting stories. I can never get enough of them!"

Ben chortled. "Why thank you, lad."

"Would you ever consider writing an autobiography?

"You know something, a lot of people have suggested that to me over the years, but no one has ever done anything about it."

That was British-accented music to my ears.

"Well, Ben, I'd like to do something about it, if you don't mind."

Brian Lewis was initially dubious. Ben had suffered some bad publicity, and was suspended by CBS, due to some debat-ably politically incorrect, off-the-record statements. He'd also had a resulting turn battling booze in the Betty Ford Clinic.

So…I had to invite Brian Lewis to the party.

I convinced him to fly us from Michigan down to Ben's home near Asheville, North Carolina to meet Wright. It was a risk because I had only met Ben in person once or twice.

After a turbulent, sideways flight on a small connector plane from Atlanta, it was smooth sailing the rest of the way. We found Ben in his sprawling, tasteful mountain home. His house overlooked the Kenmure Golf Course; Ben was looking over the British Open broadcast on his big screen television. He was drinking coffee as we piled onto the couch and big easy chair next to him. The ABC cameras switching from player to player, scene to scene at Royal Birkdale Golf Club triggered Ben's memories, and he reeled off story after story. It was as if we had our own, personal color commentator! Eventually he switched off the television and Lewis and I just peppered him with question after question…and the gregarious limey reeled off tale after tale.

The coffee finally got to Wright, and he excused himself to go to the loo, or, water closet, as he might call it.

I looked at Lewis and asked him how he thought it was going and for his impression of Wright now that he'd met him. Lewis leaned over to me and said, "We are not leaving this house without a deal!"

I smiled. "Welcome to the party!"

The ensuing experience became my most entertaining collaboration. Working with Wright, a very colorful Englishman with a powerful, British Churchillian voice and a heart just as big, was rewarding, personally and professionally. The resulting book, *Good Bounces and Bad Lies* was Wright's personal account of his amazing career hobnobbing at great resorts and cocktail parties with professional golfers and celebrities and his worldwide travels memories of covering the Masters Tournament and all of the sport's most important events.

A life spent mixing big time sports, major personalities, and network television is a potent combination, and the book was a rollicking, honest look into that fast-paced show business lifestyle.

In order to collaborate on the book with Ben, I conducted fifty hours of interviews with him at his mountain home in Flat Rock, North Carolina. I recorded the interviews on cassette tapes and transcribed every word of them. I also interviewed many of his friends and colleagues to collect their stories about Ben, which I them had him retell in his own words. I did my best to capture Ben's style of speaking in the writing, editing, and organizing of the stories and chapters. Of course, he had the final word on what went in and what was left out. I was happy to hear Ben found the process of examining and retelling his life cathartic and we have been the fastest of friends ever since. In fact, I served as best man at his wedding to his current wife Helen Litsas; Ben served as best man at my most recent and previous nuptials!

I remember driving him to the church for his big day in Greenville, South Carolina. We were in our tuxedos, and it was my job to get him to the church on time for the wedding.

"So," I said in a dramatic voice while slapping his knee, "are you nervous?"

"Nervous?" Ben scoffed in his booming voice. "I've done this four times before! It's not the weddings that make me nervous – it's the divorces!"

The book was honest, also covering Ben's bouts with booze, wives, and the aforementioned career glitch. For being a proper and polite Englishman, he was a very candid, outspoken fellow, which is what made him successful. But sometimes it made people mad…or jealous.

Good Bounces and Bad Lies was very candid, sold well and got plenty of media attention, including a review on the front page of the *USA Today* sports section (with Ben's photo.)

One of the triumphs of my writing career occurred in one a newspaper review of the book. Tom Knott's review in the August 2nd, 1999 edition of the *Washington Times* provided a compliment no writer could ever hope for: Knott compared our writing to that of Ernest Hemingway and F. Scott Fitzgerald! Yes, our names next to those literary giants we admired and emulated! What a rush! Can you imagine that?

In the interest of disclosure, I have to reveal the context in which the comparison was made within the *Washington Times* review article. Tom Knott wrote:

... Wright stuck his foot in his mouth, as people do on occasion, only he refuses to remove the foot from his mouth unless it is to have another drink.

Wright does not qualify as desperate. Desperate is the ghostwriter, somebody by the name of Michael Shiels.

Hemingway, Fitzgerald and Shiels/Wright.

American literature approaches the end of the century on a curious note...

Obviously Knott's article was tart and sarcastic. But find me another writer who has had their work compared Hemingway and Fitzgerald! I was thrilled! Thank you, Tom Knott!

This writer has now sat at a table next to Dutch Leonard and had his name in the same sentence as Hemingway and Fitzgerald!

COACH BO SCHEMBECHLER'S THRONE

I included one of my favorite behind the scenes radio stories in my first book *"J.P. McCarthy…Just Don't Tell 'em Where I Am."*

Have you ever seen backstage or behind the curtain of performance or show? Once in a while, when you invite yourself to the party, you get a chance to do just that.

Bo Schembechler was the legendary coach of the University of Michigan Wolverine football team. He was known as a tough, no-nonsense guy with a gruff, passionate way about him, but, being from Ohio, he also had a Midwestern likability.

As producer of the *J.P. McCarthy Radio Show*, I often had to track down guests early in the morning and try to get them on the phone to be interviewed. Because the topics for the program were based on fast breaking news events, not all of the interviews were arranged ahead of time. This meant it was my job to sometimes wake people up or catch them by surprise.

Early one morning, J.P. wanted me to get Bo Schembechler on the phone for a radio interview. I didn't have a scheduled interview with Bo, but it was time to invite him to the party. I rang his Ann Arbor home phone number. Bo's wife Millie answered the phone, so I wished her good morning and quickly told her who I was and why I was calling.

"I'm sorry to call so early. Is Coach Bo home?"

"Uh, yes. He's here somewhere. Let me try to find him for you," she answered.

I could then hear the faint buzz of the cordless phone as she apparently went through the house looking for her husband. I heard her whisper my name just before Bo himself came on the line.

"Mike Sheeeiillsssss….eh?" he growled.

"Hello, Coach. Nice to talk to you, too!"

"You know what I'm doing right now?" Bo asked.

"Coach, I'm not sure….?"

"I'm sitting on the head!" he pronounced proudly.

I overcame being speechless quickly enough to ask, "Coach, can you talk to J.P. on the radio while you do that?"

"Heh, heh, heh. As long as you don't tell anybody," he answered.

So, in this case, if you were listening to the radio and hearing J.P. McCarthy have a conversation with Bo Schembechler, I suspect you were lucky your "theater of the mind" probably didn't have you imagining Bo on his throne!

LLOYD CARR TO THE RESCUE!
THE POWER OF THANK YOU NOTES

Lloyd Carr was one of Bo Schembechler's assistant coaches. But long before I had ever dreamed of meeting Bo Schembechler or producing a radio show, I was a high-school sophomore serving after-school detention alone at about 3:30 p.m. in the office of Sister Nancy Marie at Our Lady of Mount Carmel High School. I must have been up to some attention-getting mischief that day, maybe setting off the fire alarm, skipping morning Mass, doing an impression of a teacher, or getting caught with my hand in a proverbial cookie jar of sorts. I was never a vandal or dangerous, but I was creative in my quest to make high school just a little more fun.

Seated at the chair in front of the principal's desk, I was minding my own business, waiting-out the minutes in the quiet school by reading something, when a tall, thin figure appeared in the door.

"Is this the principal's office?"

"Yes, this is Sister Nancy's office. But she stepped out a few minutes ago. I don't know where she went, but I don't think she'll be gone long."

"Thank you," he said, sitting down on another chair.

We waited in silence for awhile. The man then asked me, "So, young man what it is you are doing here at this hour of the day?"

Now I felt embarrassed. "I'm serving detention."

"Detention, eh?"

"I'm afraid so."

In a non-judgmental manner, he talked logically with me and asked me questions about my choices and behavior, which provoked me to think about what it all meant. It wasn't a lecture, but rather, an analysis and dialogue.

"Do you play sports?" he asked me.

"Football, baseball, and golf," I answered.

Then he introduced himself and shook my hand.

"I'm Lloyd Carr. I coach defensive backs for the University of Michigan Wolverines football team."

Gulp.

I knew he wasn't there to recruit me – he was there to see one of our senior defensive backs – but I was in awe of the legendary head coach Bo Schembechler and the Wolverines. My father took me to the Wolverines opening game – a rainy affair against lowly Northwestern, if you can imagine that – when I was in eighth grade, and I decided before I left that giant bowl of a stadium in Ann Arbor that I would take up football when I became a high school freshman. I saved newspaper clippings from every Wolverine game and watched every second of the Sunday morning *Michigan Replay* show each week. I bought a blue hoodie and blue cap emblazoned with an "M" just like Bo. When J.P. McCarthy would present his annual "Michigan vs. Ohio State" radio show on the Friday before the big game, I would pretend to have a stomach ache so I could stay home from school.

Now here I was sitting in my tiny high school with a giant coach from the mighty Michigan! It was ironic because I was embarrassed to let Lloyd Carr, presumably a disciplined man, who demanded excellence, catch me serving detention; but I also knew that had I not been serving detention in that office, I never would have met him.

You bet your bottom dollar when I got home that day, I invited myself to the party. I looked up the address of the football office at the University of Michigan Athletic Department and sent Coach Lloyd Carr a letter to tell him how honored I was to meet him, how much I appreciated our talk, and wishing him well next season.

Can you imagine the excitement I felt when, a week or so later, I got a letter with a big maize "M" in the corner of the envelope above the return address? It was, indeed, an encouraging letter from Carr. In the envelope, he'd also sent a brochure for the Michigan Wolverine Summer Football Camp for high school players, scheduled for July. I asked my parents for the fee, and they dropped me off in Ann Arbor for the weeklong camp. I got to live in the South Quad dormitory, where the Wolverine athletes stayed and spend the days being coached by the Wolverine assistant coaches. We were also given a special address by Bo Schembechler himself followed by a photo session! The highlight of the week was when we ran out of that famous tunnel and spent an afternoon practicing in the 100,000-seat Michigan Stadium.

I attended that summer camp two years in a row, and continued to exchange letters with Coach Carr.

Near the end of each school year, Our Lady of Mount Carmel held a Sports Banquet for all of the teams and their families at the local Polish Roman Catholic Union Hall. I could hardly believe it, but Coach Carr accepted my request to come speak at the banquet. My Class D Catholic high school had only 300 students, and we'd never before had a big name speaker for the banquet. You can't imagine how proud I was. I was only a junior in high school, but I was able to convince a Wolverine Football coach to appear.

It was that night that Coach Carr and I had a private chat. I wasn't big enough to play college football, but he knew I had aspirations to one day be a high school teacher and football coach.

"If you come to the University of Michigan, would you like to be a student manager with the football team?"

It was like a dream come true! He was offering me the chance to study under Bo Schembechler and be right there, with the team, on the sidelines, for all of the action. It was the opportunity to be a part of one of the most organized, successful athletic programs in the world, and a major resume builder. Of course I accepted, and applied to the University of Michigan.

It was a gray, rainy, unpleasant day, though, when during my senior year, I had to drive to Ann Arbor, to Coach Carr's office, to show him the letter from the University saying I'd failed to gain admission. I was a solid B+ student.

Coach Carr walked me over to the admissions office and got me an immediate appointment with an admissions counselor, which I greatly appreciated. The result, though, was the result I deserved: go to another university for a year to get your grades up, and then re-apply the following year.

I was always in a hurry with my career, and this decision – a rude awakening – rightly or wrongly – effectively ended my desire to be a teacher and coach. It altered my life's path when I was accepted into Central Michigan University's Broadcast

Communications School. Sometimes, when I think about clichés such as "when one door closes another opens," and "everything happens for a reason," I realize this was a perfect example. Sure I might have been happy as a football coach. But the experiences I've had as a writer and media personality have been priceless.

Coach Carr, in his endless generosity, cushioned the blow for me by leaving me sideline passes for every Wolverine home game for a few years. I'd drive from Mount Pleasant, and later, the University of Detroit, and finally, the University of Michigan-Dearborn, to stand with the team and watch Bo and his staff up close every single game and go into the locker room after ward. We remained pen pals over the years, and I have saved all of his letters of encouragement.

Only once did Lloyd Carr ever ask for a favor in return. I was working as J.P. McCarthy's producer at WJR, and in my Fisher Building office one afternoon, when the phone rang. It was Coach Carr, who by then had been promoted to defensive coordinator under head coach Gary Moeller, who'd been named head coach after Schembechler retired.

"I understand that Placido Domingo is coming to do a show at the Palace of Auburn Hills?" he asked me. "I'd really like to go to that show, but it is sold out. Do you think it would be difficult for me to buy some tickets?"

Of course I called Marilyn Desjardins, the amiable public relations director at the concert venue, and we provided Coach Carr with terrific seats.

Ironically, in 1995, I was living in West Bloomfield, Michigan, very near a swank restaurant called Excalibur. My wife at the time and I had a gift certificate for dinner at Excalibur, and had planned to dine there one spring night. As the day grew longer, and twilight approached, we didn't feel like getting dressed up, so we scuttled the plan and stayed home.

That was the infamous night that Wolverine head coach Gary Moeller and his wife happened to be in the restaurant, with disastrous results. Moeller had apparently over-imbibed, and got into a passionate dispute with his wife, creating a scene that the police officers called to the scene caught on tape. Moeller's slurred, emotional agony was painful to listen to, and very embarrassing for Moeller and the University. I've often wondered what might have happened had I been in that restaurant that night and able to call Coach Carr to get him on the phone with Moeller. I had an acquaintance with Moeller, too, since he was a frequent guest on the J.P. radio show and we talked off the air on the telephone before each interview.

But as a result of the highly publicized incident, and despite Carr's loyal protests, Moeller was fired and Lloyd Carr became the head coach of the Michigan Wolverines.

When Coach Carr guided the 1997 Wolverine team to an undefeated regular season, I attended the Rose Bowl game on New Year's Day with my friend Art Wall. As the sun set on the San Gabriel Mountain, the marching band was playing *Hail to the Victors*, and Coach Carr was being carried off of the field on the shoulders of his players after beating Washington State to win the National Championship and complete a flawless season. Lloyd Carr had done what no Michigan coach in the modern era had been able to do. A nice guy finished first – and first in the nation, at that!

"It'll never get better than this," I told Art. And I stopped attending University of Michigan football games. It wasn't anything against big blue. It's just that a rare pinnacle had been reached, and I wanted to remember that season, and that moment, when I thought about my association with the Michigan Wolverines. My fandom would ride off into that golden southern California sunset.

I, did, though, attend Lloyd Carr's last game as head coach – the 2008 Capitol One Bowl, on New Year's Day, in Orlando, Florida. I stood on the sideline behind Coach Carr, just like I had with Coach Schembechler 20 years earlier thanks to Carr, and watched the final seconds of his upset win against the Florida Gators, and his coaching career, tick off the clock.

"I always knew you'd be successful since the first day I met you," Carr told me in a post-game radio interview. Ironic, since he first met me while I was serving detention for being a bad boy!

It had been a magical ride for me and my maize and blue mentor and since the afternoon fate put us both in Sister Nancy's office, and a thank you note gave lift to our friendship.

Now that I live in East Lansing, Michigan, I am getting to know Michigan State Spartan basketball coach Tom Izzo and his wife Lupe. Izzo, who was and is very loyal to his mentor Judd Heathcote, has surpassed his former boss and created a winning dynasty of Final Four appearances, an NCAA championship, and flat out victories at MSU.

Izzo, like Carr, attended Northern Michigan University, and has gone so far as to say, "I'd like to be considered the 'Bo Schembechler' of basketball in Michigan.'" Now that may rile Spartans who don't like being compared to their rivals in Ann Arbor, but it's an honest assessment of Schembechler's legacy of consistency, toughness, a strong graduation rate, discipline, and a scandal-free, economically successful, respected athletic program over the long haul.

Before the 2010 Big Ten Tournament, I conducted one of my interviews with Izzo. I sprung the phrase, "pressure makes diamonds" on him, which he seemed to like.

"I might use that saying with the team," he told me. His team handled the pressure well that year, making it all the way to the NCAA Final Four.

What does the phrase, "pressure makes diamonds" mean?

Under continental crust, diamonds form starting at depths of about 90 miles, where pressure is roughly five Gigapascals and the temperature is over 2,000 degrees Fahrenheit.

You might think of that phrase – pressure makes diamonds – the next time you're feeling the pressure in business or life. The pressure could very well mean it's your time to shine.

One my favorite "Izzo-issms" came in May of 2010 after the coach played himself in a fundraising stage show called "Izzo Goes to Broadway." In the show, Izzo and his wife and children sang, danced and otherwise acted out a lighthearted, musical version of his life. The MSU players, dance team, cheerleaders and even Sparty the mascot all had cameo appearances. Though it may sound campy, the performance was off-Broadway quality and dynamic.

After the show, when Izzo bounded off of the stage, having pulled off a credible performance. Obviously he was not a professional singer, dancer or stage actor, but he put on a great show and had experienced a great adrenaline rush.

"When you get a chance to step outside the box, I say step outside the box!" he said.

This is great advice that fits very nicely with the theme of this book. Step outside the box. Invite yourself to the party!

DUMMY OR IDIOT?

I had written a book called "*Golf's Short Game For Dummies*" which was released internationally by a publishing company called John Wiley & Sons. The *For Dummies* series of soft cover books was a pervasive marketing icon in any bookstore. With the same yellow and black cover for each title, the four *Dummies* books promised basic, fundamental information on most any subject. The series was first launched into public awareness by the title: *Computers For Dummies*. When personal computers first became commonplace, many people were vexed about how they worked, how to use them, and what computers could do. After the success of that book, Wiley began demystifying other subjects in precisely the same format: *Wine For Dummies, Auto Care For Dummies, Painting For Dummies, Home Repair For Dummies*, and *Chess For Dummies* to name a few.

My book, commissioned at the publisher's request, was about the short game: chips, pitches and putts, needed in golf: *Golf's Short Game For Dummies*.

I was very pleased to have written such a high-profile title – the book appeared in stores all across America. My collaborator was Michael Kernicki, a very well respected PGA professional and friend who has taught golf and managed some of America's finest golf clubs.

About two years later, my then literary agent, Jacky Sach, of New Jersey, contacted me. She had a question.

"The publishers of another series of books, called *The Complete Idiot's Guide To*… is looking for someone to author *The Complete Idiot's Guide to Golf Rules*," Mrs. Sach asked me, knowing I had experience as a golf author. "Are you interested in writing it?"

"Sure," I answered. "I've always been somewhat of a student of the rules of golf. I'd like that. Yes, count me in. Invite me to the party."

"Good. I'll tell them you're up for it and get back to you," she said. "Thanks, Michael Patrick."

About two weeks later my phone rang. It was Jacky Sach.

"Michael, I'm calling about the *Idiot's Guide to Golf Rules*," she began.

"Yes, Jacky?"

"Well, the publishers loved your credentials. They were excited to move forward with you," she said. "But then they noticed that you'd written a *For Dummies book*…and they consider that a conflict of interest."

I could only laugh out loud. How could I take myself seriously after that? My self-aggrandized career as a writer and author had come down to a debate over whether I was a "Dummy" or and "Idiot!"

STRANDED WITH THE ROCKET ROGER CLEMENS

I was being sent to Jamaica for one reason and one reason only: to play eighteen holes of golf with the superstar Major League pitcher Roger Clemens in a celebrity players event and, in the process, interview him for *Golf Magazine*. Trouble was, "The Rocket" also had a reputation for being difficult with the media. I imagined I would have a tough time with Clemens, who used his intense stare to intimidate batters while towering over them on the mound.

Was I nervous about meeting Clemens? You betcha! After all, he'd made seven World Series starts for the Red Sox and Yankees, and one for his hometown Astros. He was in Montego Bay to let his hair down after a long season and have some fun playing the Cinnamon Hill course at Rose Hall. I imagined the last thing he wanted was to be badgered by questions from a print journalist.

As I flew down to Jamaica from my connection at Miami Airport, I recalled a bad experience I'd had with another superstar athlete – Buffalo Bills quarterback Jim Kelly. I was producing the *J.P. McCarthy Show* live on location at the NFL Cadillac Golf Classic, a PGA Seniors Tour event at Upper Montclair Country Club in New Jersey featuring star golfers and professional football players. The radio show was set up under a tent between the driving range and the first tee. As producer, it was my job to convince players, whether they were Senior Tour or NFL players, to stop at the tent to be interviewed briefly on their way to the first tee.

Jim Kelly, also very tall, was hitting practice shots with his caddie and an entourage of pals around him watching. In between his practice shots, when he'd stopped to chat with his friends, I invited myself to the party, which was my job, and approached Kelly.

"Excuse me, Mr. Kelly. I'm producer of the *J.P. McCarthy Radio Show*. Cadillac, the event sponsor, brought us here to host the show live from near the first tee," I explained. "Would you mind, on your way over to the tee, stopping for just a few moments to speak on the air with J.P. McCarthy?"

Kelly turned back to the tee and hit another practice shot while I stood there waiting for an answer. After his shot, as he pulled another ball toward the tee with his golf club, he asked, without looking at me, "J.P. McCarthy, eh?"

"Yes, right over there by the tee," I quickly answered.

"*Well fuck J.P. McCarthy*," Kelly pronounced, to the amusement and delight of his chortling friends. I stood there, in the light rain, startled at his callousness. I walked away thinking he was a pretty mean fellow, which is what I expected from Roger Clemens when I was on final approach to Montego Bay for the golf event.

Jamaica can be a fun place to vacation, but it is not a fun place to fly in and out of. Long waits to claim checked baggage on the way in…and long waits to check bags and get boarding passes on the way out are the norm. So, as I got off the American Airlines flight, passed through immigration, and reached the baggage claim area, I anticipated a 45-minute wait. As I began to tug a magazine out of my carry on bag, I noticed a very tall man wearing a visor and shorts and his wife approaching the luggage belt. It was Roger and Debbie Clemens, who'd probably been up in the first class section on my flight, waiting in quiet desperation for their luggage, too.

I knew, instinctively, it was time to invite myself to the party.

I had been worrying about when and where I would be introduced to Clemens, and whether, at the golf course, I'd have another Jim Kelly situation on my hands. But there was the mighty Clemens, The Rocket himself, a giant celebrity, forced to wait for his luggage, just like the rest of us mere mortals. Suddenly I was not in a locker room, dugout, or even a golf course. I was not invading Clemens' space at all. We were on common, neutral turf – the best place to meet him in a very casual manner.

I approached the luggage belt next to Clemens, paying him no mind at all, and pretended to be totally focused on watching the very few bags riding by on the slow belt. He did the same, mainly, but he knew another person was standing there in the same predicament, so, that was step one in breaking the ice.

Step two is another old technique I learned when you're nervous about approaching someone famous but want to get to know them: don't speak directly to them, but rather, befriend whomever they are traveling with, or at the cocktail party with, etc.

"Have you been waiting long?" I asked Debbie Clemens.

"Oh, yes, about 20 minutes now I guess," she said.

"Ah, you were on the American Airlines flight from Miami, too, eh?"

Now I had two things more in common with Roger Clemens than I did when the day started: we were both waiting for luggage and had both had been on the Miami flight.

"I've got golf clubs somewhere in this airport and I sure hope they show up," I told Debbie, knowing, of course, that Roger did too. Presto! Now we had three things in common!

A superstar like Clemens has an ego. There is no denying it. So as much as celebrities say they don't want to be bothered by fans, it does bother them when someone doesn't recognize them or they find themselves not at the center of attention. Roger Clemens could hear every word of my conversation with his wife. I knew the longer I conversed with Debbie, the sooner Roger would feel compelled to insert himself into the conversation – meaning he would actually be coming to me first instead of me approaching him. That meant I obviously would not be rejected. He'd invite himself to the party.

Which thankfully, he did.

During the 45-minute wait we introduced ourselves, commiserated about the luggage situation, talked about the golf courses we were about to play, which hotel we were staying in, and about our home states of Texas and Michigan. We talked about Debbie's new designer clothing line. We talked about the weather. Previous vacation experiences, you name it. I didn't say a single thing about baseball.

This technique also worked the time I was at the Punta Cana Resort's Tortuga Bay in the Dominican Republic. I was invited to a small, intimate cocktail hour by the resort's founder, Frank Rainieri, and his wife Haydee, in their stunning, open-air, oceanfront home. The great worldwide singing star Julio Iglesias and famous clothing designer Oscar de la Renta lived on property and were friends with the radiant and generous Frank and Haydee, so there was some buzz that they might be at the house. This was a party to which I was thrilled to be invited!

I wasn't too concerned with Iglesias, because I'd met him before when he came to the radio studio in Detroit to promote a concert and his new hit song, a re-release of "Crazy." Two things I remember about Julio Iglesias when I met him at seven a.m. that morning: he was exceedingly warm and friendly…and he reeked of smoke. I guess that's how his amazing voice had such velvety texture.

I was so eager to meet Oscar de la Renta, though, that I bought one of his designer shirts in the resort's shop, and brought a felt-tip permanent marker hoping to have him ink his distinctive, iconic signature on the shirt he designed. What a great gift it would make, but I'd have to "invite myself to the party" to make it happen.

I spent a lot of time talking to the vivacious and striking Haydee, who collaborated with de la Renta on the gorgeous interior design of the Punta Cana Resort's most stylish lodging. She was clearly talented, and a lot of fun. We stood near one of the natural stone ponds that ran through the expansive villa. When she noticed her friend Oscar making his way up the long breezeway into the house, I showed Haydee the shirt. She loved it.

"Mr. de la Renta would never autograph a shirt he designed, would he?" I asked. "He wouldn't want to deface it like that, I bet."

"Who?" she asked with a laugh. "Oscar? Of course he will."

"I'm not so sure, Haydee. His signature is a carefully managed, perfectly scripted, valuable marketing symbol."

"Oscar!" she called out enthusiastically. "Oscar, can you come over here please? Oscar!"

De la Renta was friendly but not effusive. He agreed to sign the shirt with the marker, though which he did by stretching it over one of the artsy sculptures in the room.

Oscar de la Renta would do anything for Haydee, but I've always wondered if he would have autographed the shirt had I alone asked him to.

Back in Jamaica, bumping into Clemens and his wife Debbie at the Half Moon Resort all weekend was friendly and familiar after our airport baggage icebreaker, and when it came time for our round of golf and interview, there was no tension at all. And the day after we all returned to our homes, Clemens was happy to call into my radio show and talk about what a good time we had.

"You could play golf with my friend former President George Bush," Clemens teased me. "He plays very fast and so do you. You don't even take a practice swing. You just get right up and hit it, just like the President."

Pretty good endorsement there, I thought!

The *Golf Magazine* Q&A turned out nicely, too, as Clemens was candid and comfortable in answering all of my questions:

MPS: Do you get nervous on the tee?

RC: "I've been hit in the leg by a batted ball going 130 miles-per-hour. And if you can handle losing in New York, you can handle anything. Just like pitching, I go out and 'trust my stuff.'"

MPS: When you traveled with the Yankees, did you take your clubs on road trips?

RC: *"When you play for George Steinbrenner you age in
dog years. The American League cities are great for golf,
but "The Boss" didn't want golf clubs carried onto the
charter flights. It didn't make sense, though, because we
just rented clubs at the courses."*

Q: *Do you play golf on game days?*
A: *"Look, any smart manager would rather have his guys
playing golf in the morning instead of staying out late the
night before chasing tail and waking up at 3:00 p.m. and
taking batting practice half-asleep. With game day golf at
least you're loosened up by the time you reach the stadium."*

I was in a similar situation when *Golf Magazine* asked me to
interview actor Kurt Russell over eighteen holes, which I did, at
Cliffs Valley Golf Club in Traveler's Rest, South Carolina. Because
of his Disney movie background and reputation as a nice guy,
Russell was nowhere near as intimidating as Clemens or de la
Renta. He and Goldie Hawn spend their summers in the lush
lake country north of Toronto, Canada, so, even though he was
a child star, he had a Midwestern friendliness about him. He
even had Vezina Trophy-winning Don Edwards, who won the
award for goaltenders when he was with the NHL's Buffalo
Sabres, with him.

Russell even opened up to tell me a story he'd never revealed
before.

"I was about twenty years-old and about to shoot the best
golf score of my life. Then, out of nowhere, on the last hole, I
snap-hooked my drive left into the LA freeway and out of
bounds. I turned around and there, about twenty yards away,
was a goose. The goose had a look on its face that seemed to say,

"What the hell was that!?" I was enraged, so I threw my driver at the goose and hit it and knocked it out. So I ran over to the goose, and there, while I was bent down trying to revive this dead goose, my friends were saying, 'Wow, if golf makes you that upset, you really should quit the game.' I did. I quit on the spot and didn't play again for more than twenty years."

Ironically, Russell became known as an avid outdoorsman and supporter of gun rights for hunters, but that time, he hunted geese with his driver!

SNUGGLING WITH
MORGAN FAIRCHILD

Glamour will get the best of anyone! As a television and radio producer and writer, I've been lucky to meet many celebrities, famous politicians, successful businesspeople, superstar athletes, authors, actors and actresses...from Kevin Costner, Vice President Dan Quayle, Alice Cooper, Kurt Russell, Senator John McCain, George Herbert Walker Bush, Donald Trump, Cheech and Chong, Roger Clemens, Mia Hammond, Damon Wayans, Julio Iglesias, Larry King, Ed McMahon, Sparky Anderson, Magic Johnson, Paul Anka, and Lou Holtz, to name a very few.

During my entire career, I have prided myself on my professionalism around these well-known people. In preparing them for an interview – or interviewing them myself – I never, ever asked for a photograph or autograph for myself.

With...one exception.

I made one, single exception.

Morgan Fairchild.

I was definitely going to invite myself to her party.

Remember Morgan Fairchild? She is a striking blonde Emmy Award-winning actress and supermodel who became America's iconic platinum blonde long before Pamela Anderson. She appeared on television in *Dallas*, *Falcon Crest*, and on *Mork and*

Mindy to name a few shows. She'd also been in some small movies, and dated Senator John Kerry and Johnny Carson for a spell.

In June of 1997, I successfully scheduled Morgan Fairchild to come be interviewed, in person, in WJR Radio's Detroit studio on the 22nd Floor of the Fisher Building.

I decided if there was ever a time to break my rule about photos and autographs, this was it! It was, after all, Morgan Fairchild.

My sleep was restless the night before. I wore my smartest jacket and a tie which was carefully chosen to match my blue eyes. I was nervous as a cat that morning, though, and as the show proceeded, I kept one ear on the lobby door. I jumped when the receptionist called to alert me that Morgan and her assistant had arrived...and off to the lobby I went to meet, greet, and usher in the world famous Fairchild. She was radiant, as I might have expected, even at eight o'clock in the morning: blonde as could be, perfect, even makeup, piercing-yet-inviting eyes, and an elegant, simple robin's egg blue suit and skirt. She was friendly, too. We made small talk during the short walk from the lobby to the studio. Her voice was distinct with a slight gravel texture, but I couldn't name her pleasant perfume.

I showed Morgan into the studio and her assistant followed along carrying Fairchild's purse. I thought I was doing very well; exhibiting all the poise, charm and confidence I could muster.

"We're in a news break," I explained. "It will last about seven more minutes and then the host will come back in and we'll go back on the air and get started. The segment will last about ten minutes, and then we'll get you back on your way."

"Thank you," said Morgan, who I could see was about to choose a chair in which to sit before I stopped her.

"Ms. Fairchild, I'm sorry. I've never, ever done this before, but it's such a pleasure to meet you...so I wonder if you wouldn't mind having a picture taken with me?"

Morgan Fairchild could not have been nicer in her response. She agreed with a smile.

"Where would you like to do it?" she asked, gently taking the camera from my hands and handing it to her assistant.

In an inviting fashion, I motioned to the wall behind the microphone next to the window showing the city skyline below. She walked in front of me toward the obvious spot, and, when we reached the wall, it was at that moment Morgan Fairchild went above and beyond. The slender, perfectly proportioned and coiffed superstar, snuggled up close to me, shaped herself into the form of my side, and had me put my arm around her back. What a sweetheart!

While the assistant fiddled with aiming the camera, I looked down, and, to my horror, noticed an unbelievable faux pas! I could not believe my eyes. At that stage, having been with Morgan Fairchild for more than five minutes, I am certain she must have noticed what I'd only just realized. I decided there was nothing else I could do but address the matter immediately in a straightforward fashion.

"Morgan," I whispered while pointing downward, "look at that."

She looked down and was standing so close wrapped against me I could feel her begin giggling.

"Can you believe it?" I asked her. "I was so nervous about meeting you this morning that when I got dressed I accidentally put on two different loafers!"

There they were – one black Gucci loafer and one penny loafer.

And I thought I'd been "Mr. Smooth!"

Over twelve years later, Morgan Fairchild was back on the radio with me…this time via telephone.

We played the song Peaches and Herb song *Reunited* in the background, and I welcomed her to the show.

"We have that song playing in the background because I have a little story to tell you about a time I met you," I told her.

"Uh, oh," she said. "Was I okay?"

"Oh man, you were terrific. It's a good story. I was producer for the *J.P. McCarthy Show* in Detroit."

"Yes…"

"When I produced this show, a lot of celebrities and famous people came on the show. I made it a practice never to ask for a photograph or an autograph or anything because I thought it was unprofessional. You were there to do business, right?"

"Honey you're the only one," she said, laughing.

"Everybody wants a little something, huh?"

She laughed more.

"Well, I violated my rule for you. You're the only person. There were presidents who came though there and everything. But I said to myself, 'Morgan Fairchild is coming. I'm going to have to break my rule.'" You were as kind as can be."

"Oh, good!"

She laughed uproariously when I reminded her about the two different loafers. So we all had a good laugh about it all over again!

"It's nice to talk to you, again," she said. "Are you wearing two different loafers today, too?"

"No, Morgan, I have the proper shoes on today...but it doesn't mean I'm not nervous, darling!"

Again, we all laughed.

Of all the producers and showbiz people she'd met during that decade, the dope with two shoes is one she remembered.

I learned that sometimes being "Mr. Smooth" isn't all it's cracked up to be. Sometimes just fessing up to your shortcomings and being sincere...being yourself...is the best thing you can be!

MASTERS MOM

Isn't it amazing how the small voice of a child can be the loudest imaginable?

I covered the Masters Tournament, in Augusta, Georgia, a number of times as a freelance writer. While the grounds inside the famed golf club are pristine, the surroundings in Augusta are not always as manicured and idyllic.

My first trip to cover the Masters was a somewhat gritty visit. As a member of the Golf Writers Association of America, I knew I wanted to participate in the annual Wednesday morning meeting in the club's media center, walk the course, and, in the evening, attend the GWAA Awards Dinner that evening in downtown Augusta. Both of those gatherings would feature the world's greatest golf writers and editors, important personalities, and famous players. So, as a rookie writer and a newbie to the Golf Writers Association, I was determined to network at those events.

So I invited myself to the party.

I didn't have a hotel reservation. I was naïve and, perhaps optimistic, thinking I would simply pop into town and pick a hotel. On a tight budget, I drove overnight timed my fourteen hour drive from Michigan to arrive in town early Wednesday morning and go straight to the golf course. With my media credential, I got to Augusta National just after dawn, and followed my plan for the day to the letter. After walking the glorious course all day in the sun and watching some of Jack Nicklaus and Gary Player at the famed Par-3 Tournament, I was getting sleepy. After all, given the long overnight drive, I had been awake for more than twenty four hours. I decided it was time to find a hotel, catch a nap, shower, shave, and get a jacket and tie on for the evening reception and dinner. I hoofed it back to the front parking lot and began my quest.

Now you will hear of people who have been to the Masters talk about the charming Partridge Inn in Augusta. It is, as described, a picture postcard, southern-style inn with a popular porch. But after the quaint, tiny Partridge Inn, most of the hotels in Augusta, especially on Washington Road near the golf club, are of the standard chain variety, ranging from Holiday Inn to Best Western and the like.

Exhausted, sun burned, and spent, I learned that afternoon that the only thing harder to score than a ticket to the Masters is a hotel room in Augusta during Masters week. All of the nearby, obvious choices were sold out, even though they'd charged inflated prices and insisted on four-day minimums. Without the Internet, I wearily drove from hotel to hotel to hotel only to get the same answer at the front desks: "no room at the inn."

I began to panic because, at minimum, I needed a place to shower and get dressed before the important dinner event! I could sleep in my car if all else failed, but I certainly couldn't shower in it. The clock was ticking, and so were my prospects for a nap before dinner time.

Finally, somewhere south of the club, in a dodgy part of town well separated from any of the festivities of the Masters, I walked into Days Inn that presumably had seen better days: faded, peeling paint, worn carpets, and streaky, smudged windows. The good news was, this fleabag had a vacancy. The bad news? Even this broken down barracks was charging $240 for the night. Desperate and nearly sleepwalking, I resigned myself to the fact that it would only be for one night and checked in.

I parked my car next to the door of my room and, with just enough time to shower in the tiny bathroom, went off to the reception and dinner, where I spent time holding myself up long enough to shake hands with CBS Sports' Jim Nantz, PGA of America CEO Jim Awtrey, LPGA Tour stars Se Ri Pak and Karrie Webb, and as many other dignitaries as I could.

By the time I got back to the room at ten p.m., I fell into, or, given its hardness, onto the bed. The pillows seemed as thin as the walls, and, from the next room, any chance of a peaceful slumber was suddenly disrupted by the plaintive wail of a child and the shrill retorts of her mother.

"Mommy, I'm thirsty."

"Be quiet and go to sleep."

"But mommy, I'm thirsty!"

"Did you hear me? I said go to sleep now!"

A moment or two of silence was interrupted by an ongoing repeat of the same argument. The child became more and more insistent. The mother got angrier and angrier.

"Mommy, please, I'm thirsty!"

"Listen to me now. I mean it. Be quiet, stop asking, and go to sleep!"

I couldn't take it any longer…so I invited myself to their party.

I threw open my covers, slipped on some shoes, and marched out of my hotel room. I dragged myself down the breezeway around the corner to the front desk, where I got change for two dollars. I then went to the vending machine and bought a can of Hawaiian Punch. Quietly then, I walked back past my room, around the corner and placed the can of punch in front of the hotel room housing the mean mom and the thirsty child. I knocked on the door and then ran back around the corner into my room and jumped into bed in time to hear the mother open her room door. Then I heard her door closing... and the sound of the can popping open.

Then...blissfully...I heard nothing...for the rest of the night!

In subsequent trips to Augusta for the Masters Tournament, I became a bit more savvy about where to stay and how to manage the week. People sometimes ask me which was my favorite Masters Tournament? That answer is easy.

Instead of staying in an overpriced hotel, I was invited to stay in a rented home near the golf club with two colorful golf professionals Michael Kernicki, from Wuskowhan Players Club; Dick Stewart, from Kalamazoo Country Club; both past-presidents of the PGA of America's Michigan Section, and their friend Tom Weibel, from Grand Rapids.

Who needed a wake up call? At 6:30 a.m., we were all awakened the sound of Dick Stewart's footsteps running up and down the stairs in his underwear, and the sound of his voice shouting, "Mr. Gene done made a two on #15! Mr. Gene done made a two on #15!"

This was in reference to Gene Sarazen's famed double-eagle on the par-five 15th hole in 1935 during the second Masters Tournament ever contested. Without the aid of television, the only way for members in the clubhouse to know what was happening on the course was via the "bush telegraph:" people running around the course telling each other what happened. "Mr. Gene done made a two on #15! Mr. Gene done made a two on #15!"

We all stumbled down the stairs in search of coffee, tea, or maybe an eye-opening Bloody Mary, and switched on the television. The local Augusta cable system, as a public service, was running a crawl on the bottom of screen: "*Masters Tournament first round play previously scheduled for today has been postponed due to wet course conditions as a result of heavy rains. First round play will begin on Friday morning. Augusta National Golf Club is closed for the day.*"

At first, we were disappointed. No golf action. But, the more we thought about it, we came to realize the rainout meant this meant would be a full day on the town with each other and the thousands of golf fans and people in the golf industry who now had nothing else to do! It was an all-day party at Augusta's watering holes such as the Partridge Inn and the French Market Grille. It was like a tailgate party without a football game to get to! And it all wrapped up at a party thrown by the Irish Tourist Board in a private home that evening.

That…was my favorite day at "The Masters!"

KEN VENTURI'S COMPLIMENT

There was a great deal at stake for me, professionally, during one of my visits to Augusta National Golf Club for The Masters Tournament. Ken Venturi, the 1964 U.S. Open champion, had, since his the end of his competitive playing career in the late 1960's, been the main color analyst for golf telecasts on CBS Sports. I had always been a fan of Venturi's on-air performance. For thirty five years he overcame stammering to deliver an emotional, judgmental, straight-shooting, staccato style, whether he was working with play-by-play hosts Pat Summerall or Jim Nantz. I was also very taken with the story of Venturi's story. He'd been a student of the great Byron Nelson and Ben Hogan. As an amateur young golfer, Venturi led the 1956 Masters through three rounds but shot eighty in the final round to finish as runner-up. I could relate to that! As a touring pro, Venturi won fourteen times. In 1964, just as he was about to give up and quit golf, he battled near-fatal heat exhaustion in humid summer temperatures over a thirty six hole final to win the U.S. Open outside Washington D.C. Venturi famously revealed that his doctors warned him that if he went out to finish the final that day, he might die. "It's better than the way I've been living," he told them. He'd also said that he was in such a state that doesn't even remember a single shot of that final round. He only remembered picking his ball out of the hole at the end and seeing his playing partner, a young Raymond Floyd, crying for him.

"My God, I have won the Open," Venturi said.

The underdog drama, plus the combination of golf and show business Venturi represented appealed to me, so I invited myself to the party.

Venturi was nearing retirement, so I began pitching him on the idea of collaborating with him on his autobiography. I tracked him down and introduced myself to him at the 1999 PGA Championship in Chicago, where I pitched him on the idea of a book. Venturi, in a darkened trailer at the CBS production compound behind the golf course, told me he'd consider the idea in the coming year, and then told me a few of the compelling stories he'd like to tell in the book, which I took as a very good sign. During his deliberation, I sent Venturi notes, and penned a number of stories and columns about him in the various publications for which I wrote, including PGATour.com. I made sure to run into him or stop by the broadcast booth to offer a quick "hello" when I found myself at the same PGA Tour event as Venturi. I also presented my credentials to Venturi's agent, Barry Terjesen. Even Jim Nantz, CBS Sports' lead play-by-play man, Venturi's broadcast partner in the booth, put in a good word with Venturi for me.

And I waited.

The following season, on Tuesday evening of Masters week, I invited myself to the party by dropping into the lively and crowded French Market Grille, a popular spot in Augusta, to have a Jameson Irish Whiskey. CBS Sports director Frank Chirkinian was part owner of the restaurant, and, when I walked in, I noticed the entire CBS golf announce team, including Chirkinian, seated at a big table in the front with plenty of drinks in front of them. Venturi, Nantz, Bobby Clampett, Pete

Kostis, and the rest. I waved to Venturi, and he gestured wildly with his arm for me to come over. When I arrived, Venturi took his hand off of his glass of Crown Royal to shake mine.

"Hey, hey Frank. Look who's here," he said, shouting across the table to Chirkinian. "Do you know who this is?"

Chirkinian nodded, and Nantz jumped in. "Of course we do, Kenny. It's Michael Patrick Shiels, the golf writer from Michigan. Good to see you Michael Patrick."

"Yeah, yeah, he's the author, the writer. The one I told you about," Venturi said, waving them off and turning to me.

"Listen," he said, "I know you want to write my book with me. You've got me thinking."

"Thank you, Mr. Venturi. It would be an honor to do that," I said, as he took a drink of his scotch.

"I want to tell you something, though," he insisted, his voice increasing in volume to the point that some of the others at the table leaned in to see what had Venturi all riled up. He looked me dead in the eye with an intense stare. "I've read what you've written about me. I've seen your work. You are very talented. In fact, you have huge talent! Your writing is excellent. I know, I've read the things you've written about me, kid!"

I was nearly speechless, but I managed to thank Venturi.

"Come and see me tomorrow at lunchtime at the golf course. We'll talk," he told me.

At that point I didn't need a drink – I was on a real endorphin high! My adrenaline was through the roof and I could swear my feet didn't touch the floor as I made my way out of the restaurant and into the spring Georgia night! I had never been paid that high a compliment for my writing from such an important person. I was just flattered that he'd bothered to read my articles, let alone compliment them like that! For the rest of the night I called everyone I knew and told everyone I ran into what Venturi said. What a professional rush. I could hardly wait to see him the next day...and backstage at Augusta National. What a setting!

The next day, near noon, I strolled through the front gate at Augusta National, up Magnolia Lake, around the antique clubhouse, under the big oak tree, and down part of the tenth fairway, turning left at the Butler Cabin, and made my way beyond the par-three course to the CBS production compound, which was hidden back in the woods.

I walked into the door of the makeshift CBS offices and found Venturi, sitting all alone on a couch, eating a sandwich and potato chips off a paper plate. He looked up and me.

"Hello, Mr. Venturi," I said, smiling. "Thanks for inviting me over. Is it a bad time?"

He nodded, still chewing, and looked at me with his piercing eyes.

"Thanks for inviting me over," I said. "Is it a bad time?"

He gestured for me to sit down.

Easing onto a chair, I said, "First of all, Mr. Venturi, before we get started, I just want to thank you for what you said last night. Really, it meant a great deal to me, and I will never forget it."

Venturi looked up from his plate.

"What did I say?"

"Excuse me?" I asked.

"Last night. What did I say to you? What did I say?"

It's impossible to describe the sensation of complete deflation I felt at that moment. Obviously the Crown Royal, and not Ken Venturi, gave me those genuine compliments twelve hours earlier at the restaurant.

Ken Venturi ended up releasing his book, titled *Getting Up and Down – My 60 Years in Golf* not with me, but with a writer named Michael Arkush, in 2006. In the controversial book, Venturi, among other things, accused Arnold Palmer of cheating. If you look Venturi's book up on Amazon.com, the very first two customer reviews include these comments:

> -*"Wow. Ken Venturi should have never allowed this book to go to print. Did he not realize how he paints himself in his own autobiography as a bitter, selfish, whiny, excuse-making old coot? On virtually every page he shows himself to be as self-centered and clueless as they come."*

> -*"Somehow as good as this read was with all the fascinating stories and incidents, I thought it was slightly "I oriented" too much."*

> -*"The whining drunk shows his true colors. Should have been off the air at least 10 years before they finally showed him the door. What a low-life ... if you're broke, it's your fault. And, if you lost the Masters vs. Arnie, it's because you didn't play well enough to win."*

In the end, was I better off not writing Venturi's book? Or would I have done a better job of helping him present his memories in a more sensitive fashion? Neither I, nor Ken Venturi, will ever know.

I had a somewhat similar incident when I was a radio producer at WJR in Detroit. Bill Bonds, the legendary but controversial, local television news anchor had been eased off of television following years of erratic behavior, often having to do with drinking, including an episode where he challenged Detroit Mayor Coleman Young to a fistfight on the air.

He was hired by WXYZ AM 1270 to host a morning radio news talk show. I decided to invite myself to the party and see what was their plan was, so I sent a note to the program director at WXYT simply wishing him well in his endeavor with the larger-than-life Bill Bonds.

A few days later, the program director called and asked to meet with me. During our meeting, we talked about the possibility of me jumping stations to produce the Bill Bonds Morning Radio Show. He seemed very excited at the prospect, and was about to make me an offer. I have to admit I found the idea intriguing. After all, I'd already worked with two Detroit broadcasting legends – Dick Purtan and J.P. McCarthy – so it would have been quite interesting to add the only media star remaining to my stable of iconic bosses.

"My only concern is Mr. Bonds' longevity," I said to the program director, in a subtle reference to the erratic behavior and boozing stories that ended his television career.

"Bill is very committed to this show. He's got it all straightened out. You can ask him about this," he offered.

There was no way I was going to ask an accomplished, veteran media journalist like Bill Bonds to assure me, a lowly young producer, that he had his personal issues settled. I told the program director that would be out of the realm of appropriate protocol.

"Then let's just have lunch with him so you can see for yourself," he suggested.

A week or so later, I met the program director at a dark seafood restaurant owned by Chuck Muer in suburban Detroit at eleven a.m. We happened to arrive at the same time that morning, so we walked in together, spotted Bonds at a booth, and we both slipped into the seat across the table from him. Bonds wore a fuchsia-colored golf shirt. He was unshaven with his toupee on, and drinking coffee out of a small cup.

After the introduction and very brief pleasantries, Bonds, in no mood to waste time, got right to the point in dramatic fashion.

"Kid, I have to ask you a question. Do you want to want to work for the great Bill Bonds?"

I smiled at his third-person reference and began to mumble something about how I'd grown up watching him anchor the news when he cut me off.

"Because I am a wonderful talent," he said, his voice growing louder and his gestures more demonstrative. "You have the opportunity to work for Bill Bonds. You did it for J.P., and you can do it for me. I need you, kid. I need you to do for me what you did for J.P. This is the opportunity of a lifetime for you to work with Bill Bonds!"

Over the next ten minutes, in between sips from his coffee cup, Bonds essentially repeated those sentiments over and over, in various versions, with amounts of emphasis wild enough to have other patrons of the restaurant peering over. His questions to me – or rather, challenges – seemed to insist upon an immediate answer, though he never really allowed time for me to speak. Anything I did say was in an effort to calm him and quiet him down. Then, suddenly, when it came time to order lunch, Bonds got up from the table. "I'm going to go, now. But you think about what this would mean. And what we could do together. You and Bill Bonds!"

With that, he was off. The wild-eyed tirade was over. Since the program director was seated next to me in the booth, I slowly turned my head to the left for the first time to see his expression.

"Well, I guess that isn't quite what you expected," he said to me.

"On the contrary," I said, "that is exactly what I expected."

We had a quick lunch, finished by noon, and when the bill came, in addition to our two lunches, it included two double-vodkas Bonds had before we arrived.

WXYT offered me the position within a week. They asked me how much I was making at WJR and how much it would take for me to jump over and become Bill Bonds' producer. To be polite, and to avoid turning down the job offer of a broadcast legend, I purposely priced myself beyond what I imagined their budget to be. I felt this allowed Bonds to save face and not feel snubbed by a young guy like me.

Bonds' run as a morning radio host turned out to be short-lived.

ON THE AIR...INVITING MYSELF TO OTHER SHOWS

Sure, I've hosted my own syndicated radio show and performed radio reports on various programs, including Jane DrGrow's *Travel Queen Radio Sho"* and, for about ten years I have appeared regularly as travel correspondent on *The Golf Club Radio Show* with Danielle Tucker, which is syndicated by Danielle's husband Rick on stations throughout the Hawaiian Islands.

I've also appeared as an invited guest on countless shows across the United States and beyond.

Sometimes, though, I've invited myself to the party... unannounced. From time to time, to amuse myself on long, boring drives, I've phoned into other radio shows when they asked for listener opinions or questions. Of course, for these playful calls, I have always used the assumed name "Peter Franks," which is the alias Sean Connery's secret agent 007 James Bond used in *Diamonds Are Forever.*

My technique is to string along the radio host as long as I can by sounding genuine and credible, and then surprising the host by turning the call upside down with an outrageous twist. For example, one Saturday in the late morning I was driving through Michigan when I came across a homespun-style talk show offering advice for Valentine's Day. The host was asking about gift ideas like flowers, chocolates and jewelry. I couldn't resist.

"Peter, in Bay City, welcome to the show. Would you like some advice for Valentine's Day?"

"Yes, thank you. I need some romance advice, please," I said, trying to deepen my voice in a very serious, Barry White-type fashion. "I have a very, very important date tonight and I want to improve my chances of making sure it goes well."

"Alright, what would you like to know?"

"Well, as I said, I want this to be a very memorable night, if you know what I mean, so…I'd like to know if it's true that certain foods such as oysters, chocolate and wine can make a woman more, you know, how can I say this on the radio? Libidinous. You know what I mean? I want to be sure she's totally turned on by the time it's time to turn in."

"Well, Peter in Bay City, I am not entirely sure about the chemistry behind all of that, but…."

"Hang on then," I said, "can you advise a restaurant for me?"

"Sure. Maybe then you can ask the chef about your food questions," the host joked. "What kind of restaurant are you looking for, Peter? Do you like a certain type of cuisine or atmosphere?"

"Yeah, the most important thing about the restaurant, to me, is that it be dark. It has to be discreet. I don't really want to be seen, because, you know, my date, the lady I am taking out for Valentine's Day, is not my wife."

"Hoookay, that's enough! Thank you, Peter, for your call and…good luck to you," the host said, cutting off my call.

While driving through Metro Detroit one evening, I worked up another "Barry White voice" and invited myself to the party of a radio show which was giving advice about cars and automobile maintenance.

"Let's go to Peter in Livonia. Do you have a car care question?"

"Yes, yes I do. Thank you for taking my call. I have a 1999 Buick Regal. Have you heard anything about a recall for this car due to the shock absorbers?"

"No, I don't believe so, but we'd have to check with General Motors. Are you having a problem with the shocks, Peter?"

"Yea, well, the back end seems to bounce and be very loose when I drive."

"Have you taken it to a mechanic of the Buick service department to be looked at?"

"No, no, man. I thought I'd call you first because, well, I am kind of embarrassed to go to the dealer or the mechanic."

"Embarrassed? Why, Peter?"

"Well, I think I may have caused the damage to the shocks. I may have worn them out."

"What makes you say that?"

"Like I said, it's kind of embarrassing, but I still live with my parents so my girlfriend and I spend a lot of active time at night in the back seat of that Buick, if you know what I mean. I just wonder if all of that vigorous bouncing and climbing around all over each other night after night might hurt the car?"

"Hoookay, Peter, let's leave it there..."

"Because, you know, I ain't proud of this but she's a big girl. She's not a small woman at all and when she gets moving..."

"Let's cut him off right there. Peter thanks a lot for your call...."

When the book I co-authored with Ben Wright, *Good Bounces and Bad Lies*, was published, *USA Today* sportswriter

Christine Brennan penned a column in her paper criticizing the book. Wright was a celebrated golf commentator for CBS Sports, and the book, his autobiography, was a candid, inside look at the high living, celebrity lifestyle of network television, its announcers and big time professional sports. It described the practical jokes, jocular carousing and brushes with fame one would expect from life on the road as a TV star. It also dealt frankly with Wright's resulting trip to the Betty Ford Rehab Clinic. *The LA Times* described the book as "maybe the best sports book ever written." But since the book also dealt with the bout with political correctness that cost Wright his job at CBS – Wright had been misquoted with some incorrectly attributed comments about golf, women's anatomy, and the lesbian element on the LPGA Tour hurting corporate sponsorship – Brennan, a devoted women's rights advocate, was appalled, and decided to tee off on Wright. She failed to appreciate the humor or honesty in the book, wrote a high-handed column admonishing Wright for the drinking stories in the book and characterized him as a misogynist boozer. I remember chuckling when I read the column because Brennan closed it by writing "do the sports world a favor and don't buy this book." I knew that, despite her efforts to disparage the book, a line like that would more than likely encourage people to run to their local bookstores to see what all the fuss was about (which they did.) Her preachy, judgmental columns often complained about women being slighted, for instance, by Augusta National Golf Club or network television's coverage of women's sports, including the Olympics.

About a year later, I was driving down from Michigan to celebrate, ironically, Wright's birthday at his North Carolina home when I got a delicious, irresistible shot at revenge. As I passed through Toledo, Brennan's hometown, I heard she was about to appear on WTOL TV-11's *Live at Five* interview segment to promote a book she'd written. The station was inviting viewer calls with questions for Brennan. I quickly grabbed my mobile phone to invite myself to the party.

The segment's host, longtime Toledo news anchor Jerry Anderson, was interviewing Brennan on camera when he took a caller.

"Peter in Sylvania, you're on *Live at Five* with author Christine Brennan."

"Thanks, Jerry. Great show. First time I've ever phoned in."

"Thank you. Welcome. You have a question for Christine?"

"Yeah, Christine, welcome home to Toledo."

"Thank you, Peter," Brennan said, smiling.

"I have read so many of your columns in *USA Today*. I almost never miss your work."

Brennan was still grinning, pleased with the praise. "Thank you, again!"

"Oh, you're welcome, Christine. I find you to be a very consistent writer. In reading all of your columns, it seems to me that they all seem to reveal a certain, distinctive quality about you."

"Really?"

"Oh yes definitely. After reading your columns, I think it's evident that you really, really, badly need to get laid."

As the frozen smile drained away from Brennan's face, Anderson jumped in quickly and cut off the call saying, "Well, Christine, sounds like one of your fans there!"

Occasionally, on the radio show I host, I will punk my own guests or listeners. Betsy DeVos, former Michigan Republican

Party chairperson, is the wife of Amway heir and philanthropist Dick DeVos. The DeVos family also owns the NBA's Orlando Magic. The DeVos family are legendary business entrepreneurs devoted to the Grand Rapids community. We asked Betsy to phone into my radio show when she and her husband Dick decided to donate $22-million dollars to the Kennedy Center for the Arts. We had a nice phone chat on the air about why they decided to invest that kind of money in the arts when I followed up with this question:

"Mrs. DeVos, speaking of the arts, have you been over to see the world-famous Chihuly blown glass exhibit being shown this month at Frederick Meijer Gardens?"

"I haven't been over there yet but I am going to go. Dale Chihuly's glass artwork is amazing and I hear they are setting attendance records this month."

"Your family is famous for being entrepreneurial, Mrs. DeVos. I have an idea. What if we created and marketed the world's first 'Chihuly Hooka Pipe?'"

Mrs. DeVos was taken aback but laughed along with the joke.

"Well, it's an idea, alright," she said. "And from what I understand about Dale Chihuly he'd probably like that idea!"

"Well then, I've got my 'angel investor!' Glad to hear you're in!" I teased her.

After that interview some people couldn't believe I'd spring that spoof on an accomplished, serious woman like Betsy DeVos.

"Is nothing sacred to you?" they asked me. But my sense is, it made me more human to Mrs. DeVos, and that she was much more likely to remember me through that joke than any other polite question I might have asked. In addition, it certainly created more buzz from the listeners: "Can you believe he asked her that?"

Dick DeVos, for his part, was involved in me punking myself on the air once. During his run for Governor, DeVos, the Republican nominee, was about to engage in his first televised debate against his opponent, the Democratic incumbent Governor Jennifer Granholm. Because one of our scheduled guests apparently had cell phone trouble and didn't ring in on time for a live interview, I was left to "fill," that is, fill the time left in the segment by talking, for five minutes. Five minutes may not seem like a long time to you, but try, sometime, talking, all by yourself, for five minutes, with almost no warning.

My forced monologue, which ended badly, went something like this...

"Dick DeVos has been telling everyone who will listen that he is a businessman not a 'Harvard-trained debater' like Governor Granholm. What he is doing is trying to lower expectations heading into this debate. But you've got to be careful when someone is trying to lower expectations because you might let your guard down and end up getting a sucker punch in the nuts..."

I looked through the studio glass into the booth where the audio engineer, Paul Keehn, and the producer Amanda Wall, had a stunned looks on their faces. I don't normally talk like that even when I am off the air! When I realized what I'd just said, all I could do was chuckle and say, "Excuse me. I meant to say nose."

When the interminable five-minute fill was over, and we entered the commercial break, Keehn, while laughing hard, managed to ask me, "Did you really just say that Dick DeVos was going to sucker punch Jennifer Granholm in the nuts?"

I guess I did.

The first time I interviewed Michigan's Secretary of State Terri Lynn Land on the radio, I found her to be quick on her feet and deftly able to manage the interview and answer my questions. I even told her so when I bumped into her shortly later at a cocktail party.

"Oh that's easy," she told me proudly. "My staff has taught me all of the tricks about how to handle an interviewer and a tricky question. I know all of the techniques."

I nodded as Secretary Land revealed her media training and I tried not to smile. I thought about how she was going to be very sorry she told me this, because I considered it a challenge. Henceforth, every time she has been on my radio show, no matter what agreed-upon topic she is there to discuss, I pitch Madam Secretary a curveball question mixed in. I deal her a real joker in the deck. One of her assistants told me that after three appearances of getting these curveball questions, Secretary Land hung up the phone and, in puzzled frustration, asked, "Why does he do that?"

"Because he is an imp," she was told. But if Secretary Land is reading this book, she now knows the real answer.

During an interview she'd requested on motorcycle safety, I asked Terri Lynn Land if she knew who is credited with inventing the motorcycle?

"Uh, no I don't," she said. "So, why don't you tell me?"

I told her it was Gottleib Daimler. What I didn't tell her was that I got the question right off of the page of talking points and press material her staff had sent me to prepare for the interview she'd requested!

During another interview with Secretary Land, I asked her a surprise question about nationally-syndicated radio personality

Golf great Gary Player on Maui,
just before he jumped on my shoulder!

With Oscar de la Renta…while wearing a Ralph Lauren jacket!

Rocket Roger Clemens in Jamaica, safely away from the airport!

Backstage with Paul Anka and Dr. Christine Tenaglia

The Best Man at
Ben Wright's wedding

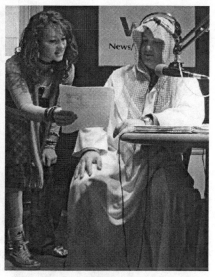

On the air…in Middle Eastern
garb! MPS has traveled to Dubai,
Oman, Abu Dhabi and Israel

Interviewing Jack Nicklaus after a bottle of Boone's Farm wine

Party Animal!

Signing autographs at
a charity event

Young MPS

On stage with CBS Sports star Jim Nantz at the Final Four

Wild bash or bad dream?…
at Turnberry Hotel,
Ayrshire, Scotland

In front of The Big Island's
Painted Church

Don Imus. Imus typically had some of the nation's most important politicos as guests on his radio show, including U.S. Senators, presidential candidates, and network news anchors. At the time, though, Imus was in serious hot water for making politically incorrect, insensitive, racist comments about the Rutgers University women's basketball team by describing them as "nappy-headed ho's." Some of his regular political guests and big-name elected officials were, therefore, walking the line between being loyal to Imus – really fearing to incur his wrath – and protecting free speech, or appeasing their constituents.

"Secretary Land," I asked, "if you were invited to be a guest on the Don Imus Show, would you agree to be interviewed by him?"

"Well I don't know anything about his radio show because I've never heard it," she answered. "I only listen to you in the morning, Michael Patrick."

Touché, Secretary Land. Touché!

During a springtime radio interview with the marketing director of the Beaver Island Ferry, I got a little mischievous. It was April of 2010, during the height of the Tiger Woods sex scandal. It was a nice enough interview about how, that very morning, scheduled ferry service to Beaver Island, in Lake Michigan, would begin again – a sure sign of the arrival of spring. After the woman finished telling me that it takes two hours for each ferry crossing, how much the tickets cost, and what the attractions are on Beaver Island, I lifted an eyebrow, played it as straight as possible, and asked, "Has Tiger Woods ever been on Beaver Island?"

"Why no," she answered. "I don't think I have ever seen him on Beaver Island. But we have a nice little golf course, so I bet Tiger Woods would love to come to Beaver Island."

My producer Amanda went running from the studio with her hands over her mouth trying to muffle her laughter.

Through my chuckling I said, "Yes, I bet you're right. I bet Tiger Woods would like Beaver Island."

Yes, I have played tricks on my radio listeners occasionally. There was a period of political debate about the fate of the suspected terrorists and enemy combatants being held by the United States at the military holding facility at Guantanamo Bay in Cuba. Some felt that the Guantanamo Bay facility should be closed because it was unfair to the prisoners who did not have the same judicial rights they would have were they held in a prison on the U.S. mainland.

I had someone pose as a guest and invited listeners to ring in. The fake guest claimed to be from the fictional Atlanta-based Coalition to Relocate the Guantanamo Bay Prisoners. During my "interview" with him, he touted, in his fake southern accent, not only the moral reasons to move the prisoners, but the economic benefit to the state that agreed to accept and house the detainees.

"We propose that Michigan, given its current struggling economic condition, would be an excellent location to relocate the Guantanamo Bay prisoners," said the guest, "and we are collecting signatures from Michigan residents to support that cause."

"Where," I asked, "in Michigan, do you propose housing the Guantanamo prisoners? Wouldn't it be expensive to build a facility?"

"Not at all," he answered. "Michigan doesn't need to build a facility. You already have a location which is perfect from a geographical standpoint. It is remote. It is a cold-weather site, which will frighten the Middle Eastern prisoners from escaping since they have never been in frigid temperatures. The proposed site already has a military fort, and it is logistically impossible to escape from."

"What is the site?"

"The perfect Michigan site to house the Guantanamo Bay prisoners is Mackinac Island."

I then invited listener calls, and, if you've ever been to Mackinac Island, a pristine, quaint, treasured tourist island in the Straits of Mackinac, you can imagine the result. For the rest of the hour irate callers shouted at the guest and hounded him with protests and questions such as, "Are you out of your mind? Have you ever even been to Mackinac Island, sir?"

"Certainly," he answered. "The terrorists cannot escape the island, much in the tradition of Alcatraz. And you could make their barracks have windows so the intrigued tourists can view them praying to Mecca."

I never let anyone in on the gag until now, but it was a perfect example of the power of radio when you touch a nerve.

On one occasion I was interviewed on Radio Kerry, in the southwest of Ireland. I had hosted my American St. Patrick's Day morning radio show live from Doonbeg, and so the Irish radio host, Deirdre Walsh, host of *Talkabout*, wanted to talk with me on the phone about my impressions of Ireland. During the interview, I mentioned casually that I would be playing golf at Tralee Golf Club later that day. Following my round at Tralee, the club's receptionist Mona came up into the clubhouse pub to tell me someone was downstairs asking for me.

"Who in the world would come here looking for me?" I asked absentmindedly, while I trundled down the stairs through the club lobby and out the front doors. There I found an elderly couple waiting for me.

"Mister Shiels," the older gentlemen began, taking off his cap and extending his hand. He then introduced his wife, who wore a scarf over her head. He explained that they'd heard me on the radio earlier and wanted to meet me.

They'd invited themselves to the party!

"We live two miles from this golf club but we've never visited it before," he said. His wife then asked me if it was true I was from Michigan, because her brother was a priest named Father Shields who had lived in Michigan. Hearing this question, I quickly called my twelve year-old son Harrison down from the clubhouse restaurant, too, and introduced him to the couple.

"Harrison, can you tell these nice people where you go to sixth grade?"

"St. Regis Elementary School, in Bloomfield Hills, Michigan," he answered, standing in the evening twilight outside Tralee Golf Club.

"And can you tell them what the name of your lunchroom at St. Regis?"

"It's the 'Father Shields Room," he answered.

"Who's picture is on the wall in that room?" I asked Harrison.

"There's a picture of Father Shields."

"Really? Would you like to meet Father Shields' sister?" I asked him.

The woman was smiling from ear to ear as we then told her about the school and about how the late Father Shields had been beloved as the Pastor. She'd never been to America.

We took pictures and I felt a tear well up in my eye due to the magic of the moment.

We weren't related because Father Shields had a "d" in his last name – unlike our last name of "Shiels" without the "d" – but that evening, in a remote location in western Ireland, thanks to the power of radio, we felt like family.

OUTSMART A CAR DEALER WITH TIGER WOODS IN YOUR TANK

The mighty professional golfer Tiger Woods chose to play in the PGA Tour's Buick Open, at Warwick Hills Golf and Country Club, in Grand Blanc, Michigan, almost every year because he had an endorsement deal with the automaker. Woods appeared in Buick car commercials and had played out of a golf bag with a big Buick logo on it.

I covered the tournament for various publications, including PGA Tour.com and the *Observer & Eccentric* Newspapers.

While working on a story about the perks Buick offered players to entice them to compete in the event, I interviewed Roger Adams, who was the general manager of the Buick Division for General Motors. Adams explained to me that each PGA Tour player was given complimentary use of a new Buick courtesy car for the six days they were in for the Buick Open.

"What happens to all of those new cars after the tournament is over?" I asked Adams.

"They are all sent to local Buick dealerships to be sold at a discount as low mileage program cars," he explained, standing with me beside the media tent behind the clubhouse.

"What's Tiger Woods driving this week?"

"A supercharged black Buick Regal, fully loaded, with heated seats and the top sound system available," he said.

I asked him what Buick does with the car Tiger Woods drove during the week? I assumed Buick did something special with the car.

"It goes back into the fleet with all the rest of the Buicks to be sold through the dealerships," Adams told me.

I sensed an opportunity to invite myself to the party!

"Let me ask you something. If you guys will pull Tiger's car out of the fleet after the tournament, I will buy it from you," I told Adams, handing him my business card. "Deal?"

"Sure," he said. "That should be no problem. We can take care of that for you. I'll have someone call you as soon as the tournament is over."

He seemed pleased to make a sale.

I was pleased to make a deal to get such a unique souvenir as the car that Tiger Woods drove.

The timing was very good, too, because I had reached my "tipping point" with the used Jaguar XJ-6 I had been driving. Sure it was a gorgeous car: British racing green with a tan leather interior. It was built in the last year of the authentic, Coventry, England-made editions before Ford Motor Company bought the brand. So that Jaguar cost more to maintain than it did for me to own it, literally. I spent more in repairs than I did in payments. Door handles broke off. The gas tank had to be replaced. There was even a kill switch that activated when you hit a pot hole too hard. Driving to Florida was like a moon shot! I broke down twice on one trip from Michigan to the Sunshine State: in Toledo, and then in Orlando. If I were running for President, my whistle-stop campaign to the nation's Jaguar dealers would have secured their votes.

When the driver's side window stopped half-way up during a Florida monsoon, I pulled into the Fort Lauderdale Jaguar dealer and waited for their initial assessment. Of course, just getting an estimate meant a ninety dollar bill for an hour's labor to take the door apart. The Jaguar technician emerged the service area and approached me in the lobby.

"Sir, your power window motor on the driver's side is burned out. It's fried, and the gears of that motor have seized up, which is why the window will not go up or down."

"How much will it cost me to fix?" I asked. It was a question I had come to fear asking with the Jaguar.

"Well, sir, you have two options," the technician answered. "To replace the power window motor will cost $850. Or I can just put the window up permanently for $250."

Window went up…but that was the last straw. I knew I had to make the Jaguar extinct.

So on this summer day at the Buick Open, I walked over to check out Tiger's car…which would soon be my car. Due to the tremendous attention paid to Tiger by autograph seekers and fans, tournament security officials had backed the Buick up to the clubhouse locker room door and gated it with waist high aluminum fencing so that he could emerge from the locker room, jump in, and speed away without being barraged by the crowds. I had a media credential which allowed me to go into the locker room, though, so I got a quick look at the car and, just for the novelty of it, I stuck around for a few minutes to watch Tiger Woods drive away in "my car."

The tournament ended with a Tiger Woods win on Sunday. By Tuesday, I got a phone call from someone within the Buick headquarters office in Detroit. He wanted to talk about my purchase of the car.

"Congratulations! I understand you've decided to purchase a Buick," he said.

"Yes, thanks. Glad you called. What is the next step?"

"We're going to get you going here. Just one question, Mr. Shiels. If it were the same type of Buick Regal Tiger Woods drove, but not the exact car, would that be o.k. with you?"

"Uh, no, not really. I wanted to buy Tiger's car."

"Well, this car would be exactly the same. The same model, the same color, everything identical to the one Tiger drove."

"That wasn't really the idea," I insisted. "I am a golf writer. The novelty is having Tiger's actual car. Mr. Adams himself promised me that car."

"Here's the problem," he explained, "we had two identical versions of that car for the PGA Tour players in the Buick Open courtesy car fleet. One of them went to Al Serra Buick in Flint, and the other one went to Zubor Buick in Taylor. We're just not sure which one it was."

I suspected that someone else wanted the car or Buick had decided the car was more valuable than to just sell it to me at the program car discount.

"So," he said, "we really can't be sure which one is the Tiger car anyway."

"The Tiger Woods car is either at Al Serra Buick or Zubor Buick?" I asked.

"Yes, Mr. Shiels."

"And you're not certain which?"

"Right. I'm sorry sir. We just can't be sure. We don't know which one it is. So…"

"I know which one it is," I stated, interrupting him.

He sounded startled. "You do?"

"Yes, I do. I am certain."

"Just how would you know which Buick was Tiger's when we don't, Mr. Shiels?"

"Easy," I answered, "I wrote down the VIN number."

There was silence on the other end of the phone.

"You did? You wrote down the VIN number?"

"Yep. Sure did. Right there at the golf course. Right before Tiger hopped in it and drove away. I watched him do it," I said. "So, you get me the VIN numbers of both cars and I will tell you which one it is. I am not bluffing. And, by the way, don't bother cleaning the interior. I'd like you to leave anything Tiger might have left on the seat in the car."

What could he say? I had actually outfoxed a car dealer! One of the major accomplishments of any person's life!

Sure enough, when I picked up the car at Al Serra Buick, only a few miles from the golf course, it had notes written to Tiger Woods in the front seat and some of his tournament literature and fliers, etc. There were 500 miles on the odometer.

It didn't improve my game at all, but, for a few years, I drove Tiger Woods' car.

The following April I read a news story about how someone had bought the courtesy Cadillac Woods used at the Masters Tournament in Augusta...and auctioned it on EBay for $200,000! They obviously invited themselves to the party, too!

THERE ARE, IN FACT, BAD QUESTIONS

The old adage: *"there are no dumb questions – only dumb answers,"* is not necessarily true, I have found. Especially in the modern age of blogging, there are plenty of would-be "journalists" who manage to obtain press credentials and make their way into media rooms or interview situations. Instead of inviting themselves to the party, they're crashed the party!

I am living proof.

I was in Melbourne, Australia visiting hotels, wineries, and golf courses, including Royal Adelaide, Royal Melbourne, and New South Wales Golf Club, with my now late friend Cass Colbourne, a golf professional and travel operator from San Diego. Waiting in the lobby of the Langham Hotel in Melbourne one morning, the concierge, in small talk, mentioned the "big game."

"What big game?" I asked.

"Tonight. Aussie Rules. At the stadium," he said. "For you Americans it would be similar to 'Monday Night Football.' All of Australia will be watching."

"Do you mean Australian Rules Football?"

"Of course, mate. It's the only real football there is. Rugby is just legalized brutality. American football is like armored chess. And soccer? Soccer is like Irish Dancing with a ball!"

I decided the Monday Night Football of Aussie Rules in Melbourne was a party I simply had to invite myself to. I gave the concierge my business card. "I'm about to take a day trip down to the Mornington Peninsula and the Yarra Valley to visit wineries all day. But could you possibly phone the media relations office at the stadium, give them my status as a visiting American journalist, and ask them for two media credentials for tonight's game?"

I had to convince concierge, and explain to him again what I wanted, but when I returned to the hotel late that afternoon, the media passes were waiting for me in an envelope. Cass and I walked to the stadium and were shown to the media elevator, which zipped us up into the expansive press box of the gleaming, contemporary stadium, which was buzzing with excitement.

The large press box had windows looking out over the field and an impressive buffet spread of meat pies and other delicacies for the media members covering the game. Cass and I each grabbed an oil can of Fosters Beer.

"Let's check out the rest of the press box," I suggested. Wearing our media credentials which read "Michigan Talk Radio Network" around our necks, we made our way down a long hallway of doors running the length of the press box.

"Look," I said, "there's the network TV broadcast booth. Let's see if we can peek in the window."

As we peered though the thin, vertical rectangular strip of window in the door, a producer spotted us and opened the door.

"You need anything?" he asked.

"No, no," I answered. "I work in broadcasting in America and was just checking out your broadcast facility."

"Michigan," he said, pronouncing it with a hard "ch," after noticing my name on the credential lanyard. "C'mon in, mates!"

With that, in the middle of the Australian national television telecast, we were not only taken into the broadcast booth, but seated directly behind the five announcers and given headsets on which to listen to the feed! Can you imagine trying to do that at the Superdome during a New Orleans Saints Monday Night Football game?!

Each of the commentators and play-by-play men managed to give us a wave as they called the frantic action below, which included injured players crawling off the field or being carried off on stretchers while the game kept going!

One of the Aussie commentators described a strategic play during the game by pronouncing, "That play was as evident as a dog's balls!"

I told him that if I said that on the air in America my career would be toast…with vegemite on it!

Golf Magazine decided to publish a monthly feature in the magazine called *"This Interview is Over."* The editor gave me some questions they'd like to have answered, and sent me to Asheville, North Carolina, to interview former U.S. Vice-President Dan Quayle, a fine golfer, who was participating in a celebrity pro-am at The Cliffs Valley Golf Club. His love for golf and involvement in it was well documented. I invited myself to the party by contacting Quayle's office a week early to request a five-minute interview. His secretary got his permission and instructed me to meet him on the driving range at 9 a.m.

When the day came, I was excited, and I approached Quayle, who was hitting balls, in a very respectful fashion.

"Good morning, Mister Vice-President. I am Michael Patrick Shiels, for *Golf Magazine.*"

"Yes, yes," said Quayle, extending his hand and smiling. He was an immaculate golfer and gentleman, wearing a fawn-colored cashmere sweater and linen trousers. He could not have been friendlier to me while I asked him five or six simple golf related questions. His answers were thoughtful, and he seemed excited to be talking a about golf. Quayle told me about courses his loved in his home state of Indiana, and some of his best golf memories of playing while he was in office. We had a nice rapport and it was a very pleasant conversation in the morning sunlight.

Then came my final question:

"Mister Vice-President, you know of Peter Oosterhuis, the former Ryder Cup player who is now one of the golf commentators on CBS Sports' coverage of the PGA Tour?"

"You bet I know him," Quayle said. "I watch golf on tv and I have met him on a number of occasions."

"Could you please spell his last name? Can you spell Oosterhuis?"

Dan Quayle froze. The smile left his face and he narrowed his eyes squinting at me. "Now why would you ask me that question?"

Before I could answer, he turned away slowly, and went back to hitting practice balls. The interview – which was the desired effect of the feature – was *over*.

Obviously former Vice President Quayle was offended by my mirthful but childish spelling bee question – which harkened back to an unfortunate incident he endured misspelling the word "potato" in front of school children when he was in office.

I was standing in the back of a tent at Warwick Hills Golf and Country Club after the conclusion of the Buick Open. The victorious golfer Tiger Woods was seated on a small stage in front of a room of reporters seated on folding chairs. This convenient press conference scenario happens after every PGA Tour event. The writers and media members raise their hands and ask questions of the champion. Tiger was answering on a wireless microphone.

The questions being asked that day were all quite standard inquiries about Tiger's round and his win, until, a man stood up in the middle of the room and asked this question:

"Your comments about a windy day today is a perfect segue into this inquiry. I know that you know that for some time now materials with origins in the aerospace industry, i.e. titanium, have been used in club construction. In fact your own club constructors have to contend with the same material physics as do aircraft and automobile manufacturers, such as weight, structural rigidity, elasticity, tension uniformity and deformation. Current regulations with the PGA permit day-to-day club performance characteristics modifications but no changes once the clubs are in play for a given round.

The question is, as the science of club making advances, would you advocate rules modifications that permit real time adjustments based on club conditions, and player performance, and, if unlimited design and construction resources were placed at your disposal right now what would be your criteria for a perfect driver?"

Woods, who patiently sat through this question, looked at the questioner and finally spoke:

"Could you repeat the question?"

The room full of reporters, who had been holding their collective breath, erupted into a rousing burst of uproarious laughter. Next question!

That wasn't the first time I'd seen someone embarrassed in a press room.

South African Gary Player won more worldwide golf titles than any other player and, during his career, won all four Grand Slam titles: Masters, U.S. Open, British Open and PGA Championship. Flying millions of miles on airplanes to do it, the small but mighty Player had to remain fit as a fiddle to withstand the travel.

Since I was a teenager, I had been a big fan of Player, even dressing like him on the golf course, in all black, to emulate him. I'd studied his instructional video and rooted for him in tournaments.

Then, as a golf writer, I'd been in press rooms, and bunkers, many times with Player, and once walked eighteen holes with his wife of more than fifty years, Vivienne, interviewing her while she watched him compete in Tampa. For whatever reason, though, Gary Player and I struck up a casual conversation in the clubhouse at Kaanapali Golf Club, in Maui, after the first round of the Senior Skins Game. While convivial, his tone turned quickly serious.

"The next time I see you I want to notice that you've lost some weight," he said from under the black bill of his cap. "You are killing yourself and shortening your life by carrying around that extra weight."

Gary Player then proceeded to clasp his hands together and hike himself up onto my shoulder.

"Walk across the room, now, with me hanging on you," he insisted. So right there, in front of Fuzzy Zoeller, radio host Danielle Tucker, and everyone else in the room, I trudged across the room while Player hung as much weight on me as he could.

"That is what it's like to carry around an extra thirty pounds. It's dragging you down, man!"

He meant well. So I went and immediately bought the book he recommended, *The China Study*, at the Borders bookstore in nearby Lahiana. It is essentially a vegetarian diet.

Jack Nicklaus was giving a press conference in the media room at the Renaissance Hotel at the World Golf Village in St. Augustine, Florida, before the Champions Tour's Legends of Golf event. Similarly, Jack was seated on a stage with a microphone, answering questions. At the start of the press conference, the first questioner asked Nicklaus simply to describe the state of his game.

"Horrible," said Jack. Then he remained silent for dramatic effect, before elaborating on his answer.

About seven questions later, another reporter began his question, "Jack, I know your game is horrible right now, but…"

"Well it's not 'horrible,'" Nicklaus interjected, cutting him off.

There were a few quiet snickers from some of us in the room as the reporter dropped his pen and notepad and tried to respectfully recover. It was obvious that Jack Nicklaus did not mind describing his own game as horrible, but he sure didn't like the sound of anyone else characterizing it in that way!

Nicklaus has steely blue eyes, and for as nice as he has always been to me, I did get caught once in the glare of his tractor beams. I was producing a radio show with Rick Smith, the young PGA Tour teaching guru from Michigan who made a name for himself by helping Nicklaus with his swing for a spell late in Jack's career. Smith also coached two-time U.S. Open winner Lee Janzen, Greg Norman, and other major champions, including Vijay Singh. Smith, also a budding golf architect, designed three golf courses at Treetops Resort in Northern

Michigan, and I knew that Nicklaus had visited him there to see the courses, tweak his swing, and go hunting. I attended a Nicklaus press conference at the Ford Senior Players Championship, in Dearborn, planning to record some comments from Jack to play on Rick's radio show. After the common question and answer session, Jack was walking off the stage, and he agreed to answer a few questions for me on tape.

"Jack, I know you've worked with Rick Smith on your swing. He's designed golf courses up at Treetops Resort. You've a golf course architect, so I'm wondering what you think of Rick Smith as a designer?"

Nicklaus stared into my eyes, and then, finally, answered dismissively into the tape recorder: "I haven't really seen any of Rick's golf course design work, so I can't really say."

I froze. That was not the answer I expected. After all, I had seen photos of Nicklaus and Rick Smith walking the holes up at Treetops. His visit was well-documented!

Nicklaus stared at me blankly, and the silence was awkward. I knew he'd challenged me and was likely wondering what I would do next. Was I supposed to call "bullshit" on American sports icon?

After letting me squirm for a moment, Nicklaus pointed his finger into my chest for emphasis. "You tell Rick Smith that when my son Gary tries to reach him and leaves a message for him, he'd better call him back."

Then Nicklaus smiled, winked his famous wink, and walked away.

My very first experience interviewing the Golden Bear Jack Nicklaus, though, was nerve-wracking for different. I was twenty years-old and producing cable television shows for the public access channel in Dearborn Heights, Michigan. I received notice of a nearby press conference featuring Nicklaus, PGA Tour Commissioner Deane Beman, and Ford Motor Company executives. They would be announcing the creating of the Tournament Players Club of Michigan, on Ford land near the company's "Glass House" headquarters in Dearborn. Nicklaus would design the golf course, which would host a major senior tour event.

This was a party I felt I had to invite myself to, so I did. I applied for media credentials, and since I was from the local community, I was granted not only access to the press conference, but also a four-minute, one-on-one television interview with Nicklaus!

Only one year earlier, at the age of 46, Nicklaus had won his record sixth Masters Tournament and was the biggest star in golf. Yes, I was thrilled to get the interview…and yes, I was nervous as a cat.

So, when the production crew made their way over to the press conference with the cameras and equipment in the television truck, I did what I thought would be the best solution to calm my nerves: I stopped at the local party store for a "spooker." No number of bottles of Opus One I've consumed in my later years can make up for the embarrassment of admitting that I bought a bottle of Boone's Farm Strawberry Hill apple wine in that party store. I wasn't even old enough to legally purchase it, but I unscrewed the cap and drank. it before I arrived at the press conference. A couple of Altoids® breath mints later, I was ready for Jack!

After the speeches were given and announcements made, Nicklaus came over to our mobile television set. Jack and I sat in director's chairs while technicians used two cameras to record our interview. As I think of it now, I can only wonder what the superstar must have thought about having to be interviewed by a 20-year-old kid for a local cable channel, but Nicklaus could not have been nicer or more gentlemanly. And he even gave me some very thoughtful answers to my questions.

Why did he choose to focus on golf?

"It was the only sport that I didn't need anybody else to do. I didn't need anyone to throw me a ball or catch it. I could do it by myself all I wanted," Nicklaus said.

Then I hit him with what I considered to be my curve ball question:

"In an article in *Golf Magazine*, Bob Cupp said you have an excellent memory, and that if you were asked, you could remember what club you hit for your second shot on the seventeenth hole of the third round of the 1967 British Open. That was twenty years ago. Is he right? Can you remember?"

Without hesitation or any hint of surprise, Nicklaus not only told me which club he used (2-iron), but he also told me what golf course it was, how many yards he was from the hole, who the leader was – and how many shots behind the leader he stood at the time he hit the shot!

I was a little clumsy after the interview ended when I presented him with that copy of *Golf Magazine*, with him on the cover, and asked him to autograph the cover.

"It's for my father, Art," I said. "He's a big fan of yours and I remember him watching you on television when I was growing up. You could be fifteen shots out of the lead and he'd still be rooting for you."

Nicklaus, while signing the cover, paused and looked me right in the eye.

"You know, I'm not sure I've ever been fifteen shots behind," he said.

"Right. Sorry, Mr. Nicklaus."

As for the Boone's Farm wine spooker I drank before the interview, I hate to admit this, but I have watched the videotape of the interview many times – I still have it – and I appear to be remarkably smooth and calm!

Even the Hall of Fame radio host J.P. McCarthy, who was rated #1 in Detroit for over thirty five years, used to tell me, "I can do a lot of things, but I can't drink and talk at the same time" when I tried to offer him a vodka and orange juice during his St. Patrick's Day morning show.

It was in the same year of the Nicklaus interview, 1987, that I was picked to be the lead play-by-play man for Continental Cablevision's live high school football coverage. I loved football and loved producing the pre-game shows with highlights and music, but live play-by-play was new to me, and seemed a little daunting. No one really teaches you how to do these things, but into the booth I went, keeping a hybrid of CBS Sportscaster Brent Musberger and Hockey Night in Canada's Rom McLean as a style to emulate. To be honest, though, the first game I called, Annapolis High School at Dearborn Heights Crestwood High School, was a night game near a Red Lobster restaurant. So I met a pal there and drank a couple of Long Island Ice Tea spookers. While it definitely relaxed me, it taught me a valuable lesson, because midway through the first half, in a remedial wooden press box high above the bleachers, I had to take my bladder to the bathroom badly! I watched the game clock crawl on, secretly cursing every time out, incomplete pass, or out of bounds run. I made a run of my own when the band took the field at half time, I had to hurry down the bleachers, out onto the running track, down past the end zone of the football field, and into the restroom, which was in the gymnasium of the school building. Believe me, I started the second half relieved… but winded!

Booze got its revenge on me, again, some years later, when my brother and I went to Shanty Creek Resort, in Northern Michigan, to play my first round ever on the Arnold Palmer-designed course called "The Legend."

The night before our round, in the resort's bar called Ivan's, I did way too much "wine tasting." The eight a.m. starting time we had was not very conductive to the condition I was in. Truthfully, I was angry with myself, because I had been very excited about finally playing The Legend course.

When my brother and I arrived at the first tee, the worst thing possible happened: we were paired by the starter with a very nice, respectable, elderly couple. The first hole of The Legend course is a steeply downhill par-5, so I figured if I could just get the ball started with my first shot if would roll a long way down the hill, which would stop me from embarrassing myself in front of the older couple and give me time to rest in the cart. But when I stood over the ball, I could barely keep my balance. I took a very slow, cautious, tentative swing and the club head of my driver missed the ball entirely, passing over the top of it by no less than ten inches! My next smack at the ball found the club head hitting the turf well behind the ball, skipping forward, and foozling the shot about twenty yards down the hill.

I was mortified. I felt as if I were about to weep until I heard the old lady say, "Don't you worry, young man, we were all beginners at one time. You'll get the hang of it."

Ha! I had been playing golf since I was in the sixth grade! After four holes of fresh air, ice water, Advil and circulating blood, I started to get my sea legs back and actually made a putt. I overheard the old man whisper to my brother, "Looks like your brother has finally worked off some of those drinks from last night, eh?"

Another occasion comes to mind in which I had no business being on a golf course. It was nine a.m. in The Algarve region of Portugal. Europeans often dine very late, which means any after dinner drinks and entertainment run even later. A screenwriter named Robb Bradley and I had spent the evening inviting ourselves to the party! We sampled local nightclubs, bars, and cafes in order to write travel stories to help readers decide what to do if and when they vacation in The Algarve. We lost track of time, which, if you'd been at these nightclubs, would seem perfectly understandable. Imagine our surprise when the bartenders in the nightclub insisted it was last call. The surprise wasn't that it was last call – the surprise was that closing time was six a.m.! The morning sun had emerged before we came out the front doors of the dark yet dazzling nightclub.

By eight a.m. we were on our way to Quinta de Lago, a resort and residential golf club that has been characterized as the Augusta National of Portugal, and has hosted important professional golf competitions. We arrived in the clubhouse restaurant where we were scheduled to have coffee with the club manager. Since we were journalists, the manager wanted to brief us on the history of Quinta do Lago and the area. After about two minutes of our chat, which was mainly his monologue, I looked down, in between head bobs, and noticed that I had been scribbling unreadable words on my paper as I tried to take notes.

"Com licenca, desculpe," I said, excusing myself and the apologizing. I told them I'd be right back and headed for the restroom.

Once in the stall, I sat down on top of the toilet lid. My eyes were closed even before my sleepy, sore head listed over and rested on the cool metal of the tissue dispenser mounted on the wall. The next sound I heard was knocking on stall door and Robb's voice.

"Michael Patrick, are you in there?"

Thirty five minutes had passed since I'd gone into the restroom!

Red-faced and back in the club restaurant with the manager, I mumbled something about "last night's fish stew." He didn't press the matter. So out to the golf course we went on a bright, sunny, warm morning.

As we sat, legless, red-eyed, pale and drained in our golf cart on the right side of the second fairway, I looked up in horror. There, about two hundred yards away, galloping directly toward me along the tree line, was a majestic white stallion! I grabbed Robb by the arm with urgency.

"Robb, tell me you see that horseman on the white stallion too!?"

"Huh?" he said, squinting in the sunlight.

"Just look," I urged, "down there."

He put on his aviator sunglasses and stared for a moment as the white horse drew nearer. "Yep. That's a horse all right."

I exhaled, more relieved than you can imagine. A posh golf course is no place to see a white stallion, and I, for a moment, in the depleted condition I was in, thought that I was about to meet my maker. I actually thought the horseman of the Apocalypse was coming for me!

Later I learned the Quinto do Lago's resort facilities included an equestrian center, and that the horseman had just wandered a little of the wooded trails.

The next day, after a proper night's rest, I attended the grand opening ceremony of the Victoria Clube de Golfe in nearby Vilamoura. The high-profile course was designed by Arnold Palmer, and Palmer, the golfer they called "The King," was on hand to perform a golf clinic on the practice range, followed by a press conference, and then he'd be the first to play the course in a spectator exhibition. There was also a media tournament scheduled.

Palmer had finished the golf clinic portion of his itinerary, and was seated in front of a microphone at a table on a stage in the clubhouse ball room, facing sportswriters from across Europe. Bradley and I, along with Californian Al Peterson, and Orlando-based Ken Carpenter were the only American golf and travel journalists in the room.

Palmer, macho man that he is, had a beer in front of him, and was taking questions. One of the English writers stood up and asked, "Mr. Palmer, as a golf course architect, what is your opinion of designing waste bunkers into a golf course?"

Palmer was quick to answer definitively. "I think waste bunkers are exactly as their name implies: a waste! They really have no place on a golf course. They're confusing to the players and a nuisance for the course maintenance people. So I am against waste bunkers."

"Then why did you put them on the seventh and eighth holes of this course?" the reporter followed up.

Palmer, who was listed as the architect of the course, looked at his design team standing in the back of the room, and then back at the reporter. "Did we? We'll, we're just going to have to do something about that!"

The room filled with laughter since Arnie was charming, but the cloak had obviously been lifted on the myth that Palmer had designed the course himself. In fact that it was possible Palmer – the architect – had possibly never even seen the course before. To suggest that a major construction change be made to a golf course on its' opening day was outrageously cheeky!

But, after all, he was Arnie, and nobody really minded suspending their belief about "his" design too much.

When Palmer then went out to play the inaugural round on the new course, the European PGA Tour had arranged a fun media tournament for the journalists in attendance. Robb Bradley, Al Peterson, Ken Carpenter and I competed, and mixed in with the European journalists. Carpenter, who only brought a few clubs on the trip, was constantly borrowing clubs from other players – a rules violation – and had some other peculiarities about his golf game. So when, at the evening banquet, he was announced as the winner and given an etched glass vase as his trophy, Bradley and I were both chagrined. But the more Carpenter then bragged about his victory, the quicker chagrined escalated into being aghast.

A shuttle van took us back to the hotel, and Carpenter, pre-occupied with getting back to his room to blog about his win on his website, accidentally left his trophy vase in a rectangular, white cardboard box under the seat.

"Shhh," I told Bradley and Peterson, quietly snatching the box and whispering, "Meet me in my room."

Once we gathered in my hotel room, I carefully removed

the etched vase from the white box, and replaced it with two of the hotel's water glasses.

"What are you up to, Shiels?" Bradley asked.

"I think I know," Peterson said grinning.

"Al's going to be sure to get Ken his trophy back," I said. "He will be so relieved."

Then I took my 9-iron from my golf bag, stuck it in the box, and smashed the water glasses in the bottom of the box. I closed and resealed the top. When you shook or even slightly moved the box, you heard the unmistakable sound of shattered and broken glass shifting all over and grinding inside.

We knew Al was the gentlest of the bunch, and that he could deliver the box with a straight face. We wanted to be in on Ken's reaction, though, so we made Al carry my small reporter's mini-recorder in his pocket.

When Al brought the tape back, here's what we heard…

Knock, knock, knock…

Door opens.

"Al, it's late. What's up?"

"Ken, you forgot your trophy vase in the van. The driver brought it to the front desk. They didn't know which one of us it belonged to, so I picked it up and brought it up."

"Oh, wow. Thanks! I didn't even realize I had left it."

Al hands the box to Ken. The noisy shattered glass shifts inside.

"What happened, Al?! Oh my God what happened?!," he asks, shaking the box. "Did you drop it?"

"No, Ken, I didn't drop it. I don't know what happened, but it doesn't sound good. Where did you have the box?"

"On the floor of the van," Ken said, sounding resigned and disgusted. "Thanks, anyway. Goodnight."

Door closes.

The three of us probably listened to the tape six times, laughing our asses off, before we decided we shouldn't let Ken go to bed depressed. We called room service.

"Do you have any sausages or hot dogs?" I asked.

"We do, sir, yes. We have hot dogs on the children's menu."

I then asked room service to bill my room, but to send to Ken a single, uncooked hot dog, covered by a lid on a silver platter. No garnish. A solitary, raw hot dog. And for the server to please deliver the phallic symbol with the tape recorder in his pocket. It took some convincing, but they did it. "A special late night delivery from Mr. Bradley and Mr. Shiels," the room service waiter said after wheeling the service cart into Ken's room.

Then he lifted the silver lid to display the wiener!

Ken stammered and sputtered and asked the waiter, "What is the meaning of this?!" But he got the subtle message when the waiter then reached in the little cabinet under the linen below the top of the cart and pulled out his etched glass trophy, safe and sound.

3

Invite Yourself
To the Road
Travel Tattles!

ROMANCE ON THE ROAD

I am an amorous travel writer. I fall in love with almost every place I visit. The thrill of arriving at a new destination feels, to me, as if I have been introduced to a glamorous and mysterious stranger. We shake hands.

We make eye contact.

For those first moments in a new locale, my senses are heightened, just as they are when having a glass of wine with a potential new friend. I tread lightly through the streets as I would a conversation, excited, yet politely restrained. I catch a whiff of perfume at the same time I notice the jewelry. My head is turned all the while I know that there is so much more beneath the surface – so much I will never fully know.

As if the entire town is a party to which I have been invited… or invited myself.

I put on a jacket and tie my first evening in Paris before gliding out of le Warwick Hotel on Rue d'Berri. I felt the historic "City of Light" deserved my respect through proper attire on this, my opening night. Indeed, I felt as if I were in a Broadway show when, moments later, I stood in the middle of the Champs-Elysees, gazing up the avenue at the Arc de Triumph and down, through the clipped chestnut trees, glittering shops, and street-side brassieries toward the obelisk in front of the Place de la Concorde. The Eiffel Tower, appearing delicate and bejeweled in lights, was also visible. No one would wish to be undressed for such an occasion!

Thus began my tradition of dressing up on the first night in a new world city: Istanbul, London, New York, Lisbon, Monte Carlo, Jerusalem, Tokyo, Beverly Hills, San Remo, Dubai, Auckland, Sydney, Toronto, Glasgow, New Orleans, Honolulu, Bangkok, Las Vegas, Washington D.C., and Seoul...it was splendid to meet each of you!

My love affairs with many places have resulted in a mental scrapbook of priceless occurrences.

I discovered white port in the town center of tiny Sintra, Portugal – an insanely romantic, storybook setting in the hills below a gleaming, ornate palace tucked amid the pink rooftops. Lord Byron, in 1809, described Sintra, the summer home to the Kings of Portugal, as the world's most beautiful city. I was sure to tell her that she was, by toasting her with port, during my visits.

A representative of the Societe des Bains de Mer – essentially the Monaco tourism authority – once took me inside the stately Monte Carlo Casino a few hours before its late afternoon daily opening for a tour. A casino official brought out a rack of gaming chips so we could stage an authentic photo shoot for the magazine story I was writing, ala 007 James Bond in a white dinner jacket, at the Baccarat table. *Was this really happening to me?*, I wondered to myself. It was.

I loved sitting outside Mabel's Lobster Claw, a simple restaurant frequented by former President George H.W. Bush, after a satiating lunch of a lobster roll and blueberry pie, in the northeastern seaboard village of Kennebunkport, Maine. My room at the nearby Cape Arundel Inn provided a picturesque view of Walker's Point, where two First Families have frolicked on Bush's famed speedboat, Fidelity IV.

I've covered seven Space Shuttle launches from inside the Kennedy Space Center in Cape Canaveral, Florida. I stood as close to the launch pad as any civilian is allowed to watch from – right there next to the big clock across the pond you see on television.

It seemed that all of Glasgow had boarded trains and buses to come to the soccer stadium at Parkland Ground in order to see the Scottish National team take on Lithuania. Thousands of fans welled up with emotion while singing their anthem, The *Flower of Scotland*, and then, at half-time, they crooned along with the Scottish pop band "The Proclaimers" then they performed their hit *I'm Gonna Be (500 Miles)* on the field below. I have a "when in Rome" policy, so I had a meat pie and placed a bet on the game, both from the same window at the concession booth under the grandstand!

Was I really standing atop the landmark Sydney Harbor Bridge looking *down* at the white, billowing roof of the world famous Opera House only hours after taking a two-day, sleeper car train trip across the Australian Outback?

It was hard to believe I was, in my sandals, walking in the footsteps of Jesus Christ through the Old City of Jerusalem, in Israel, where the most important symbols of the world's three major religious are virtually adjacent to each other inside the walls.

I stood at the top of the iconic seven-star Burj Al Arab Hotel, shaped like a massive sailboat, on the Dubai beaches of the Arabian Sea in the Persian Gulf. Later that day, after being driven over the desert dunes to lunch in Oman, I met an Italian couple on holiday. He was a police detective in Rome and she was a movie star in Italy, and had been in some films with her friend Claudia Gerini, essentially the Pamela Anderson of Italy, who played, among other things, Pontius Pilate's wife in Mel Gibson's *Passion of the Christ*.

"Claudia Gerini," I exclaimed, even though the actress spoke no English. Then I pointed to my heart and hit my chest with my open hand. "Claudia Gerini make my heart go 'boom, boom, boom!'"

"No, no, no," she said shaking her head and wagging her finger. "Claudia Gerini il diavolo di amore!"

I looked at her blankly, but I could see in her expressive eyes and the grasping motion of her hands she wanted me to understand her.

"Claudia Gerini…sex devil!" she blurted out.

"Ah," I said nodded emphatically and thumping my chest with my hand again, "Claudia Gerini diavolo di amore! BOOM, BOOM, BOOM!"

My next two bucket list trips, if given the opportunity, will be to experience the stylish architecture, classic cars, and Cuban cigars in Havana. My friend Catrine Medewar, jeweler to the stars, has also promised to take me to Beirut, Lebanon – once considered the "Paris of the Middle East."

A can-do love for travel makes it all so.

I never expected to be in these places, or in these situations. But when it came time to leave, I did so with a bittersweet sense of melancholy. I would love to do it all over again. Of course, as in any romantic relationship, I can only remanufacture the golden, spontaneous moments in my mind, but returning to places I've visited feels like going back in time.

In most cases when you are nostalgic for something, you are actually nostalgic for the "you" you were at the time it happened. Who were you then? How did you feel? What was important then?

If I stand in a certain, memorable, unchanged spot, it is as if I can almost have a nostalgic visit with the "self" I was long ago. It's a spirit that will always linger and will always call me back, even if only for a moment, because, after all, there are other places in this big world with which to fall in love.

FEAR AND PARENTING
IN LAS VEGAS

"Vegas?!" his mother shouted "Are you crazy? That's no place for you to take my son!"

No place embodies the ultimate father and son trip like Las Vegas! …Except when your son is eight years-old.

Nonplussed, little Harrison and I winged it to Sin City for a long weekend. After all, I had heard about how Las Vegas has made efforts to become family friendly, so I figured we could play golf and splash around in the swimming pool all day, and then take in the lights of the Strip by night. What kid wouldn't be wowed by the white tigers and colorful, fiery exploding volcano at The Mirage?

Now before you consider phoning child protective services to report me, you should know that I never gambled once on the trip. And we didn't even stay at a casino hotel on the Strip. But the glitz and glamour began immediately when Harrison wanted his photo taken with the limo driver holding the sign with his name on it at McCarran Airport.

And you should have seen the look on the young man's face when we were led into the giant two-bedroom sweeping suite at the J.W. Marriott in Summerlin. One push of a button opened the automatic drapes and revealed a 180-degree panoramic view of the Strip, behind the patio hedges, six miles below. The hotel management and public relations team, Jamie Land and Lisa Roughley, had left a welcome tray of nacho chips, beer, root beer, and fancy chocolates, which Harrison dug into. After that it didn't take him long to explore the suite and come back asking me, "Why are there two toilets in each of the bathrooms?"

He giggled his ass off, and so did I, when I explained what a bidet was, and demonstrated with my pants on.

My Vegas scheme was working very well when we rented a cabana for the day in the desert sun beside the J.W.'s massive swimming pool. We played countless games of Marco Polo in the part of the pool which winded under a waterfall and rock cave. Harrison lived large, ordered kiddie daiquiris and smiley face-cut French fries to the cabana, which had soft chaise recliners, a cold water mist machine, and a television. Sleep came easy that night after a sun-splashed day.

By day, we tooled around through the Red Rock Canyon, and played eighteen holes of golf on Pete Dye's fantastic, dramatic Wolf Course at Paiute Golf Club, where the highlight of Harrison's round was an up close inspection of a large lizard on one of the cart paths. On another day we played golf at Angel Park and TPC Canyons too, where we were paired by coincidence with television star John Daly, the host of *Real TV*.

But the lights of Glitter Gulch beckoned, beginning with dinner at the Capital Grill overlooking the new Wynn Hotel. Harrison endured the gourmet dinner well, but with the lights in his eyes. My plan, though dubious, was working. He was enthralled by the pirate show's explosions in front of Treasure Island. Harrison's jaw hit the floor watching the magic show and trapeze acrobats at Circus Circus, which also featured an amusement park with a Sponge Bob Squarepants ride. He won a stuffed animal in the neon glowing arcade at Luxor, or maybe it was Excalibur. He gazed at the lights from high atop the Stratosphere Tower. When his neck craned at the Freemont Street Experience animated light show, I was certain Vegas had been stimulating for Harrison.

Then it happened.

While walking across from Caesar's Palace, Harrison noticed a man walking along the street handing out little fliers. His bright yellow t-shirt had a message emblazoned on it: "GIRLS TO YOUR ROOM – $30."

"Dad," said Harrison, tugging on my arm. "What does it mean: 'Girls to your room $30?'"

"What's that?"

He pointed at the man and repeated, "Girls to your room: $30."

Time seemed to stop. I thought as fast as I could.

"Cleaning ladies," I finally blurted out. "That man is advertising for cleaning ladies. They come and, you know, clean your room."

"Gee," he said, "Can we call my mom? I should tell her about this."

Oh no, I thought to myself.

"Why do you want to tell your mom!?" I asked Harrison.

"Because the lady who cleans our house charges her 75 dollars!"

THE TOO-FRIENDLY SKIES

Noel and Trish LaPorte are a vivacious, colorful couple who own a number of popular bars and restaurants in Michigan, including Dublin Square, East Lansing's Irish Pub, and Los Tres Amigos, a Mexican Restaurant.

Noel is a sharp, very alert, and funny guy who also has a reputation as a super lobbyist in Michigan's state capital. He specializes in gaming, commerce, associations, taxation, transportation, and retail issues.

The vivacious Trish is quite the operator herself, often seen at special events, charity functions, and political meetings.

The LaPortes are wired in everywhere, even Las Vegas, where they're connected at the sophisticated Red Rock Resort and Casino, which is owned, in part, by actor George Clooney. While standing at the back bar in Dublin Square, Noel and Trish told me about their recent trip to the Red Rock in Vegas.

"We were thinking we might run into George Clooney or some of the other celebrities that turn up at the Red Rock," said Trish, then she and Noel recounted a conversation they had after some drinks on the flight to Las Vegas:

"Noel honey, maybe we will see some celebrities."

"It's certainly possible, Trish. I've seen Clooney there before."

"That's so exciting," said Trish, sipping her Sugar Free Red Bull and Rum.

"What celebrity would you really like to see, Trish?"

"More than anyone?"

"Sure, yes."

"Oh, Noel I just don't know what I would do if I saw Brad Pitt! I'd be just beside myself!"

"You're crazy for Brad Pitt, eh?"

Trish tossed her hair and joked, "I might have to leave you for him!"

"Well," Noel answered. "Why don't we make a deal in case it happens?"

"What do you mean?"

"Each of us can select one person that, if we happen to meet in Las Vegas, we're allowed to have a hot night with, no questions asked. What do you think?"

Trish laughed. They both laughed. Then she called his bluff.

"Okay. Okay, I will go for that if that's what you want. One person. We can select one person, Noel."

"Okay, Trish…so who is your one person? Who are you selecting?"

"I'm taking Brad Pitt. You know that. He's mine. Brad Pitt."

"Okay, good," said Noel. "If you happen to run into Brad Pitt in Las Vegas, you can have a night with him."

Trish smiled.

"And what about you, Noel? If I meet Brad Pitt, I can have a night with him. Who can you have a night with if you meet them? Who are you selecting?"

Noel grinned and said, "The first cocktail waitress I see."

Game over!

The moral of the story? Never, ever try to out-bluff a lobbyist!

MAY THE IRISH ROAD
RISE TO MEET YOU

The Irish countryside is a wild and wooly affair, as anyone who has piloted an automobile over its winding roads is fully aware. Unforgiving stone walls line the narrow, bumpy routes, which are often clogged by tractors, bicyclists, and herds of sheep and cattle. The twists and turns of the mountain passages are treacherous, or "lethal enough" as the Irish might say.

Absent of the pervasive directional signs and traffic control devices American motorists have come to rely upon in the United States, the Irish still prefer tricky roundabouts and the occasional arrow pointing toward the next town with a message like *Cahirciveen 9* or *Killorglin 2.5.*

Following a round of golf at the Arnold Palmer-designed Tralee Golf Club in Adfert, Country Kerry, I prepared to settle in for an evening's drive up through the mountains and out onto the Dingle Peninsula. The peninsula is a rocky, cloud enshrouded slice of goat-covered heaven that juts out into the pounding Atlantic Ocean. Dingle is a place where soul inspiring rainbow sightings are commonplace among the Irish-speaking inhabitants.

I'd planned to lodge in Dingle Town, a colorful, remote fishing village known for its pubs and very traditional musical entertainment.

Enchanted with a mandarin twilight and the good fun I'd had on the scenic Tralee golf course, I was feeling quite content and relaxed. I wheeled into a petrol stop, climbed out of the automobile, and approached the attendant, who looked to be passing the time in the doorway of the station.

"Good evening," I began. "I wonder if you might give me directions up to Dingle Town. What is the best route to get there?"

"You're going to Dingle Town, yes?" asked the attendant who eagerly nodded while squinting the setting sun from his eyes. "You need directions?"

"Yes, thank you," I confirmed as I watched him peer down the road. He was paused in thought, obviously considering the routes and options before he answered. I could tell that he looked as if he'd decided on a solution when he nodded his head and once again employed his brogue.

"First of all, if you're really set on going to Dingle Town," he advised, "I wouldn't start from here!"

WE'LL ALWAYS HAVE PARIS

But Paris was a very old city and we were young and nothing was simple there, not even poverty, nor sudden money, nor the moonlight, nor right and wrong, nor the breathing of someone who lay beside you in the moonlight.
— Ernest Hemingway, *"A Moveable Feast"*

It was a warm night in the City of Light. I was covering the Paris Auto Show – Mondial de l'Automobile – and one of the major manufacturers held a reception for executives at the opulent French Automobile Club, which is housed at a prestigious location at the foot of the Champs-Elysees near the French President's residence and the Ritz Hotel. The club occupies 10,000 square-feet of space in a classical, stately building attached to the world class Hotel de Crillon. Commissioned in 1758 by King Louis XV, the Crillon is one of the oldest luxury hotels in the world. Sadly, the Crillon was chosen as the headquarters by the invading German army during the Second World War. On a happier note, it was also the site where the French became the first nation to sign a document officially recognizing the sovereignty of the United States of America.

Staying in the Crillon, which I was, was like living in a sumptuous palace with antique furniture and 17th century tapestries. The price, at over $1,500 per night, is princely, but the auto industry at the time seemed to have deep promotional pockets.

Before we went to the reception at the nearby Automobile Club, my friend Greg Francis and I stopped for a drink in the small, dark piano bar in the hotel. We were sitting at a low, round table enjoying some wine, listening to the piano player, and readying ourselves for a night on the town. My back was to the bar, arm's reach behind me, and I caught a whiff of a freshly-lit cigar. It smelled like a very good one, perhaps a Cuban Cohiba, so I turned around to try to see the label. It was the smoker, not the cigar though, that drew my attention. Billy Joel, dressed in all black, was sitting alone at the bar with his Cohiba! He had been in the news for attending the fourth wedding of his second wife Christie Brinkley. The singing superstar caught me looking, took a draw on his cigar, and nodded. Just as I gave Joel a casual "hello" back, the piano player stopped playing and left the keyboard for his break. Sensing an opportunity to invite myself to the party, I motioned toward the piano and said to Billy Joel, "Well, how about filling in for a few minutes during his break? You are the 'Piano Man' after all."

Joe's eyes smiled, but his mouth didn't. "That will cost you $100,000," he said.

"Charge it to my room," I joked.

We all had a good laugh, and then left him in peace with his cigar.

This was already a memorable night and something told me it would get even better.

The reception was up on the Automobile Club's third floor. After what happened at the Crillon, I found the reasonably affair to be stuffy and perfunctory, though the champagne was exceptional.

"There's my boss and his wife," Greg said to me. "Let's go say hello. I'd like to introduce you. Remember, be nice." He dragged me over, where I shook hands with the dry fellow and his very plain, stiff wife. From behind her spectacles, she was unsmiling, quiet as a mouse, trying, apparently to behave in an appropriate, dutiful fashion for her rigid husband. Trying to make conversation with these two Americans was pained at best.

While the four of us stood there, Greg and his boss began to speak to each other about a business matter, so the woman and I naturally drifted a few steps away to look out the tall windows into the night. Down below, alight, was Place de la Concorde, a grand, paved square with a towering obelisk in the middle and the Tuileries Gardens to the left.

"What a beautiful view," she said, tugging back the sumptuous draperies.

"Yes, indeed," I said to her. "It's too bad. We're too late now but just think; at one time you could stand in this window and watch the beheadings."

She turned her head slowly toward me with a look of horror and disgust on her face and then drifted away from me.

Greg sensed something had gone horribly wrong, so he swept over and asked me what happened. "Never mind; don't even tell me," Greg relented. "I can tell it's just time to get you out of here."

At last, we were inviting ourselves out of this party and getting back out on the town! Once out the front door and onto the Place de la Concorde, I explained to Greg that, in fact, King Louis XVI, Marie Antoinette, and thousands of others, including 1,300 in one summer month in 1794, had faced the guillotine!

We went below the street to board the Metro and rode the subway train to Pigalle Place, the red light district which is home of the famed Can-Can dancers of the Moulin Rouge cabaret. Picasso once lived in this Montmartre neighborhood, but we were there for the nightlife.

Greg and I slipped into a dark club for a drink. The hostess, oddly, seated us separately at booths on opposite sides of a small dance floor. Before I knew it, a curvy, young, blonde French girl in a flimsy, satin, white mini dress slid into my booth next to me. I looked across the dance floor where Greg was being joined by a sparsely dressed dark haired woman who would, unlike the blonde, would not have finished in the top-50 of the Miss America Pageant.

Once we calmed down, in it was all rather enchanting. The affectionate blonde spoke no English, and I spoke very little French, but we found a way to communicate. It was all very cozy. She drank champagne. The waiter would occasionally come and top off her glass. She'd pretend to understand my English…and my broken French attempts, until she finally got frustrated and she led me onto the dance floor. We were the only two on the floor, and slow dancing very closely, when I heard Greg shout, "Hey, you look like Ted Kennedy out there!"

"Very funny," I said, my necktie all undone and askew.

"You about ready to go?" Greg asked me from his booth.

"Never," I joked, dipping the blonde for emphasis.

Greg subtly gestured toward his companion and frowned. It was time to get him off of the hook. I bid my blonde playmate adieu – Merci, Madamoiselle – and waved for the waiter. "L'addtion, s'il vous plait!" I said, asking for the drink bill. Greg and I stood waiting for the tab near the Maitre d' stand. I was handed the tab, and, after reading it, decided I needed more light, so I held it close to my eyes and squinted, and then slid it under the small lamp on the stand.

"What's the matter?" Greg asked.

"Nothing, it's just that I can't possibly be reading this correctly. Or, my U.S. Dollars to French Francs conversion is way off. Math is not my thing, you know."

"Let me see it," Greg said, taking the bill from my hand. "It's 13,195 francs," he said flatly.

"What does that convert to in U.S. Dollars?"

Greg's eyes looked skyward as he worked the figures. Then he looked me square in the eyes and didn't speak.

"Well?" I asked.

"It converts to $2,500 U.S."

"Very funny."

"No, MPS, I am serious. It's $2,500."

"C'mon," I said, leading Greg over to the short, older French woman near the front door who appeared to be the manager.

"Pardon, Madam," I said. "Uh, mon l'addition grand, uh mon l'addition petite."

"I speak English, as well," she said, cutting me off. "What are you trying to say?"

We then had a small caucus with her, explaining that we'd only had two vodka drinks each, and that the bill couldn't possibly be over 13,000 francs.

"You bought the girls' drinks, too," she explained.

"A little champagne?" I asked with the sound of dubious protest in my voice.

"It was very good champagne," monsieur. "The girls drink very good champagne."

Greg then tried the "we didn't know" plea, which fell on unsympathetic French ears.

"Madam," I said, "surely you must know we did not intend to spend that much money. And the waiter never asked our permission to refill the girls champagne glasses."

"13,195 francs, si vous plait," she said without flinching.

It was at that moment I became a big believer in ESP. Greg and I, without saying a word or even looking at each other, bolted. We both ran for the door, sprinted into the street, and down the steps of the nearest Metro Station we could find. Heaving breathlessly, and without speaking, we left the train at the first stop, and climbed onto a line heading in a totally different direction. I guess we thought we were confusing anyone who might have been chasing us, and throwing them off of our scent, so we rode the train to the far outskirts of town, and then boarded yet another subway train back into the Arc de Triumph area from an opposite direction.

Once we caught our breath, we began laughing like silly schoolchildren at an amusement park.

It wasn't long before we emerged from the subterranean tunnels below and were back again on the big stage of Paris that night. Finding our sea legs and straightening our ties, we strolled down the Champs-Elysees, which was bathed in light and teaming with people walking in stylish shoes.

Our feet were aching from our Olympic sprint in wingtipped, hard soled shoes, so we sat down at a sidewalk table in front of the famed Fouquet's cafe. Founded directly on the most famous avenue in the world, Fouquet's, founded in 1901, has served the likes of Charlie Chaplin, Maurice Chevalier, Winston Churchill, Jackie Kennedy Onasis, Franklin Delano Roosevelt, and Marlene Dietrich…and now, Greg Francis and Michael Patrick Shiels.

"Greg, it's silly for us to sit across from each other. Let's enjoy the view together," I suggested. It wasn't the view of the Arc de Triumph, or the stylish French architecture, or the Eiffel Tower, or even the obelisk way down the street back at the Place de la Concorde. I was talking about the view Fouquet's is known best for – the parade of people watching as the coiffed damsels in haute couture and dapper Dan's stroll, and troll, the glittering street. I turned our twp four-top, sidewalk tables to face the street, and positioned Greg and I next to each other facing the sidewalk and street. I also left two empty chairs on the street side easily accessible in case anyone wished to join us.

Unlike Americans, I find that most French people will happily say "hello" and smile at you when they pass you on the street. The well-dressed women, particularly, seem pleased to be noticed, so when you greet them, nod or even give them a compliment, they most often will give you a knowing, flirty smile back. It's very sophisticated and subtle. They know. You know….and they know you know.

So if Greg and I, with a bottle of Pouilly Fuisse and four glasses on our table, caught the eye of women walking toward us far enough down the sidewalk, we could smile, get smiles back, and by the time they were about to pass our table, we would gesture to invite them to sit down and join us. It was all in good fun. We were inviting them to our party.

Sure, we heard a lot of friendly "No, merci!"

And, "Bonsoir."

But we also met some nice people and chatted pleasantly with them when they paused for a moment without sitting.

Until, that is, three women took us up on our offer around midnight. Suddenly we were like the dog chasing the car who didn't know what to do once he'd caught it! (Which would be an ongoing feeling for the rest of the night!)

The exotic, dark, Nadia, and Zola, from Algeria, and their friend Lattice, from Trinidad and Tobago (the definite third wheel), sat down across from us and sipped the wine we poured for them.

"Bonsoir, Je m'appelle Michael," I said, and then did what I could to introduce Greg.

They stylishly dressed and friendly, but again, spoke almost no English, so the conversation was a challenge. There were, however, lots of smiles, and another bottle of Burgundy vin blanc. All of this happening under the moonlight and violet sky, virtually in the shadow of the majestically lit, Arc de Triumph.

Not wanting the night to end without another good story to tell, I decided to invite myself, and Greg, to the party. I gathered all of the French I could possibly remember.

"Michael je t'aime Nadia," I said pointing to my heart and then toward hers. "Nadia je t'aime Michael?"

Nadia, in black, with intense brown eyes, medium to short black hair, and sharp Middle Eastern features, smiled and nodded.

"Greg ja t'aime Zola," I then said, pointing gesturing toward Greg's heart and then Zola's. "Zola je t'aime Greg?"

Tiny Zola, with a big head of curly brown hair, soft features, full lips, and a clingy pink and black patterned spandex dress, also smiled back and said, "Oui."

"Merci," I said to the ladies, and then I turned to Greg.

"Okay," I said cupping my hands, "Foreign relations are

moving right along. We've just chosen paired off and established that we love each other."

He waved his hand. "They don't know what you're talking about."

"Je t'aime, Greg, is the international language of amour," I said. The girls heard the word "amour" and started giggling. "See?"

"Whatever," Greg said. I considered that a challenge, so I continued trying to conjure up French words.

"Nadia and Zola, go taxi l'hotel le chambre," I suggested pointing at the four of us and then down the street.

Nadia and Zola nodded in the affirmative. "Oui."

"Did you see that Greg? They said 'oui!'"

"Aw, they don't understand what you're saying," he insisted.

"Un minut, si vous plait," I said to Nadia, Zola and Lattice, with a shrug. I then grabbed Greg's mobile phone, rang up the hotel, and asked for the concierge.

"I am a guest at the hotel. Can you translate French to English for me?"

"Certain oui, Monsieur."

I handed the mobile phone to the girls, and they spoke animated French to him for a moment. I listened for the concierge after they handed the phone back.

"You are asking the ladies to come back to your hotel room, yes?"

"Oui. Merci, Monsieur. Au revoir."

I handed Greg his phone. "Looks like they're invited to the party," I said.

So off the five of us went in two taxis back to the hotel, up the elevator and into my room on the concierge level. We all kind of stood awkwardly around or sat on the bed. Lattice sat on one of the only chairs in the room near the window. She seemed to know she had only a supporting role. What to do now?

"Champagne," I said, opening the mini-bar and pouring everyone a bit from the bubbly split bottle. That seemed to help, but the language barrier was hampering this party. "Music! Everyone loves music!"

I grabbed the television remote and searched until I found a music channel.

"MTV!" Zola exclaimed.

Nadia smiled. Lattice was expressionless, looking out the window. Greg was looking antsy. It was nearly 2 a.m.

On the television, MTV was playing music and showing runway models walking up and down a stage showing off fashions. The ladies seemed very interested in it.

"Zola...runway!" I suggested, waving my arm backwards and forwards to suggest the narrow passage between the two beds was a makeshift runway. She smiled and leapt up, walking between the beds like a model, priming her hair, twisting, smiling and posing. We all laughed and gave her applause.

"Nadia...runway!" I said, again motioning. Nadia, too, enjoyed the silliness of pretending to be one of the models.

Suddenly a random French word came to mind which I thought could be useful at this moment: "sans"...which translates to mean "without."

The music was playing, the models walking on the television, and the champagne still flowing, when I shouted out, "Zola, runway, *sans top!*" and tugged on my own shirt. The ladies giggled. When Zola reached down to tug her one-piece mini dress over her head, Greg jumped up.

"Hookay, I am outta here," he pronounced.

"What are you crazy, Greg You're going to leave me here with this party getting started?"

"It's late," he said, heading for the door. "We have an early appointment tomorrow at the automobile parade, don't forget."

By the time Greg's hand reached the doorknob to leave, Zola's little hand touched his shoulder. Startled, he turned around.

"I go...you. We go," she said pointing at him and the hallway. The next sound I heard was the door shutting. They were off to the privacy of Greg's room on another floor.

With Zola gone, Nadia looked at me seductively.

"Un minut. Pardon moi," I said, holding up one finger and slipping into the bathroom. I checked my hair, freshened up a bit, dab of cologne under each ear, and reentered the room. I was reaching for my champagne glass when my "Spidey sense" went off. Some of the incidental items in the room seemed out of place. I am a very tidy traveler, so it was easy for me to spot anything amiss.

Nadia then excused herself to go to the bathroom. She was in there for some time. I looked at Lattice, who stared at the television, expressionless.

Nadia then called me into the bathroom. Again, I noticed my dop kit in a different spot than I left it. The towels were moved around.

Nadia, apparently, didn't take into account that, though I may have been exuberant, I was still a savvy traveler. I had quickly, without anyone seeing me, locked my wallet, passport, and wristwatch in the closet safe as soon as we all got into the room.

Now, looking at Nadia in the bathroom, I felt a very "James Bond 007" kind of satisfaction over this Chess game. After all, I'd outsmarted treacherous gypsies who seduced me and were now clearly intent on robbing me.

It was time Nadia, the dark, mysterious beauty, and I had a tete-a-tete.

She leaned against the counter with a serious, pleading expression with her brown eyes. Then she managed to express to me that she needed taxi money for the three girls to get home.

"Can you give francs?" she asked me.

I stared at her and squinted.

"Oui," I said. I made them both stand outside the room in the hallway while I retrieved just enough francs for a short cab ride. I gave Nadia the money, and with that, she and Lattice went down the hallway toward the elevator.

I went to the phone and dialed Greg's room.

"I can't talk right now," Greg said. "Zola got sick. She's been barfing up champagne. Hang on…someone's at the door. Hey, I've got to go. Nadia and Lattice are here to take her home. I want to get her out of here. I'll call you in a little bit."

With that, before I could say anything, Greg hung up the phone.

I shrugged, undressed, put on a white hotel robe, and collapsed on the bed.

Ten minutes later I was awakened by the phone. It was Greg.

"Okay, they're all gone," he said.

I scratched my head and yawned. "Why don't we have breakfast and review the evening's events," I said, as the morning's first light was just barely coming through the window at 5:30 a.m. "I will call room service and order it for two to my room. Meet me here."

Greg agreed but reminded me that I'd have to come to his floor and get him because I was on the concierge floor – a room key was needed for the elevator to access my floor. I told him I was on my way. Since it was so early, and I figured the hotel would be quiet, I slipped out into the hallway and over to the elevator in my robe and slippers. I had a big surprise when the elevator doors opened, though. A family of tourists, with three small children, and their luggage were on the elevator. I figured they must have just arrived on the overnight flight from New York and were going up to their room.

"Bon jour!"

I nodded, smiled, and sheepishly squeezed into the elevator, stinking of booze and perfume, and stared straight ahead.

The doors opened and I quickly stepped out to where Greg was waiting for me in the hallway. He took one look at me in my robe and said, "Look at you! Who the hell do you think you are, Frank Sinatra!?"

"Shaddap Dago," I said, pushing the elevator button so we could get back to my room. We found breakfast awaiting us, and sat across from each other at the table in the room next to the east-facing window, eating croissants and drinking tea.

"Well, they were wolves in sheep's clothing I guess." I said.

"What do you mean?"

"They were mutton dressed as lamb. Beautiful, but dangerous. Thieving gypsies."

Greg insisted he didn't know what I meant. And I explained to him my account of how they'd tried to clean out my cash and valuables.

He started laughing at me and put down his tea cup.

"Well, those girls must have seen you as an easy mark, I guess. My Zola had nothing to do with that. She truly liked me."

"What happened with her, anyway?" I asked, while putting jam on a croissant.

"She held my hand in the elevator, walked her little self in front of me all the way to my room. We talked for a little while and the next thing I knew, she got into bed."

"She didn't ask you to take a shower?

"No."

"I see. It wasn't like that up here."

"I know, because Zola was really into me. She wasn't like the other two. She was sweet. But right then she got bed-spins, I think, because she leaned over and looked as if she were about to start barfing up champagne over the side."

"She did drink a lot for being such a tiny, young girl."

"I sat patiently with her to see if she would be okay, then she went into the bathroom. Right about then the other girls came, thank goodness, to help her. They gathered her things and her clothes and took her away."

I nodded, and finished my croissant. Greg and I toasted each other with our tea cups to salute having an interesting night in Paris and making it to sunrise. He left and went back to his room. I closed the drapes, and fell into bed.

Within a moment, a ring of the bedside phone awakened me.

"Hello?"

"It's Greg. I'm back in my room," he said, in a tone that was both staccato and glum. "Yeah…it looks like they got me for 500 francs."

I hung up the phone and laughed myself to sleep.

The following night, during a much more mellow early evening, Greg and I were strolling way across town near the Seine on the Left Bank, in the quiet Saint-Germain-des-Pres area. We passed a serious, professional looking woman in a tan trench coat as we turned a corner. We said a polite hello, as did she, but then she stopped.

"Excuse me. You two," she said, speaking English with a French accent, "you are Americans, yes?"

"Oui, Madame," I answered.

She looked us in the eye, up and down, and squinted before slowly nodding her head. We got chills when we heard her next question. "Wasn't it you two I happened to see last night very late on the Champs Elysees?"

"We were there last night, yes," Greg said.

"I thought so," she said. "I saw you. I would advise you two to be much more careful with the company you keep."

She didn't smile, but she politely bid us "adieu" and continued on her way into the Paris night.

DANCE FEVER AND ISLAND FEVER ON MACKINAC

It was late in Horn's Bar, a popular saloon on quaint Mackinac Island, Michigan. I had worked my way down into town from a political/business conference at historic Grand Hotel to catch some of the nightlife.

There was a band playing rock music on the small stage near the front of the bar, and a big group of people were dancing.

I decided to invite myself to the party.

I walked up on to the dance floor, slipped into the middle of the crowd, and started dancing. Very soon, a cute, sexy young girl danced over my way, right next to me, and smiled at me. I kept dancing, and smiled back at her. This was getting really good, I thought.

Then she danced a little closer to me, leaned in, and looked into my eyes.

"What're you doing?" she asked, speaking up so her voice could be heard over the music.

"What?"

"What are you doing?" she asked again, looking in my eyes and still grooving.

"Dancing," I answered.

"Are you sure?"

Then she giggled and danced away.

Ouch!

INSIDE THE GATES OF EXCLUSIVE BEL-AIR

Frank Chirkinian was the most innovative director in the history of televised sports. He was about to retire from a long run at CBS, and I knew he'd have a great book in him. I wanted to collaborate with him if he decided to write a book, so I invited myself to the party by contacting him and courting him.

Chirkinian invited me to discuss the matter with him at his home in Bel-Air, California. He asked me to meet him at ten thirty in the morning at the prestigious Bel-Air Country Club. I pulled up in the cobblestone driveway and gave the valet attendant the keys to my tiny rental car. He parked it amongst the Bentleys, Porsches, and Jaguars. Upon entering the club, I was shown to the famous round table near the windows in the corner of the clubhouse overlooking the swinging bridge and the canyon and course below.

Chirkinian, wearing a lavender cashmere sweater and Italian loafers, welcomed me, and we sat at the round table chatting about the concept of a book and a potential deal. As we talked, one by one, Bel-Air members came off the golf course and greeted Frank. Some of them sat down at the big round table.

Though I was focused on Chirkinian, I noticed that suddenly I was surrounded by the some very famous and powerful people, including ABC sportscaster Al Michaels, who in addition to hosting *Monday Night Football,* made the famous "Do you believe in miracles…yes!" call of the U.S. Olympic hockey team upsetting the Soviets in the 1980 games at Lake Placid. Next to Michaels sat the singer-songwriter Mac Davis, who'd had hits with *Baby Don't Get Hooked On Me,* and *Lord, It's Hard To Be Humble.* Davis also did some acting, co-starring with Burt Reynolds in North Dallas Forty.

Davis was wearing a white golf visor, with the letters "O T F I G" emblazoned on it. I had never heard of a company called "OTFIG," so I couldn't resist inviting myself into the conversation.

"What is 'OTFIG?'"

"'O-T-F-I-G' describes my golf swing," he answered. "It stands for *'Over The Top…Fuck, It's Gone!'*"

ISTANBUL NOT CONSTANTINOPLE...
TURKISH DELIGHT!

During my visit to exotic, intriguing Istanbul, Turkey, I decided to invite myself to the party with some locals. I found myself posing questions to Turks when I felt the situation was right. When I found someone who could speak English, I made conversation.

"Who do you think is the most famous American?" I asked.

"Bill Gates," was one of the answers I received.

"Bill Clinton," was another reply I often heard. One fellow even mentioned Tiger Woods, even though there are only eight golf courses in all of Turkey.

The most interesting exchange came while sipping Turkish coffee at a café and smoking apple-flavored tobacco from an ornate nargile water pipe. A young Turk next to me named Paul Wolfowicz, the former Deputy Defense Secretary who was heading the World Bank, as the most famous American. Hearing that answer, I wondered how many Americans had even heard of the bureaucrat?

I felt the Turk's answer gave me the opportunity to talk more about politics, so I asked him about then President George Bush. He shook his head and, at first, hesitated to say anything. But after I encouraged him to talk more, he said, "I know that Bush and Condoleezza Rice are not evil people. They have families and children, so I know they're not evil," he said. "The evil ones are the men who run the oil companies: BP, Texaco, Exxon. They're the evil ones!"

Curiously, while emerging from a tour of Topkapi Palace, I encountered a line of at least 150 Turkish school children waiting in line to enter. It was probably my clothes, or maybe my accent, but the students, who were probably ten to twelve years-old, began smiling, waving, reaching out, and shouting to me in excitement as I passed. I felt like the President or a rock star, working the rope line and shaking hands.

"I know all about America," some of them insisted. They recited the names of states, mentioned cowboys and told me their own names!

The Bosphorous River divides Istanbul, placing half of the city in Europe and half of it in Asia. From a commercial plaza full of kiosks and shops near the Kempinski, I boarded an inexpensive, busy ferry and crossed the river, then walked all the way down the river and boarded a boat to Maiden's Tower, a twinkling, lighthouse-like fortress on a small island in the middle of the river dating back to 408 B.C. Maiden's Tower, which was featured in the James Bond movie *The World is Not Enough*, now houses a café and observation deck. I felt like I was in a 007 movie!

And while I clearly was in a somewhat unusual environment, at no time did I feel threatened or uncomfortable...despite recent anti-American poll results.

LURKING IN KEY BISCAYNE

It was an idyllic Sunday morning on Key Biscayne, Florida. My brother Robert Shiels (it's always good to take golf trips with your own meteorologist) and I were walking a very natural section of beach in the state park near the Cape Florida lighthouse. The windless morning was sunny and clear. Though the sparse European sunbathers were topless near the sea grass dunes, we could more easily see the stilt houses built off shore on aquamarine water that was as flat as glass.

To cool off, we varied our route into the water, plodding slowly at almost waist-high level. Talk about relaxing. As if on cue, two-foot long, skinny silver pencil fish, a pair at a time, swimming parallel to the shoreline, began playfully jumping out of the water in joyful, graceful arcs as the sped along.

Sounds peaceful, right?

About a week later I was sitting at an oceanfront tiki bar on the Galt Ocean Mile in Fort Lauderdale. When I overheard a fellow near me say he was a fisherman, I invited myself to the party and asked him a few questions while I finished my Corona. I told him the story about the Sunday morning at Key Biscayne because I wanted to know what kind of fish those silver darting fliers that were skimming along were.

"You say they were jumping out of the water right beside you?" he asked.

"Yes, it was really neat."

He looked at me, and took a swig of his Red Stripe. "Do you know why fish jump out of the water?"

"No," I said. "Why?"

"…Because something is chasing them."

I gulped. "What chases a fish that is two-feet long?"

The fisherman grinned ominously at me.

Suddenly my memory of that idyllic morning was tarnished as I could just about hear the theme from the movie *Jaws* playing in my head!

LAUNDERING FRENCH MONEY
IN NAPA VALLEY

It wasn't easy, but I scored a lunch reservation for two at Chef Thomas Keller's world renowned French Laundry restaurant in the Yountville area of Napa Valley, California.

Getting a reservation at French Laundry is nearly impossible. The reservation phone line opens on a certain day in September, and within forty eight hours, the entire year of lunch and dinner reservations for this organic, gourmet opus is sold out. I can't say how, and it took three-month's notice, but I got myself invited to the party.

The exterior of the little restaurant, a turn of the century stone building, is quaint and understated, with ivy and creeping roses covering a trellis as you pass through a small courtyard to the door. Once inside, the plain, white tablecloths sit in plain rooms with no artwork on the walls, plants or flowers. Chef Keller wants nothing to distract from the presentation, aroma, or taste of his food.

Sitting down at the table felt like a privilege. A waiter brought the menu.

"Would you like to start with a glass of champagne?" he asked.

"What a fine idea. We're celebrating being at what some consider America's finest restaurant," I said.

Two glasses of French bubbly were on their way…all the way from Reims to our table. Examining the wine list, I noticed the Brut in the slender glasses on the waiter's tray were $44 each. I gulped.

Naturally, in a gastronomic experience such as this, each course should be paired with a wine. At $20-$30 per-glass and nine courses on the way, the meter was running, and I was about to become a teetotaler! Then I noticed the prix fixe price for the Chef's Tasting Menu was $250 per-person, not including wine.

I am quite certain, at that moment, when I could virtually feel the blood rushing out of me, that I turned as white as the linen tablecloth.

The three-hour lunch went on, though – a ceaseless stampede of tiny, artsy food items on large plates:

Cauliflower Panna Cotta

Moulard Duck "Foie Gras Au Torchon"

Pacific Kahala "Amandine"

Maine Lobster Tail "Pochee Au Beurre Doux"

"Aiguillette" of Liberty Farm Duck

Bouillon-Poached Elysian Fields Farm Lamb Rib Eye

(The Japanese Wagyu Sirloin required a $100 supplement)

"Chaput Grand Foin"

Persian Lime Sorbet

…and, for dessert, "S'mores"

Or

"Charlotte Aux Poires Et Aux Dates"

…I chose the S'mores.

The total bill? …A house payment, a flight to Europe…or lunch at French Laundry.

KOREAN CAR BOMB

Jeju Island is a resort destination below the Korean peninsula. There I was...on the veranda of Nine Bridges Golf Club, following a round at the brand new course on the island. The club was ultra-exclusive, with a $500,000 membership fee. So fancy were the various buildings and adjacent villas that all of the service elements were below ground and connected by tunnels, so none of the members or guests ever saw a kitchen, or an office, or any rubbish whatsoever. Instead of a halfway house, the golf course had two elaborate stone buildings after each six holes so golfers could sit and enjoy invigorating fruit drinks, Soju whiskey, sushi or even shark fin soup.

Fellow golf writer Evan Rothman and I had just had the honor of playing golf with the club president – a Korean man they affectionately called "Georgie." On one of the seventh green, we noticed a large, tarantula-like spider walking across the green. Georgie, nonplussed but with little hesitation, walked over to the spider and stood over it. Then he pulled his divot-repair tool from his pocket, and, like a Ninja Warrior throwing a Chinese star, whipped the divot tool down with a quick flick of his wrist. The pointy tines of the tool went right through the center of the spider!

Evan and I, standing next to each other, went slack-jawed at the impressive, deadly accurate feat! We watched as Georgie then picked up the tool and turned it upside down at eye level to examine the spider – it's eight legs wiggling like crazy.

I grabbed Evan by the arm in horror. "He's not going to eat it, is he!?"

Georgie flung the wounded spider into the nearby jungle of trees, and we played on.

Evan left Georgie and me with the American public relations woman, Ann Victor, on the veranda following the round. Georgie's English was very broken, but we managed to communicate. We were having drinks, and I was feeling very internationally cosmopolitan learning about Korean culture and geopolitical policy issues. Once again I felt like "Bond, James Bond," right?

Georgie changed the topic and asked me in his growl of a voice, "You…shower?"

"What's that?" I asked in return?

"You shower?"

"Yes, I shower."

"You….shower with me!" he exclaimed.

I froze. And I looked at Ann Victor, the American PR woman who'd brought me there as a journalist.

"Ann," I said, "There must be something lost in translation?"

"We go," Georgie said, pointing at the clubhouse "Shower!"

"Ann?" I said, as he led me away from the table. I was trying to play it cool, but it seemed so bizarre!

"You should be honored," she said. "He wants to show you the club."

Up the marble steps we went and, once in the door, instead of turning toward the locker rooms, we turned left, through a special door. Based on what I began to observe, Nine Bridges Golf Club had two locker room areas: a smaller one for guests; and an elaborate, expansive private one for its executive members.

I tried to remain sophisticated, but I kept my eyes closely on Georgie because no one else was around at this exclusive enclave. The next thing I knew, Georgie and I passed through the locker room facilities, where he'd handed me a tiny Korean bath towel, which looked like a Michigan face cloth! I tried to cover up with my fig leaf of a towel. It looked silly when we moved, without clothing, to a large, peaceful atrium with three, large square Jacuzzi tubs cut into the slate floor. I hopped in below the water level as fast as I could, then George climbed in. I stayed on the far side of the Jacuzzi.

"George," I said, trying to send a definite signal, "I notice you have an all-female caddie corps here. They are all sweet and gorgeous. And cute, too, carrying their 'Hello Kitty' handbags."

I am completely uncertain as to whether Georgie understood anything I said, since he merely threw his head back and laughed and smiled.

"Do you know 'man's gold?" he asked.

"Man's gold?"

"Yes, man's gold what is?"

I shrugged.

He then tried to explain to me how Korean men stand in cold streams first thing in the morning and dip their testicles into the water for virility! Then he displayed how!

In the end, Georgie was just enthusiastic about showing his club to an American. Many of the others were startled to hear he took me into the private side of the club, as this was a rare occurrence. He was proud, and, I suppose I amused him, so he brought me into the club's inner circle. Though I was initially nervous as a cat, and unfamiliar with this custom, I accepted his invitation to the party.

INSTANTLY ELDERLY

Crested Butte Ski Resort is a forty-five-minute flight from Denver, Colorado. But it is at considerably higher elevation. The authentic Western town and mountain, is known for its double-black diamond terrain and it's remote, casual vibe – as opposed to the glitterati and Cartier crowd in Aspen, which is a million miles away figuratively, but geographically only twelve miles away, as the crow flies over the mountain ridge. It sounded like a party – and so I invited myself.

I had seen a doctor in Michigan a couple of days before my trip to Crested Butte, because I was battling bronchitis. He'd prescribed some medication, and off I went to Colorado, thinking some time off and fresh mountain air would be good for me.

My first hint of trouble that evening should have been when, after the bus ride up from the airport in nearby Gunnison, I arrived at my swank, slope-side hotel, which was named Elevation. The hotel had that name for a very good reason: Elevation, and the Crested Butte ski resort's base, sat at the highest elevation of any ski facility in the United States.

After a sleepless first night, loss of appetite, and absence of any strength whatsoever, I begged off breakfast and skiing to see if I'd feel better in time for the after lunch ski session. All day, I sat in my room, looking out the window at the majestic mountain, whereupon my friends were schussing through what looked to be fantastic snow conditions on a chamber of commerce day. Meanwhile, I was the Prisoner of Azkaban in my elegant room. To look away, I watched news programs on the flat screen TV and dozed in and out of restless sleep and trips to the bathroom, every step of which winded me.

At some stage, I came to realize that Bronchitis and the thin air at 9,400 feet of elevation probably didn't go well together, so I called the resort's doctor.

"Some people die from altitude sickness," he said. "This is a serious matter."

So while everyone else was enjoying some nightlife and a gourmet dinner in the gorgeous hotel's 9380 (elev.) restaurant, and looking forward to another day of skiing, I was driven forty five minutes back town to Gunnison, which was about 1,500 lower in elevation. On doctor's orders, I was checked in to a desperately tired, standard Days Inn next door to the Gunnison Hospital. A nurse met me in my handicapped access room and hooked me up to an oxygen machine. I spent the night on oxygen, television clicker in hand, aghast at my condition, and embarrassed.

"I have bronchitis, not altitude sickness," I told everyone, not wanting to seem wimpy or unable to handle ski conditions. Skiing is a macho sport for the vibrant and virulent, after all. I was only forty two years old, and had skied in the mountains – Big Sky, Beaver Creek, and Breckenridge – plenty.

The next morning came an even worse indignity. I was feeling better having had my night of oxygen at a lower elevation, but I had left my luggage and ski gear up at Crested Butte. I'd have to go back up there to get it, and spend one more night before departing back to Michigan. I was instructed to take the daily free shuttle bus from town to the resort, which left at ten a.m. from a designated spot very near the Days Inn.

I went to the spot, rolling my oxygen machine along with me. Standing in the cold, bright Saturday morning at the pick-up spot, a crowd began to assemble. It seemed the entire teenage population of Gunnison, with their snowboards and wild, colorful hats and scarves, were assembling to get on this bus. When the bus did arrive, these kids all steps aside to let me roll my oxygen machine onto the bus! They even helped me lift it.

"No, no, no," I wanted to scream! "I am not some poor, old, feeble man on oxygen! I just had bronchitis!"

But I sat there, in the seat they insisted I take while many of them stood, chagrined.

And suddenly very, very elderly.

SNAKES ON AN ICE BREAKER

I keep a rubber snake in my golf bag. Why? To break the ice, of course! And invite someone to the party!

Often when playing golf you might find yourself paired with a stranger. Or you might be playing corporate golf with a client or paired with someone in a charity event.

Sometimes a little comic relief...a little ice-breaker...is needed.

The snake, while only the thickness of a pencil and not very long, looks very, very real. If the wind blows, or with any nearby vibration, the rubber head bobs a little bit. So, when my cart partner or someone in the other power cart is away from their seat playing a shot or putting, I slyly drop the rubber snake on the floor of the cart where the victim's feet naturally rest. It's not meant to be mean, but when the unsuspecting victim returns to the cart, they typically are on top of the snake before they notice it – with hilarious results that erase any snobby pretention or stiffness.

Greg Johnson is the long time sports writer and columnist for the *Grand Rapids Press*. I was playing golf with Johnson and golf promoter Tim Hygh at Boyne Mountain's Monument Course one summer, and, coming down the watery eighteenth hole, I decided to play the joke on Greg. After slipping the snake into his cart, I noticed him across the fairway poking around for balls along the edge of the water hazard. This was absolute icing on the cake.

"Greg," I called out to him. "You'd better watch it. There are snakes around here."

"Yeah, yeah," he said, waving me off without looking up.

Well, moments later, when Greg Johnson climbed into his cart and the snake caught his eye, he got absolutely airborne in his attempt to escape from the rubber serpent!

On a press trip to Colorado, a few of us were playing the Greg Norman course at Red Sky Ranch with resort promoter Pat Peeples, a very nice lady who displayed her extreme phobia of snakes by screeching, diving from her cart, and rolling around on the ground in shock and embarrassment when her toe touched the slithery reptile.

"What kind of people are you?" she howled in a combination of tears and laughter. She was a great sport. "Oh my God what kind of people are you!?"

To put icing on the cake, I took digital photographs of this display, which, upon arriving home, I printed and mailed to her in a thank you card.

Do you think Pat Peeples will ever forget us?

I know she won't.

Tom Weibel, an attorney from Grand Rapids, was clinging to a cup of coffee on a frosty fairway at the Golf Club of Georgia one cold morning until the snake startled him and sent the Styrofoam skyward! Weibel had to duck from under a fifteen-foot shower of coffee when the cup came down!

The snake, or any choice of ice-breaker, is not always appropriate, though. You've really got to know your audience. I had the opportunity to play golf with Haley Barbour, the Governor of Mississippi, who had also served as Chairman of the Republican National Committee. We were together in a cart at Dancing Rabbit Golf Resort.

Governor Barbour and I talked amiably between shots as we played the front nine.

"I only really play golf because my wife likes it," he told me. "I was a baseball player, really. I played one year of college baseball."

"Why only one year, Governor?"

"Well, I liked to drink...and I was a Corporal in the Sexual Revolution," he joked.

At some point during the front-nine, Governor Barbour told me about his close relationship with President Ronald Reagan.

"Reagan loved 'dick jokes,'" he told me. "Every time the President would spot me at an event, he'd call me over and ask me to tell him a dick joke."

We had good fun, and I knew the Governor was a good sport, but I didn't dare use the snake trick on him. Besides, he didn't need any loosening up. He was a good ol' southern boy.

The Governor was along to show off his home state to a few golf writers from across America, so, in the cart behind us, was golf writer Anne McAndrews, from California, and Janet Leach, who headed up Mississippi's State Tourism Authority.

Somewhere in the ninth fairway, I dropped the snake into their cart. Neither of the women immediately noticed it, but when we pulled up beside the ninth green, I alerted the Governor to turn back to look at their cart, which had parked behind us. Just as he did, Leach spotted the snake, shrieked and, in her attempt to evacuate the cart, tripped and fell backwards into a huge hedge beside the cart path! Her shriek and the commotion caused two of the Governor's security officers to come sprinting down from the clubhouse with, shall we say, heightened concern. The graceful Leach was stuck in the hedge like an upside down turtle before we all helped her out. I felt a little badly about that and for causing the security team a fright. It wasn't until later that even after a scotch or two with the Governor that I felt comfortable laughing about it.

You've got to be careful with your cultures, too. The all-female caddy corps in their pink uniforms I encountered at the golf club in Pattaya, Thailand, scattered from the bag drop, screamed, and made a funny scene. But the ladies did not think it was humorous and were not at all charmed by my trick since there were, indeed, very poisonous, deadly snakes in the jungles bordering the course.

The Thai caddies got their chance to laugh at me too, though, midway through our round. After a nine-hole walk over tumbling terrain in extreme humidity, we reached the half-way house: a tiny, tented gazebo with Coca Colas, Singha beer, water and fruit. Beer was out of the question in that heat, so I drank a bottle of water, poured another one over my head. My blue golf shirt was already soaked through anyway. I also bought a banana to rebuild my perspired potassium, and as we walked toward the tenth tee, I noticed a monkey playing under a tree along the vegetation about twenty yards away from me. Every cartoon in the world teaches you that monkeys like bananas, so I unpeeled the banana and broke a little piece off of the top, which I waved at the monkey and whistled to get his attention as I walked toward the little, brown guy.

I got his attention, and he moved carefully toward me. Suddenly, though, I noticed the leaves of the thick vegetation starting to rustle violently, even though there was no wind. I found out why when, frozen in my tracks, I saw what seemed like forty monkeys broke through the trees and started brazenly making their way toward me and my banana! Though I was exhausted, I involuntarily turned and ran, which only excited the pack of monkeys and incited them to give full on chase! I came to my senses when I realized I was not going to outrun this platoon of baboons, so I, like a Detroit Lions quarterback being blitzed on a screen pass, wheeled around without stopping running and threw the banana as far as I could in the opposite direction back toward the trees. Like a biblical swarm of locusts, the monkeys answered my prayers when they all turned in unison and thundered on toward the far flung fruit!

I noticed the caddies trying not to giggle, so when I smiled at them and waved my arms the four darling ladies broke into a full chorus of rousing laughter.

THAI ME UP WITH YOUR TIE, TY?

…While we are on the subject of subject of Thailand, as a member of the Society of American Travel Writers, I have to tell you that if you get a chance to go to Thailand, invite yourself to the party and go. That's what I did, even though Thailand was a place I knew nothing about and had no plan or desire to travel to.

I met Diana Moxon when she was public relations director for the historic Langham Hotel across the street from BBC headquarters in London. When she left London to work at the Anantara Resort and Spa, in Hua Hin, Thailand, I thought I would never see her again…until an invitation from her appeared in the mail asking me if I would like to be a guest of the resort and be flown to southeast Asia by the Thailand Tourism Authority in order to cover the Inaugural King's Cup Elephant Polo Tournament? She promised the King of Thailand would be there.

Now this sounded like a party…and I was invited! It ended up being my first of two visits to Thailand. Both visits were pure adventure! The international teams were sponsored by up-market champagne, scotch and beer companies, along with automakers and banks. In between matches some of the elephants performed tricks such as painting and playing the drums. During the competition, a *mahout* rides atop the elephant and guides him while the player, also on top, uses his mallet to move the ball.

Elephants, some faster than others, may not lie down in front of the goal or pick the ball up with their trunks. The official rules state: *"Sugar cane or rice balls packed with vitamins (molasses and rock salt) shall be given to the elephants at the end of each match and a cold beer, or soft drink, to the elephant drivers and not vice versa."*

You will enjoy your trip to Thailand much more if you suspend all of your notions about life and just relax. First off, your body clock will be seriously thrown out of whack by the eighteen hours of flying required to get to Bangkok, plus three hours or more of travel outside the city, which is essential if you want to truly experience Thailand, or Siam, if you prefer. Bangkok is a big, busy, frantic city that can make you feel claustrophobic.

Hua Hin, site of the King's Cup Polo, is also the King's home city, so it is peaceful with beach resorts along the Gulf of Thailand, shopping, golf and dining. It's a three-hour drive south and to the west of Bangkok.

A similar drive to the south and to the east of Bangkok, on the other side of the Gulf, is Pattaya, which similarly, has beaches, shopping, golf and dining, but is bigger with wilder nightlife.

You are going to view sights which will seem unusual to you, like ornate temples, elephants in the street, and, early in the morning, orange-frocked Buddhist monks canvassing the town. Beware not to tear any Thai currency bearing the King's photo or step on currency which has fallen on the ground. This is considered disrespectful to the His Majesty and is a major, punishable offense. If you're at a bar, you might notice a brass bell in the front with a rope hanging from it. Resist the temptation to pull the rope and ring it – unless you plan to buy the entire bar a drink, which is what the bell signifies. And if someone in Bangkok asks you if you want to see a "Tiger Show," don't expect to see the famous golfer (even though he is partly of Thai descent) and don't expect to be taken to a zoo. Let's just say a Tiger show involves female sexual acrobatics and features projectiles.

You will also find out that Thailand is called "The Land of Smiles" because the peace-loving Thai people and friendly and smile easily. The other marketing slogan for the country is "Mysterious, Sensuous, Thailand." There is good reason for that, too.

My initial visit to Hua Hin was made easier by Moxon, who looked after me, and another Brit, Frank Gilbride, who operates Hua Hin Golf Tours. Richard Catska, an English golf photographer from Hong Kong, whom I had met in South Korea, connected me with Gilbride when he heard I was going to Thailand. When I reached Gilbride by telephone, he told me he'd come to the Anantara Resort at noon to pick me up and give me a tour of Hua Hin. Imagine my surprise when Gilbride showed up to fetch me on a moped! Fourteen hours later, at two a.m., I was returned to the resort in the back of a tuk-tuk: an automotive, three-wheeled rickshaw!

"I came to Thailand on a two week trip but ended up staying forever," Gilbride told me. After our day on the town, I could see why. Whiskey was about four-dollars a bottle. You and your mates could drink all night on a twenty-dollar bill! Hotel rooms in snazzy oceanfront resorts with swimming pools and manicured gardens could be had for seventy dollars a night! A ninety-minute beachfront Thai massage costs five dollars! I picked out the fabrics and was fitted for three suits, three dress shirts, and two pairs of shorts, all custom tailored custom for a grand total of $400! New release bootlegged DVD's of films currently showing in theaters were a dollar. Designed-brand clothing, or knockoffs of the same, abundant and so inexpensive that you could sweat through them one night, throw them away, and buy new duds the next day.

Hua Hin boasted a number of fun open-air bars. If you pull up a stool during the heat and humidity of the day, the bartender will greet you by extending a pair of metal tongs with a small cold, damp face cloth. Very civilized! Many of the bars also featured pool tables and were stocked with bar girls.

Okay, stop right there.

"Bar girls?" you ask. "What do you mean by the term 'bar girl?'"

Well, how can I explain this? Let me give it to you straight. If you thought Las Vegas was a great place for a Bachelor Party, believe it or not it's time for you to recalibrate. The bars in Hua Hun, Pattaya, and Phuket, for that matter, are often all lined up next to each other. Most of them are open to the street, so the area takes on a festival atmosphere. The bar scene is like one giant Hooters restaurant. The girls who hang around the bars are friendly, outgoing and dote on your every word, just like a Hooters waitress. Unlike a Hooters waitress, though, Thai bars girls are on the menu, figuratively. They virtually populate the bars, being playful and friendly, shooting pool, having drinks, and chatting with customers. You would never know they were anything but out for a night until the question comes, "Want to go hotel?"

It's a simple, friendly question that will sound like a tempting invitation. It's an invitation that comes with a price tag, though.

Licensed bar girls (yes, they do carry renewed licenses) ask for a fee of about twenty dollars…and that includes a "wake up call." At that price one could quickly become known in Thailand as "Two Lady Man!"

The odd thing was it was all out in the open, not in some seedy section of town. The custom is acceptable and expected. In fact, Thailand also features snazzy, air conditioned lounges, which have the feel of gleaming, dazzling casinos, except that in front of the room there is a glass covered stage. What's behind the glass? Thirty or so women in evening gowns or various costumes and dresses, each with a number pinned to their dress like beauty queens in a contest. They sit, in rows, looking into the crowd, smiling and nodding. Next to the stage is a telephone… and if a patron is in the mood, he may summon a waiter with the number of his choice. The waiter then lifts the phone to alert the woman. When she hears her number called, the glamour girl smiles with glee at being chosen! She then meets the patron in front of the glass stage and leads him down a hallway of suites where she will fix him a drink, draw a bath for them, and share other pleasantries. How much is that doggie in the window? Thirty dollars.

Did I invite myself to the party in this case?

Thankfully, Gilbride, with a dry sense of humor, gave me play-by-play commentary and analysis of the scene I was observing in the bars, and the Thai Tourism Authority actually took me to the window lounge for a drink, in the interest of journalism.

But after we went back outside to a street side bar, Gilbride let me swim on my own when a particularly stylish and striking bar girl slinked up next to me. She set a game on the bar between us. It was the old Connect Four game with the grid where you drop red or black checkers down the slots in an attempt to line up four of them before your opponent.

I decided to invite myself to the party, since she already had! The gorgeous woman who set the game down had perfectly straight, long, dark-haired and wearing a flashy, tight, red evening dress. She spoke almost no English. I spoke two words of Thai: "Good day" and "thank you," (the very minimum you learn if you travel to a foreign language country, in my opinion.)

The bar girl and I couldn't communicate much at the bar under the dark night sky beyond our smiles and our playing of the Connect Four game. With her perfume filling the air, she defeated me in every game of with deadly efficiency...and always seemed pleased with herself – but not surprised – when she won. And she always gave me a charming look that beckoned: "Try me again?"

It was fun. It was flirty. I was feeling worldly as my "James Bond 007 alter-ego" kicked in. Gilbride watched quietly from his stool behind me.

Sometimes she and I got into a rhythm of dropping the checkers into the slots, and sometimes I would pause, staring into her eyes when it was my turn, and lifting an eyebrow to play up the drama and try to read her strategy. She looked straight back into my eyes, pursing her lips or winking. Though I was enjoying the losing streak, I became intent on winning at least one game of Connect Four.

Whether or not the lady in red let me win is unimportant. The fact is I won, at last. When my winning checker fell into the slot, she stared at the board, squinted, and pretended to be miffed that she'd lost to me. And then she broke into a broad smile and nodded to acknowledge my victory. I smiled back. Romantic, right?

She reached across the game and gently placed her soft hand, with her perfectly polished red fingernails, on my hand. She tossed her dark hair.

"We go hotel?" she asked quietly.

"You'd like me to take you to my hotel room?" I asked.

"Yes," she said, in a seductive tone.

"That would be very nice," I said. "You're very sexy."

She smiled and caressed my hand.

"But let me ask you something first," I continued. "Are you one-hundred percent?"

She tilted her head and tried to smile playfully. But I could see her becoming crestfallen when I insisted on getting an answer.

"One-hundred percent? Or no?" I asked again.

She stared into my eyes for a few seconds, and then, resigned, answered, "Not one-hundred percent."

I shrugged my shoulders, smiled, and removed my hand from under hers so I could extend a parting handshake.

"No hotel. Only one-hundred percent," I said, in a slightly apologetic but definite tone. "Thank you, though, for the games. You're very sweet."

"You worthy opponent," the Thai girl said before nodding and slipping away into the night.

I turned back to Gilbride who had ordered us two more cold Singha beers, which sat on the bar in front of him.

"Jolly good, Shiels," Gilrbide said in his British accent. "But how did you know? I wondered where it was all going. How did you know?"

"No Adams Apple," I answered in a matter-of-fact fashion, concealing the fact that I didn't immediately know. It took me a while. In truth, I was relieved I didn't find out the hard way, pardon the pun! "And Frank, to tell you the truth, I was hoping I was wrong!"

"I can see why not," he laughed. "She was a darling Lady Boy."

You see, mixed in to the 'bar girls' in Thailand are the occasional 'lady boys.' Lady boys are women who, in realty, are men. They may be in the long process of surgically becoming women, or they may simply be men who are fair and slight enough to dress like and appear to be women. Thus they are not 'one-hundred percent' women. In any case, they are not aggressive and not offensive. Lady boys are just an ornate and unusual part of the adventure, but beware.

Travel writer Larry Olmsted and I visited a number of cities in Thailand, and one night in Pattaya, we decided to invite ourselves to the party. With good sport Kayla Schubert, an amiable Canadian representing the Tourism Authority of Thailand leading the way, we attended the ritual sport of Thai Boxing. The three-round fights were staged up on a boxing ring in middle of an open-air bar with a corrugated steel roof. The place was a combination of a garage and a Tiki bar. There was no seating other then the bar stools.

We sidled up to the bar and grabbed three bottles of beer while the wild sounding, piercing music squeaked out of a horn to signal the fighters into the ring. They wore colorful, long silk boxing trunks, and, before the fight started, elaborate head-dresses. There was a golden gong at the corner of the ring to signal the beginning and end of each round.

As we observed the boxers warming up and took in the scene, I was startled by the sound of a low, scratchy, rumbling voice asking me: "Who win?"

The question came from a small, wrinkled man with a grey ponytail and pointy gray goatee. He wore a black eye patch and had an elfish quality about him. He'd appeared suddenly.

"Who win?" he insisted in his growl, gesturing toward the two boxers and shrugging.

I'd noticed the Thai boxer in the red trunks was taller and seemed to have a longer reach.

"Uh, the boxer in red will win," I answered.

"Red?"

"Yes, I pick the boxer in red."

He nodded twice and his one eye looked me straight in the eye. "Five-hundred baht," he said. "Five-hundred baht."

"Oh, you want me to bet? I see."

I asked Kayla how much five-hundred Thai baht converted to in U.S. currency.

"It's about fifteen dollars, Michael Patrick."

It was a nominal amount and it seemed like an interesting experience, so I invited myself to the party by looking the little man and nodding my head. "Yes. Five-hundred baht."

He nodded and walked back to his position ringside, where he signaled the boxers, sounded the gong, and watched the action with his elbows on the edge of the ring canvas under the ropes.

It wasn't much of a fight. The red boxer was dominant, so we celebrated my wisdom with another round of Singha beers before the third and final round was over. Sure enough, after the gong sounded, the little man brought me my winnings. I picked up a cool 500 baht simple as that.

Soon enough, though, two new boxers emerged and began to warm up. And once again, the exotic, gnomish man approached me.

"Who win?"

Once again, I picked the taller boxer with longer reach.

"Yellow," I said, "the one in the yellow trunks."

"Ah, yes. Yellow," the man said nodding. He paused for a moment, then leaned in and lowered his gruff voice. "Thousand baht?"

"Thousand?"

"Thousand baht," he repeated, this time more a statement than a question.

"Alright, fine," I said. "Thousand baht."

After a nod, the man went around the ring arranging baht bets with other bar patrons. Then the man took his position at the corner of the ring. Before he banged the gong, I saw the boxer in the yellow paying close attention to him. The little man gave him an odd look, and the boxer seemed to subtly respond. I squinted and watched what was going on.

Predictably, perhaps, the boxer in the yellow shorts – the one with the height and reach advantage – was struggling badly. He was getting kicked and punched and very tentative. He landed very few punches.

"The fix is on. I've been hustled," I told Kayla and Larry. They laughed as it became apparent yellow-trunked boxer was playing pantomime pugilist. The little man was probably working his odds and signaling the fighters based on the way his bets around the room went.

In between the first and second round, I slipped over to the corner where the boxer was taking his short break and wiping his face with a towel. Keeping an eye on the little man, I called out to get his attention without waving my hands or being demonstrative.

"Hey! Psst!"

The boxer looked down and seemed to be startled that someone was trying to get his attention during the fight.

"You win," I told him, nodding enthusiastically. "You win…two-thousand baht. You win – I give you two-thousand baht!"

Now I really had his attention. After a quick glance to see where the little man was, he looked back at me. "Yes," I said just before the gong sounded to start the second round. "You win…two thousand baht."

Well, that boxer in yellow trunks, who had been sluggish and hapless, went into round two on the attack, like a man possessed, and threw a flurry of hard and fast kicks and punches! I don't know who was more surprised, his suddenly battered opponent or the little man who'd taken the bets!

After "re-fixing" the Thai boxing match, I got paid and, after having Kayla discreetly pay off the fighter, I broke even…but what a priceless experience.

We then "excused ourselves from the party" before there was trouble!

BEING INVITED TO INVITE YOURSELF TO THE PARTY… IN HAWAII

I believe it was socialite Gloria Vanderbilt who, in her autobiography *It Seemed Important at the Time*, wrote: "Look for things that shine and move towards them."

Motivational speaker Tony Robbins advised, "If you want to be successful, surround yourself with successful people."

I find both of these to be excellent advice statements.

But sometimes, like a sailboat, you have to let the winds blow you around, harness them some, and let the forces of nature and fate invite you to the party. Or is it more than fate?

I had arrived in Kona, on the Big Island of Hawaii, in January 2001, to serve as Media Director for Pro Tour Hawaii, a ten event mini tour for aspiring professional golfers. On Sunday morning, I woke up very early because I hadn't yet become acclimated to the six hour time difference. It was barely light outside. I didn't feel like firing up my laptop to work. I felt the need to get out a little. I remembered hearing something about a Painted Church somewhere to the south of where I was staying along the Kona Country Club.

I found a listing in the phone book with a small map, which I tore out and took with me when I headed to the car and hit the road to Honaunau at sunrise.

After a twisty road up and down the cliff along the coast, I found myself getting a little frustrated by the map, which was quite general and not very detailed. It showed none of the little roads that weaved through the brush. I was lost. Suddenly I found myself down on the valley floor on a narrow road which cut through high vegetation, which I presumed to be pineapple or Kona coffee plants.

The road was very remote, with no buildings as far as the eye could see, so I decided to give up on the Painted Church, turn around, and go have breakfast back in Kona. The problem was that the long road was so narrow I struggled to find a place to turn around. Then something caught my eye up ahead. It was a person. It was a very thin woman in black with a brimmed hat shading her face. The desolate road was in the middle of nowhere, yet this woman was strolling along, walking toward me as I slowed the car as not to hit her or frighten her.

"Where are you going?" she asked me when I stopped the idling car to allow her to safely pass.

I was embarrassed to be lost. "I'm just out for a Sunday drive."

"Down here? You must have been trying to get somewhere else. Where was it?"

"Actually I was looking for a place called the Painted Church. Have you ever heard of it?"

She smiled.

"Am I near it? Is it around here somewhere?"

She pointed way up the green mountainside toward the Mauna Loa volcano, told me to turn around, and gave me some directions. "It will be only a ten-minute drive," she said. Her wide-brimmed black hat shielded me from the morning sun for a second, so I stopped squinting and thanked her. "Do you need a ride anywhere?"

"No, thank you."

I drove away up the road about fifty yards, finally finding a worn spot to turn around. With the car now pointed in the right direction, I began backtracking, but was startled to see that the woman walking the road was gone. I suppose it's possible that a woman, walking in the middle of nowhere, would climb into thick crops taller than she was, but let's face it, it's unlikely. I shrugged and dismissed it.

I followed her directions to the Painted Church, though, and was immediately taken by the look of what I now learned was St. Benedict's Church. The delicate, tiny, antique wooden church was built in 1899 – the first Catholic Church in Hawaii, and three miles from the site where Captain Cook was killed. The interior was hand-painted with stunning Biblical frescos by the original pastor, and the windows remain open to allow the breeze to blow up the leeward side of the island from the ocean, visible from the church, a thousand feet below. The setting was stunning.

I walked through the graveyard that fronted the church, up the steep, broken sidewalk, and into the door of the church, where, to my surprise, Mass was just starting...at seven fifteen a.m.! Starting Mass on the quarter hour seemed like an odd time to begin, but the church was full of native Hawaiians. The Hawaiian music and hymns were very culturally organic – played on a simple ukulele, but everyone in the church sang, which was soulful and touching.

I sat down in the creaky wooden pew in the last row, enjoying the view inside the church and of the Pacific down below. The homily, or sermon, was based on one of the readings, which was the story of Samuel. Samuel had been persistently awakened in the night three times by the Lord, who needed his help to fight wickedness and spread His word. During the homily, the priest, an aging, diminutive fellow with gray hair and an Irish last name, mentioned that he was originally from Detroit – my home town!

I was beginning to feel like Samuel – as if the Lord had been calling my name – trying to awaken me in the night. After all, I was awakened in the middle of a Hawaiian night, randomly compelled to visit the Painted Church, got lost – and mysteriously redirected on the way – arrived, by coincidence, just in time for a seven fifteen Mass, and finally, the priest was of Irish descent, and from Detroit! *How many signs did I need?* I thought to myself. This time, I had been invited to the party.

The musicians and gathered broke into the next hymn:

"I will break their hearts of stone,
Give them hearts for love alone.
I will speak My word to them.
Whom shall I send?

Here I am, Lord. Is it I, Lord?
I have heard You Calling in the night.
I will go, Lord. If You lead me.
I will hold Your people in my heart."

During the song, a woman came down the aisle searching for newcomers and visitors to welcome. Spotting me (I did not look like a Hawaiian native), she approached me and placed a handmade lei over my head and around my neck. I have to admit, at that moment, I lost it. I was overwhelmed by the setting, the moment and the meaning, and began to weep big tears freely. The air, the music, and the lei enveloped me. I knew it was time for me to accept what was obviously an invitation to embrace a more spiritual existence of clean living. It was a chance to trust in fate and whatever in whatever direction I would be sent. "Is it I, Lord? Here I am."

After the Mass, I remained in the church until everyone else had gone across the lawn to the small community center for Kona coffee, which was grown in the local area. The priest, who was cleaning up the altar, agreed to hear my full confession. We sat in the front row of the empty church, and I left no stone unturned in my sins, regrets, admissions. And he gave me counsel unlike anyone before.

Finally, at the conclusion of the confession, the priest whispered reference to something which would be happening surprisingly soon in my life. I was dubious, since I deemed it out of the question, but I listened closely with my eyes closed. He put his hand on my head, gave me advice and absolution, and then, "whack," he gently slapped my cheek. "You think of that the next time you consider missing Mass."

I won't reveal what the occurrence the priest referred to was, but I will tell you that his foreshadowing proved, to my absolute amazement, to be completely accurate – within months! Also, during my silent prayer in the church, I asked for relief from a specific, physically visible chronic ailment that had affected me for a number of years. I received within weeks. You may be thinking that I am exaggerating these claims, but I assure you, whether you believe me or not, and however you choose to interpret it, this retelling of my experience is absolutely true.

We parted, and I climbed into my rental car to begin the drive back. Before I could start the engine, I was interrupted by a knock on the window. It was the older woman who had played the lei around my neck.

"Please, come have a cup of coffee with us before you leave," she insisted gently. I most certainly joined the Painted Church Parishioners for a cup of Kona.

When I did get back to my rental condo that morning, I opened the St. Benedict's church bulletin, clipped out a verse, and scotch taped it to my lap top computer keyboard:

"Trust in the Lord with your whole heart and lean not on your own understanding. In all ways acknowledge Him, and He will make straight your paths."

– Proverbs 3:5-6

Invite Yourself
To Romance

HONEYMOON WITH JIM NANTZ

Jim Nantz is one of the most accomplished sports broadcasters in the world. He is the voice you hear describing National Football League games as well as the NCAA Basketball tournament and the PGA Tour for CBS Sports. He's called the action from the Olympic Games and, in addition, has hosted the *CBS Early Show* and the Macy's Thanksgiving Day Parade. In fact, in his *New York Times* bestselling book, *Jim Nantz – Always by my Side*, he recounts anchoring the Super Bowl, Final Four and Masters Tournament in a span of just over two months!

I developed an acquaintance with Nantz over the years through our mutual friend Ben Wright, the Emmy Award-winning English golf announcer who was part of the CBS golf broadcast team for over twenty years. Wright and Nantz are colleagues and friends. Nantz is on record as calling Wright "the greatest golf announcer of our time." Wright and I have written two books together, including his autobiography *Good Bounces and Bad Lies*, which the *Los Angeles Times* wrote was "maybe the best sports book ever." I served as Best Man at Wright's wedding to Helen Litsas in Greenville, South Carolina near their home. As I drove Ben to the church, both of us in our tuxedos, I slapped him on the knee and said, "So, Ben, are you nervous?"

"Nervous?" he exclaimed in his commanding Churchillian accent, "I've done this four times before. It's not the wedding that make me nervous…it's the divorces!"

Wright, who was "retired" by CBS in 1996 when the network declined to renew his contract due to some politically incorrect off the record statements about golf and women's anatomy, was also my Best Man. We've traveled together and worked on projects for ESPN, The Golf Channel, and Crystal Mountain Resort, in Michigan. In fact, I have an autographed photo of Ben and myself which he autographed to read: "From Your Savior Ben Wright." Some people chuckle at that "savior" sentiment since Ben has been married five times and taken a trip to the Betty Ford Clinic in Palm Springs, California! There's no doubt we've been good for each other...and there's no doubt sometimes we're not so good for each other! But I am always proud when Ben tells people I am "like a son to him."

So, through Ben I first met Nantz at the Masters Tournament and, over the years, I have written magazine articles about him and have dropped in to see him at the CBS broadcast tower when he covered Michigan events like the Buick Open or the Ford Senior Players Championship. He phones into my radio show from time to time, and was good enough to come in person and spend an hour on the show when he was in Detroit for the 2009 NCAA Final Four, featuring a magical run by the Michigan State Spartans.

One winter Sunday afternoon in Michigan I was watching the Nantz and his co-hosts David Feherty, Gary McCord, and Nick Faldo provide commentary on the CBS broadcast of the Los Angeles Open while I caught up on some work. I was a week away from my honeymoon trip to Hawaii – my first visit to Maui - when I remembered that Nantz spent a couple of weeks each summer at the Wailea Resort on Maui. I figured I'd send Jim an E-mail asking if he had any travel tips or advice about

Hawaii and, in particular, Maui. I'd expected that in a few days, maybe Tuesday, I'd get a response.

But right in the middle of the CBS telecast, as Nantz and the others were calling the action at Rivera Country Club, I got an E-mail response from Jim! It was two paragraphs of ideas and places he likes to visit on Maui: the Four Seasons Hotel and a restaurant called Sarento's on the Beach! Knowing what I know about how complicated anchoring a golf telecast is – with announcers and cameras at various locations as players hit shots and putts all across the final nine holes – it was astonishing that Jim would be reading and responding to his E-mail while he was on the air and flattering that he'd choose to write back so quickly.

I printed the E-mailed information and settled back into my work. The golf telecast, and the thought that I'd be in Hawaii in a week made seeing the falling snow outside my window bearable. About twenty minutes later, I heard Nantz reading a promotional announcement looking ahead to the PGA Tour events being contested the following week.

"Next week on the PGA Tour," he said as a graphic with the tournaments and locations appeared on the screen, "the World Golf Championships Accenture Match Play Championship at The Gallery at Dove Mountain, in Malara, Arizona; and the Champions Tour Skins game will be held at Kaanapali Golf Club, on Maui...*And there'll be some other action going on in Hawaii, as well...*"

I nearly fell off of my chair!

Nantz was making a sly, double-entendre reference to my Hawaiian honeymoon right there on CBS! Mahalo!

A few months later, when Jim was coming to Detroit for the PGA Championship, he phoned-in as a guest on my radio show. I told the story, on the air, of how Jim had responded to my E-mail with travel tips right in the middle of the broadcast.

"Well, what are friends for?" he asked in response.

Then I told my radio listeners about his cheeky "action in Hawaii" comment.

Jim started laughing. "Yep, that was for you," he said. "I hope you didn't take offense! I just wanted you to know I was thinking about you!"

So when you're watching a live broadcast, remember, there might be more going on than meets the ear!

PAUL ANKA PROPOSAL...
AND DR. PHIL DIVORCE

Six engagements and three marriages – romantic occasions I took the plunge and invited myself to. Looking back I don't regret any of them because, for better or worse (if you'll pardon the pun), my heart was in each one of the matrimonial assignations.

I love hearing stories about how married couples, or formerly married couples, got engaged. After all, it is likely one of the most dramatic "invite yourself to the party" moments in a person's lifetime, whether you are the one who proposes, or the one who accepts!

Sometimes the proposals are elaborate schemes like flying banners over football stadiums, or a flash on the scoreboard during the seventh inning stretch. Maybe it's the proverbial diamond ring in the champagne glass on Valentine's Day, or Christmas morning, or in a boozy Las Vegas nightclub near one of those infamous chapels, almost every proposal involves a fella on bended knee. It's once he's actually married that she actually brings him to his knees! (Just kidding, of course!)

Perhaps the most entertaining of my personal engagement stories involves one of the entertainment industry's most success-ful singer-songwriters: Paul Anka.

Anka is best known for writing the song *My Way* for Frank Sinatra. He also wrote *Johnny's Theme* for Carson's legendary Tonight Show. Tom Jones sang his smash hit *She's a Lady* because Anka wrote it for him. The King of Pop Michael Jackson's posthumously released song *This Is It* was written in collaboration with Anka. Of course, Anka, an amazingly energetic and likeable stage performer, sang his own hits, including *Diana, Put Your Head on My Shoulder, Lonely Boy, Having My Baby,* and *The Times of Your Life,* which made a Kodak commercial one of the most enduring television advertisements of all time.

I first met Anka after his terrific concert at Pine Knob Music Theater, an outdoor venue, outside Detroit, in 1989. I was producing WJR Radio's afternoon drive show with Joel Alexander, and we held a promotion with the theater, so the public relations woman, Marylin Desjardins, took us backstage for a short "meet and greet" with the famed singer after his killer performance. He was friendly and very lively.

A couple of years later, on a summer morning, Anka phoned into the J.P. McCarthy radio show one morning. He was promoting another appearance that upcoming Sunday night at Pine Knob. As McCarthy's producer, I took the call, chatted with him again on the telephone before the interview. I found him to be very friendly and energetic, especially after he told me he'd just stepped off an overnight flight from Paris.

Desjardins kindly set me up with two front-row tickets, so I made plans to attend the show. I didn't plan what happened next. It was a warm Sunday twilight when I made my way into the show with my girlfriend Vera Ambrose, a celebrity chef whom I had met through the *J.P. McCarthy Show.* She was a blonde who resembled actress Mariel Hemingway. Ironically,

Vera had been college roommates with Mariel's sister Joan Hemingway. Joan, Mariel and their sister Margaux were grand-daughters of Ernest Hemingway.

When I picked up the tickets left for us at the theater's Will Call window, I secretly slipped the attendant an envelope, told him I was a radio producer, and asked him to get it to Mr. Anka backstage. There was a note inside, with our seat location. I was completely uncertain as to whether the note would actually even reach the star and, in fact, considered it unlikely.

We sat down in our seats and let the high energy show unfold. About thirty minutes into the performance, nature was calling. I really had to go to the bathroom, but I didn't dare...just in case. I sat tight, and occasionally wiggled.

Then, sure enough, like lightning, during the middle of a song, Anka came down off of the stage, singing all the way as he traipsed through the front row. When he reached us, it all seemed surreal.

"Are you Vera?" he asked.

Stunned, she managed to say only, "Yes."

"He wants to marry you," Anka said, pointing to me.

When she looked my way, shocked, I had pulled a ring box from my pocket, and had it open and presented.

Anka sang and danced his way back onto the stage. Occa-sionally, during a song, he would come over our way and sing words of congratulations or encouragement by incorporating them into the lyrics of the songs he was performing.

Anka actually coming down and assisting with the en-gagement was exciting, but I have to admit the anticipation I experienced sitting through the first half of that show, wonder-ing whether or not I would leave the theater an engaged man was intense! Once I sent that note back to Anka, it was out of my hands! So the engagement, in a way, was a surprise to me, too!

Flash forward sixteen years.

In 2008, I was a radio host, and I interviewed Anka via telephone to promote an appearance he was making in Windsor, Ontario:

Anka: Hi Michael, how are you?

MPS: Great to hear your voice again! Now you and I have an interesting history, you know.

PA: I remember. I think it's the first time that had ever happened to me. But you tell them.

MPS: It was 1992 at Pine Knob. I was in the front row. You came off of the stage, walked through the front row, and told my girlfriend I would like to marry her. That was such a generous thing to do.

PA: Oh, I remember the set up. Obviously I was informed. That was the first time it had happened. I have done it about six times since then. May I ask, are you still married?

MPS: Uh, I've been married two more times since then.

PA: I don't meant to laugh, but I should have been there for the other two!

I met Rose Henry in 2001, in the pink twilight of a warm, spring evening on the steps of Our Lady of Mount Carmel Church, in Wyandotte. My first words upon laying eyes on her were, "*Who…is…that?!*" Like Michael Corleone when he first spotted Apollonia in *The Godfather,* I was struck by what the Sicilians in that movie called *The Thunderbolt.*

I proposed to her on her birthday, June 21, while we shared a bottle of Dom Perignon and danced to Sinatra in her living room. It was that third engagement that resulted in my second marriage...which led me to appear on the *Dr. Phil Show*.

Dr. Phil McGraw, a superstar television psychologist, was at the height of his powers when I was invited to fly to Los Angeles to participate in a broadcast that would focus on "Newlyweds in Trouble." Dr. Phil, an Oprah Winfrey disciple and creation, had been on the air less than a year and was very popular.

A producer from the Dr. Phil Show had read the true story of my wedding, one-hour marriage, and "runaway bride" in tabloid publications. The headlines, from the *New York Post* to the *Daily Mirror*, to CourtTV.com, read:

COLD BRIDE FROSTS HUBBY

BRIDE AND VROOM!

THE REAL RUNAWAY BRIDE

...The true story of a dashing groom, dashed hopes and the bride that dashed off into infamy. Author Michael Patrick Shiels's plans for a storybook wedding to Detroit coffeehouse owner Rose Henry turned into a much grimmer story.

Their 2001 wedding took place in a quaint, seaside village in Ireland.

But by the time the champagne had been poured at the reception, hearts began breaking. The bride had changed from her wedding lace into an all-black outfit and refused to sit next to the groom.

She ignored him during the entire week-long "honeymoon" and immediately filed for an annulment upon returning to the U.S...

Over the course of a couple of days, from her Hollywood office, the producer conducted two lengthy phone interviews with me, asking all about the details of the incident. She presented the details of the tale to her coordinating producer who then phoned me and formally asked if I would come to Los Angeles and participate in the program to be taped one week later.

I was flown, coach class, from Detroit to Los Angeles and taken by limousine to Paramount Studios. Since I was on my way to Puerto Rico for a golf trip following my Dr. Phil visit, the producers were surprised when I walked into their offices carrying golf clubs and luggage.

A female producer showed me around the offices, which were unremarkable and really no different than any workplace. She introduced me to a few people, but most everyone was busy working the telephones from inside their cubicles. I was then taken into a small room where I was interviewed on camera so the producers would have tape of me telling my story, which would be edited into a highlight package used to set up my live appearance on the show. So I told my story, yet again.

After that I was a free man. The chauffer drove me to my room at the snazzy Renaissance Hotel on Sunset Boulevard, where I was allowed to stay for two nights, compliments of the *Dr. Phil Show*, which also provided a couple of meals. The Renaissance Hotel is attached to the Kodak Theater, where the Academy Awards are given out each year, and right behind the famed Hollywood landmark Grauman's Chinese Theater. Feeling like a big shooter, but without a car, I spent the evening walking down Sunset Boulevard visiting famous water holes like SkyBar and the Viper Room.

The following morning I was driven back to Paramount Studios. The producers had been very serious with their admonition that I not be late for the 10:00 am car pickup. I was on time, which was a bit annoying because we weren't scheduled to tape the episode until two thirty p.m., yet I was to be deposited at Paramount by ten twenty. As I was driven through the sound stages and sets on the Paramount lot, I looked around at the other buildings and saw a street scene of ABC's spy show Alias being shot. (No sign of Jennifer Garner, though.) We reached a big, boxy building with some steps shaded by a small black awning emblazoned with the words "Dr. Phil."

Once I passed through the door, yet another production assistant met me and took me through a maze of corridors and stairwells until we reached a dim, well-worn hallway with doors on both sides. She opened one of the doors and, voila, it was my own personal "dressing room." The dressing room was not as glamorous as it sounds – it was very plain with a mirror, makeup table, and a vinyl couch. No television, no mini bar, no amenities. I sat in there for two hours alone, and might have even dozed off once, but then my nerves began to take hold of my stomach. Like a boarded horse, I paced some, and every once in a while I would open the door and stand leaning on the frame, watching the other guests coming and going as they were taken to their dressing rooms. I wondered what their problems were. I felt like we were part of a fraternity of oddities. It was like a prison or dormitory situation.

"We're each in our little boxes until it is time for us to perform," I said to one of the prettier passing guests.

She didn't reply.

As the time of the taping got closer, activity picked up. Various producers carrying clipboards came in to check facts with me, and explain the logistics of how the taping would go. I was led into a salon-like room where makeup was applied. That's how I knew we were close to taping time.

"When will I be taken to the studio?" I asked the makeup lady.

"In about thirty minutes," she answered. "Don't worry about it. They'll come get you."

I had my reason for wanting to know the exact timing.

"Can I have a of cup water with ice?"

A production assistant brought me a large Styrofoam cup with ice and water, which I took back to my dressing room. The instant the P.A. left and closed the door behind her, I poured the cup of water into the trash can through my fingers, straining the ice with my hand. I then unzipped the small, leather bathroom kit bag I'd brought with me and pulled out the four mini airport-sized bottles of Stolichnaya Vodka I'd stashed in the bag amidst the toothpaste, mouthwash, and hair gel. This was national television, concerning a sensitive subject, in front of a live audience – I was not "going in there alone." So I sucked down a couple of "spookers." When I caught myself drinking too fast, I reminded myself that I had plenty of time and that the whole purpose was to relax. So I sat back on the black vinyl couch spread my arms out, and looked around the room.

"Doctor f-ing Phil," I muttered. "It's come to this."

I was halfway though the Styrofoam tankard of booze and caught by surprise when the door opened again a full twenty minutes before the time to go to the studio. It was Dr. Phil's chief producer with some last minute questions. I stood and pretended to be straightening my tie in the mirror in the hopes of ditching the vodka, but it was too late – she'd cut me off and motioned for me to have a seat on the couch. Somewhere in my mind I remembered that good vodka was supposed to be odorless and tasteless, and those qualities were really put to the test in this moment. I held the cup as far from her as I could without looking suspicious.

The producer sat on the arm of the couch and though she was in a hurry, she doodled on her clipboard and dawdled.

"How are you doing?" she asked, although not seeming terribly interested in my answer.

"Fine."

"Okay, well, I'm not sure how to ask you this, but are you comfortable talking about your story – I mean, is it painful for you?"

I had been gregarious with the production people for the last two days. When I started to answer, she cut me off. "Because we're thinking maybe after the newlyweds come on and tell their stories and Dr. Phil deals with their problems, well, we thought maybe we could take a lighthearted approach to your story. I mean, not to make light of it..."

"I see," I said, interrupting her this time. "I get it. You want me to be the kicker story. I'm the funny example of extreme newlywed troubles."

"Are you okay with that?"

I looked at her.

"Look, whatever you want me to do, I can do it. You want 'flippant and funny' – no problem. You want 'fractured and forlorn,' just say so."

She had the answer she needed, and began to hurry towards the door.

"Which is it?" I asked, now boldly sipping the vodka cup.

"Well, Dr. Phil is not quite sure which way he wants to take it yet. I think he kind of wants to see how it goes. But I've got to go back and tell him, so, just wait right here."

She was halfway out the door when she remembered to thank me.

I nodded. Then I drank some more.

I didn't really care which way Dr. Phil presented me and whether our chat was serious or funny. It occurred to me that I probably would not meet him before the show and that I would not know before the cameras were on me which format it was to be. I was ready in either case.

If Dr. Phil went for the laughs, and I played along, I would appear flippant and unaffected by it all. And if Dr. Phil got serious on me, I knew just what I wanted to say.

It was nearly time to go under the lights, so I tossed out the empty cup and took a swig of mouthwash from another small, travel-sized bottle. A producer, like the Pied Piper, came and fetched me from my room, leading me down the hallway, and on the way, stopping at each door to "pick up" the show's other guests – three pairs of still married newlyweds. We talked a little on the way, but small talk only, and I felt very out of place as the only person there without a "date." I knew they were wondering what was up with me, because we had not been briefed at all on each other's stories.

We spent five minutes waiting in a cushy holding room just off of the studio while the producers straightened our ties, touched up our hair, and ran lint brushes over our suits. During those five minutes, I began the resent the other well-dressed young couples in their makeup, who each had someone to playfully joke and laugh with to calm each other's nerves. I was the third-wheel in some kind of demented prom night.

We were each outfitted with a tiny microphone. Mine was clipped to my tie with a thin cord running down the sleeve and attached to a concealed battery transmitter hooked to my belt. We were then led out to the soundstage and placed behind the backdrop of the set. We couldn't see the stage or the audience, but the crowd was obviously being "warmed up" because the producers were having them clap in rhythm.

"Five minutes," a producer told us, barking to be heard over the applause.

Then it happened.

I grabbed the arm of a busy floor director who was rushing by. She was startled and looked blankly at me. Then she tugged the earphones from off of her head and leaned in so she could hear my question.

"Through that door and down the hall," she said, wasting no time. "And leave your microphone on. You only have two minutes."

Yep – it was only seconds from airtime, but after four hours of down time, and four airport bottles of vodka, I had to whizz.

I went as fast as I could, and felt kind of special that I could break ranks with the other show guests. By the time I got back, the excitement was really building in the crowd. The studio was filled with loud, pumping music: Cher's *Do You Believe (...In Life After Love)*. Cher is apparently a favorite of Dr. Phil. The audience was eating it up, too, and when the other show guests and I – the goofy supporting cast in this production – were led in to our seats under the bright lights in the front, I could swear I felt a showbiz bounce in my step.

When the audio engineer cross-faded to the well-known Dr. Phil Theme, the audience cheered and clapped even louder. Out from behind the sliding panels on the stage emerged the bald, Texas-accented, larger-than-life shrink himself, and for a moment, like the first time you actually meet a celebrity, he didn't look real and none of it seemed real. It was like literally walking into a television show.

Things settled down and the show got into its routine pattern. Two-by-two, each pair of newlyweds took their turn on stage being embarrassed and getting Dr. Phil's advice. The first couple was struggling because the husband, a young sly looking guy, was still staying out all night with his guy pals. His wife was a hottie, so I wondered why he was straying. Dr. Phil admonished him to calm down.

The second couple was dull by comparison – they were having trouble finding time for themselves because their newborn was not fully healthy yet.

The third couple was, to me, a sad story. The wife, a picture-pretty blonde with a husky Louisiana accent, had been raised by a family of Southern Baptist preachers. She married a doughy, white, dim, former football player, who was clearly hopelessly infatuated with his bride. It was embarrassing to watch their segment because the wife cried throughout it. It seems she was a virgin when the harmless lumbering sod married her, and she found out very quickly that she just didn't like sex and, although she "loved him," she didn't want him touching her – anywhere – ever. He tried to hold her hand though the segment, but she appeared bothered by that and returned no visible signs of affection. She even demonized the poor bastard for giving her love taps on her bottom when she'd pass by him in their living room. Dr. Phil suggested the husband "work on refining his approach," and advised the wife to consider sex therapy. I know I could not have been the only cynic in the audience who secretly wondered if maybe she would have liked sex if only he were more adept at it. After all, he's the only man who has ever captured her flag, so she has nothing to compare it to!

They promised to take Dr. Phil's advice and try to work things out.

As the commercial break was ending, I began to get nervous because I knew my part was next and there was no turning back now. The music swelled and the floor director counted Dr. Phil down...then pointed for him to start. Reading off of the teleprompter, the good doctor began:

"You know the promise we make when we get married: "Till death do we part? Well, how about 'Till dinner do us part?' Well, Michael didn't get a chance to be a newlywed because he married 'the real runaway bride.' Take a look:"

Two large screens on each side of the studio lit up and a vignette about my wedding story rolled. It featured some of the interview that had been taped a day earlier and lots of photographs and footage of the wedding in Ireland, since they borrowed the wedding tape from me.

The song "Here Comes the Bride" played, and I heard my own voice narrating:

"We got married at noon on a beautiful day in Ireland and by our wedding dinner at six o'clock, she wouldn't sit next to me. She said, 'The act of getting married made her realize that she can't be married.' She wouldn't spend our wedding night together in our wedding suite. I left the door open all night hoping she would come, but she didn't. It was the loneliest wedding night I imagine any groom had ever spent.

Once she decided that she didn't want to be married any-more, I thought we should stop the honeymoon trip and head back to the U.S., but she said, 'can't you be a good sport so my mother and sister and kids can have a good time and we won't tell anybody until we get home?' So, that's what I did and there we were traveling around Ireland in a van with a 'Just Married' sign on the window and everybody was festive but me. Once we got back from Ireland, she filed for an annulment and that was the last time I saw her other than in court."

The video clip ended and the camera cut to Dr. Phil, who was leaning on his elbow on the edge of his chair making a face that portrayed both chagrin, astonishment, and a touch of whimsy.

"O-K," he huffed in a sing-song voice. Then came his rhetorical question: "So other than that, how's it going?"

The next sing-song voice was my own, answering his question, due to nervousness, too quickly and in too animated a fashion, and worse yet, with a line I'd prepared and rehearsed in my dressing room. "Well, having me on a show with newlyweds is like having Jennifer Lopez on a commitment special."

"Yeah, very funny," said Dr. Phil.

"I'm the 'third wheel' here today," I insisted.

"So, I mean, how was it when you were dating?"

"Fantastic," I answered, getting down to business. "She's forty and I'm thirty five. Both from the same small town; from the same church; had small kids the same age. We had everything going in the right direction. Both independent business people. Very communicative, very passionate. I was totally duped."

"So you had no clue. What, did she just want a free trip to Ireland or something?"

The audience laughed softly, and the camera cut away to the concerned faces of women in the crowd listening intently to the story.

"Nah, people have suggested that, but I don't think it's true."

"How long did you date?"

"We dated for four months."

"Well, that's not long," Dr. Phil said with a shrug, "but it's long enough to know whether she wanted to do this or not. So, she wouldn't even stay in the honeymoon suite with you...and then it got worse from there?"

"Yeah. I thought it was jet lag or maybe the stress of having little kids around. Who knew? But I honestly thought that things would get better with time and that at some point we'd be able to work it out. Being with these newlyweds today I wish we'd had the chance to work out the problems."

"Are you wearing a wedding ring?"

The camera focused in to a tight shot of my left hand.

"Yeah, it's an Irish Claddagh ring – an Irish wedding ring."

"Is that the ring from the ceremony?"

"It is," I answered, nodding.

Dr. Phil's tone became accusing as he leaned in. "You're not married."

"No. Not any more."

"Why are you wearing it?" he asked with a touch of exasperation.

"Well, because the traditional ring stands for love, loyalty and friendship, and I'm just not ready to give up, at least, my love, loyalty, and friendship to a marriage that I took seriously."

"Did you tell the producer that if she would have you back, you would do it?"

"Yeah, I wish we were both sitting in those chairs next to you because it's the great mystery of my life, honestly."

"Well," said Dr. Phil, "I understand that you wish that were true but honestly, if she called you today and said, 'What a fool I've been. Let's go back to Ireland and consummate this marriage and do this right' you would load and go?"

"Yes, I would. Of course I would."

"Of course you would?"

"Yeah. I made a commitment."

"Okay. You didn't break the commitment. She did. Do you have a question for me?"

"Gee. There doesn't seem to be a way to repair it. The marriage is gone, but I always thought at least the relationship would survive because she told me that 'if we hadn't gotten married we'd still be happily dating.' So that kind of haunts me a little bit and it makes me wish that I'd done something different on that wedding day. Maybe I should have been more understanding or stronger for her, maybe. Maybe I shouldn't have resisted the divorce. I second-guess what I have done."

"Really?" Dr. Phil asked in that astonished pitch in which people ask that one-word question.

Then came another rhetorical question: "So maybe it's your fault?"

"Well, I might have been able to help," I said, my voice falling off, "…in…some…way."

Dr. Phil listened, looking at me, leaning in toward me with his head nodding.

"Hmm," he grunted.

He'd heard enough from me, so he leaned back, changing his posture to dispense his advice in a commanding way.

"That's an interesting theory," he said, "but I'm a real 'results-based' sort of guy. The results are, you asked this woman to marry you. She said yes. You went over to Ireland and had a beautiful wedding. She went back to the room and basically said, 'Take a hike.'"

"Yeah. She said, 'The act of getting married made her realize she cannot be married,'" I explained.

"Okay, then I would get real busy working on accepting that reality."

I nodded and mumbled an acknowledging sound that was tinged with disappointment while women in the audience nodded their heads in agreement with Dr. Phil.

"I'm telling you, if she called you and you went back into this deal with her, I promise you would be sorry that you did. Because I think the best predictor of future behavior is past behavior, and she has shown you some instability that you want no part of."

The camera closed in on my face as Dr. Phil continued.

"That's sad. And I'm sorry. And I know you feel funny, but you didn't break a commitment – she did. You're out, and I think you ought to stay out...for sure."

The stringy theme music swelled, the applause lights came on prompting the audience to clap, and Dr. Phil told the camera "We'll be right back."

"That's tough Michael," he said above the applause. "That's tough."

My pity party continued after Dr. Phil closed the show, when a number of the well-dressed women in the audience approached me to express sympathy and support, saying things like "You're too good for her," and "Someone better will come along." Down deep I wanted to collect all of their phone numbers or take them all out to dinner, but at the same time I knew each one of them were wolves in sheep's clothing, pretending to be better than my "bride" when, in fact, each one of them was probably more than capable of the same sort of emotional recklessness. Besides, Dr. Phil was waiting for me backstage. He stood with me for a photograph and shared a few thoughtful private words with me, expressing his own brand of acknowledgement and support. He seemed to really care and showed more sympathy than he did on stage.

Then a producer actually handed me a *Dr. Phil* coffee mug and sent me, exit-stage right-on my way out into the afternoon sunshine of the Paramount Studios lot. So I figure I got thirty seconds of psychological counseling and a coffee mug out of the deal.

It was by sheer luck I met my third wife, Dr. Christine Tenaglia. I had just moved to Lansing, Michigan to be morning radio show host of the Michigan Talk Network. My manager, Tim Hygh, insisted I play in a charity golf scramble tournament being put on by the Lansing Chamber of Commerce.

"Tim I am really busy working on this new show. I don't have time for golf today, but thanks," I said.

"Be there at noon," he answered.

Ugh. I showed up only seconds before the starting time at Eagle Eye golf course to play in a foursome with some clients. As soon as the golf portion was over, I grabbed my clubs and headed straight for the parking lot to get back to work. Someone who knew me caught my putting my golf clubs in the trunk.

"You're coming in to the awards banquet…at least for a drink, right?"

"Nabbed again!" I thought to myself.

So in I went to the massive Eagle Eye ballroom. Four hundred people were in the room, seated at a sea of round tables. I ordered a quick drink from the bar and mingled with a few people... keeping an antsy eye on the door.

"MPS, c'mon over and sit with us," said attorney David Lick, a senior member of his firm who is well-connected in town.

Snagged, I thought.

He took me over to a table of people I didn't know, which included one woman. When he introduced me, one of the community leaders at the table asked me how I liked living in Lansing. In the interest of making small talk with the strangers, and because, after all, I am a talk show host, I turned the question around and asked everyone how they liked living in the state capital. The answers were varied, until the woman answered.

"It's a nice place to raise a family, but not so good for a single professional woman," she said.

I immediately got up and filled her water glass.

Sixteen months later we got engaged in the Frog's Leap Vineyard in Napa Valley.

There is a centuries old Irish song called *The Parting Gluss*. It is about a man, about to leave a town, perhaps for America, perhaps to go to war, perhaps for the great beyond, but in any case, he seems to be taking stock of his life's activities. His lyrics include the phrases:

...And all the sweethearts that e'er I had,
They would bid me one more day to stay.
And all the harm that e'er I've done,
Alas it was to none but me...

That song seems to sum up nicely what I feel about my former betrotheds. It'd be nice to think they still like me enough to wish I'd stay for a bit; but if not, I hope at least that any harm in the relationship was not to them, but to me.

THE COMPLEX LIVES OF THE SIMPLE IRISH

*"To be Irish is to know that in the end the world
will break your heart."*
-Daniel Patrick Moynihan

The night had been a filling mix of music, drink, and now, air. Four hours earlier I'd filled a bowl of lobster bisque with soda bread at the Half Door restaurant on John Street. The entire front of the Half Door is painted dark green. It is in the middle of the block next to Doyle's, the entire front of which is painted red. I ate at the bar and read through the *Kerry's Eye* newspaper. After, I walked out into the near dark, turned right and headed up the hill, past An Droicead Beag, beyond James G. Ashe's, and Banc na hEireann. Past Paul Geaney's on the right and the Benner's Hotel on the left. Just next door, Patrick Hennessy was closing up his Fado antique shop. We waved to each other, and I kept on through the dusk in Dingle, County Kerry, Ireland.

At the top of the hill, I turned left onto Green Street, which runs back downhill in front of the church on the right and then on down to the marina. Dick Mack's Pub is on the left, across the narrow street from the church. The pub itself is a stubborn antique that retains its character through zero maintenance.

Dick Mack's occupies a space that first sold dairy products and tea. After Tommy Mack died, his son Dick became proprietor, and turned the shop into a leatherworks and shoe store during the day; and a public house after dark. No food or trappings. Just whiskey and porter. If any paint had been applied to Dick Mack's Pub in the last quarter-century, it was Oliver's bit of memorable prose on the alley gate next to the pub: "*Where is Dick Mack's? Opposite the church. Where is the church? Opposite Dick Mack's.*"

On this night, I went in to Dick's for a silent pint.

"Mr. Shiels," the bartender said in a low tone and with a nod.

I nodded back. "A pint, please, Jamie, sir, if you would."

"All right then, Michael."

Once the creamy pour was finished – it takes half-pours to settle properly – I put down three Euros and grabbed my dark drink of Guinness. I sat on the workbench next to the shoe shelves and old footwear across from the bar.

It's easy to stay quiet at Dick Mack's Pub. Most of the patrons speak in hushed tones. Dick Mack's is a very little place for drinking and smoking and little else. It is not there to feed or entertain. The tiny nature of the pub and its local regulars can be intimidating. Unsuspecting travelers will come through the door, immediately sense the silence and feel the gaze of the regulars. It can seem as though they might be walking into a classroom or interrupting an IRA meeting. Some visitors turn heels before they get two feet in the door. Sometimes I observed boisterous American tourists who come in and treat the locals in a patronizing fashion: as if the Dingle residents, many of whom have never even left the peninsula, are cast members in their own personal holiday adventure. For them, it's as if Dingle Town was a themed area in some amusement park called "Ireland World." The tennis-shoed tourists in denim jeans or Docker pants, Land's End coats and baseball caps will put on a Lucky Charms stage brogue and spout Irish stereotypes. They'll try a Guinness because it's the thing to do and choke half of it down because they cannot stand the taste. Next they order a Harp because it is the closest thing they can find to Coors.

On weekdays in Dingle, during the extended period I spent living and writing there, I mainly wore a tie and sweater vest. I always wear my gold Claddagh ring, and sometimes I wear a gray, flat Shandon cap. This often led the tourists to assume I was an Irish local. It was interesting to be more anonymous among my own countrymen than amongst the locals.

A thirty-something American loud mouth once stood next to me at the bar. He put his arm around me and, in order to amuse his wife, while grinning from behind his glasses, spoke in a put-on, sing-song, leprechaun tone: "And where is it then that ye hail from, laddie?" he asked me.

They waited anxiously for me to speak.

"Michigan," I answered him flatly, as their faces fell.

My apparent charm vanishes once the Yanks realize I am an American. On nights I am feeling dour and especially anonymous, I will just nod my head or grin at tourists who try to talk to me. This leaves them not sure what to do next. I wouldn't fake a brogue, though. Never.

Dick's two antique snugs make good retreats on those tourist-heavy nights. A few of us can duck in, shut the door behind us, and ignore the crowd alone with our drink.

I observed a man called Peader in Dick Mack's. He was a

middle-aged, debonair yet gruff fellow who smokes hand-rolled cigarettes in no particular hurry. I listened to Peader and his friend, Joe, speak to each other at the workbench for a long time. It was near half-eleven and we were the only three patrons remaining. Jamie was tending bar.

"Peader, did you know Neil went to sea?"

"Went to see what?"

"For fuck's sake. You know what I'm saying."

"I do. I know."

Jamie drew the shades. It was closing time.

"Jamie…," Peadar grumbled.

"Too late now, Peadar."

"But I'm in need of it Jamie, I truly am. I need one more pint."

"They're not my rules Peadar."

Peadar's voice suddenly became less gruff and more melodic.

"Now Jamie, I've never asked you for a Porter after hours. I've never before asked you for a pint after hours…I might have demanded, but I have never asked."

Jamie had already begun to draw the pint anyway.

"Come and get it then. But don't ask or demand again."

It was fair enough that Joe had another as well. Hearing this, I asked for a glass of Jameson Crested Ten over ice.

"My father used to drink that stuff, that Crested Ten," Peadar said directly to me when he heard me order it.

I extended my hand and introduced myself to Joe and Peadar.

"What do you do here in Dingle?" I asked Joe.

"As little as possible."

Joe and I toasted to that.

"Slainte."

"Slainte."

Peadar didn't bother to answer.

I told them that I was a writer, and began to speak a bit about my previous visit to Dingle.

"Michael Patrick Shiels. Shiels," Peadar said. He rolled the "l" while he rolled a cigarette. "Do you know a Jimmy Shiels from Dublin? That's where I grew up."

"No, I don't think so," I answered. "But I was told that my great grandfather…"

"Well I went to school with Jimmy Shiels."

Peadar had interrupted me, but it reminded me to listen more than to speak.

"Jimmy Shiels exploded a copper pipe bomb in the school principal's automobile. He blew that fucker to kingdom come."

Now I was listening.

Peadar lit his cigarette with a match.

"What I didn't know is that I was the one who made the bomb for him," he said.

Peadar could tell I was about to ask, so he pushed up his spectacles and continued after a long drag and puff.

"We made bombs all of the time. We blew them up in the field for just the amusement and the noise. Jimmy Shiels asked me to make a bomb for him. I figured he wanted it for the field. I procured a piece of copper pipe - about an inch wide. I made a hole the size of a nail in the middle of the pipe. Just the size of a nail, like. I crimped one end of the pipe closed. Then I filled the other end of with a mixture of sugar and fertilizer."

"Just like the bombs the IRA used," Joe said.

"They're more sophisticated now. But the point is that you crimp off the open end once you've filled the pipe and then leave a little trail of the mixture leading to the hole. You light a match to the trail. Then you run like the fucking wind because there's going to be a load of fucking copper flying all around when it blows."

Peadar's voice had risen with amusement.

"Jimmy Shiels did that to the principal's automobile. He hurt no one, but this prompted a mighty investigation."

"Did they catch him?"

"Oh fuck yes they caught him all right. They caught Jimmy Shiels. I'll tell you something. Nothing ever came of it like. The clergy wanted it kept quiet you see? The clergy intervened and covered the whole fucking thing up."

I joked aloud, having heard his story, that I surely must then be a relation of Jimmy Shiels. But Peadar took me very seriously. He looked first to see if Jamie was paying attention while he swept up, then he lowered his voice.

"You have that in you then, do you?"

"No, no. Not really." I said. "I'm harmless."

"You're a Catholic, are you, Michael Patrick Shiels?"

"I am, yes."

"But do you really believe in that shit?"

I nodded.

"With all due respect, one of these days I'm going to walk across the street to the church and ask the Canon right to his face straightaway if he really believes that shit he's telling everyone," Peadar said. Joe shook his head and puffed before Peadar continued. "All this religion came about because as human fucking beings, when we were running around naked with the lions, we had to go and fight for our food. We could hunt without fear because we didn't know the fucking difference between living and dying. We hunted and scavenged to survive. We didn't know the lion was going to eat us every time.

"Then the frontal lobe developed and we got smarter," Peadar said, pointing to his head. "Suddenly the human being could understand his own demise. The human being got fucking scared. He was too fucking frightened to hunt. But that was no way to survive, you see. At the same time the frontal lobe developed, the pituitary gland developed," he said, this time pointing to the base of his skull. "That gave the human being an imagination, and with that imagination, he had to invent something like God and an afterlife. Otherwise, he'd have been too smart ever to have left the cave to fight the fucking lion."

Jamie cleaned glasses at the bar and tried not to listen to Peadar.

"Two thousand years later we're still spouting all of this bullshit and killing each other because of it instead of killing the fucking lions."

Joe tried to change the subject my breaking into song.

"*And we all got stone-cold paralytic drunk the night the old pub caught fire!*"

Peadar shot a look at Joe.

"It's a true song," Joe said. "I know the guy who says he started the fire."

I asked Peadar if he'd read the book *How the Irish Saved Civilization.*

He shook his head no and smiled at the preposterousness of the title.

"It was very popular in America. Written by Thomas Cahill. One passage in his book explains how the Celts fought the invading Romans with the same wild abandon you say early man fought the lions with. The Irish Celts imagined that they could transform themselves to be fifteen-foot tall warriors and that they were overpowering in battle. They drank wine before fighting and believed they could transform their features into hideous, grotesque, two-headed, one-eyed shapes. They stripped and fought naked like insane, possessed savages.

"When the Romans came to conquer, they could hear the sounds of baying and piping before they arrived. When they encountered the Celts, they were shocked. The all-powerful Romans were frightened by the aggressive, screaming, howling naked maniacs."

My paraphrasing allowed Peadar to near the bottom of his pint and Joe, rarely speaking, had long since finished his. Peadar spoke.

"When Cromwell had finished taking most of Ireland, he fucking took off on a ship and left his deputy in command. It was obvious to all that Cromwell's deputy was going to bring his men to invade Connemara, if for no other reason than to find out if Connemara was just all rocks, and bogs, and shit. Whether it was worth conquering," he went on, knowing there was not another pint coming. "Well, there was a giant living in Connemara at the time. He was considered to be a giant because he was something like six-foot-seven. The average man then was about five-foot-fucking-six. So he was a giant.

"When Cromwell's deputy and his men reached the river to cross into Connemara, they looked across to the other riverbank and saw this giant sitting up on a horse.

'The first fucker that comes across this river…' well, he didn't say 'fucker,' but he shouted at them: 'I'll use my bare hands to tear apart the first man that crosses this river.'

"They turned fucking tail and got the fuck out of there," Peadar said, with his eyes smiling through his thick glasses. I swallowed the last of my whiskey. He took a drag on his cigarette.

"I am proud to say that the records will confirm that the giant I just told you about was my great, great, great, great, great, great, great, great grandfather."

"Oh, go away now," Joe said. "Go away with you now."

Since that first night in Dick Mack's back in Dingle I'd seen Peadar at his best and worst. I'd learned that he was one of the most accomplished wooden whistle players in County Kerry, and that he played mighty sessions in the local pubs with other traditional musicians who played the fiddle or elbow pipe or squeeze box. He'd known some of those musicians from his days avoiding the Garda as a busker in Dublin, when they worked Grafton Street theatre lines performing for punts. Just as they had in Dublin, the musicians in Dingle played without a stage or microphones. They just gathered in a corner, five nights, not for money but for drink, at whichever pub would have them at that rate. The deal wasn't always as easy for them to arrange as it would seem.

I could see that Peadar enjoyed the attention and was at his best during these sessions. He must have felt appreciated and useful while playing his music. Most of the hardcore traditional musicians played for themselves and to each other. Peadar did too, especially in Dingle's off-season winter months when the town was quiet. But when the tourists came, he often talked with them between the slip jigs and reels they listened to with wide eyes.

"Where are you from? Are you enjoying your holiday?"

Sometimes a tourist would bring their tin whistle and he'd invite them to join the circle and play along, or he'd encourage girls with tapping toes to step dance if there was room to do so. Peadar's mood was quickly changeable, though. One slow night at the Marina Inn, Peadar had charmed an older couple that sat near the band. They'd applauded and given their full attention to the music for the final hour of the session. I watched Peadar chat them up as he took apart his whistle and put it into the suede case he carried it in.

"Are you enjoying your holiday?"

"Yes, thank you. We enjoyed your music very much."

"Thank you. Thank you very much. Where is it that you're from?"

"Israel."

"I wish you hadn't said that," said Peadar. He turned away, the smile gone from his face.

The older couple wasn't sure they heard what they thought they'd heard. They just kept smiling and asked Peadar a question about his whistle.

"Look, you people don't belong there. You were put in there and you took land from the Palestinians that does not belong to you. You don't belong there. I'm sorry."

I watched the older couple walk out the door, fully dismissed, smiling through cold teeth.

There was not silence but a din tonight in Dick Mack's as I sipped through the cream of the pint. Peadar was not there. Joe was not there either. Joe had been taken to Limerick to take chemotherapy to treat testicular cancer. It seems that his government health insurance had delayed any treatment for his symptoms until his position on a waiting list came up. His treatment was now available, so the government had paid for his two-hour taxi drive to a Limerick hospital, where it was discovered he'd caught a hospital infection during his biopsy and diagnosis.

He was told he had ten months to live, months he said he'd prefer to spend in Dingle, drinking and smoking to the end – and taking painkillers – instead of spending his dying days in a hospital sickened by the chemotherapy. Joe didn't want treatment.

"You'll go alright," Peadar had grumbled at him. "You're going to go through five months of horrible shit if I have to drive you to Limerick myself. And, if you should make it through and you turn out alright, do you know what I'll say to you?"

"What?"

"I'll tell you to fuck off!"

The boys weren't in Dick Mack's Pub tonight, though. Peadar was probably down at the John Benney's Pub playing a session. A black and white dog was curled up on the cement floor. There was a woman at across from me at the workbench that I'd known to be a regular but had never spoken to. She was as Black Irish as a Gaeltacht woman could be. This was no shy, round, pasty redhead with freckles. She was tall and thin and pointy, with a crazy curly bush of midnight black hair exploding from her head. Her eyes were dark and her teeth uneven and shaded. Her clothing was nondescript and dowdy. She clutched a pint glass of Bulmer's cider with ice in it but didn't smoke. She had a large black Celtic tattoo encircling one of her biceps. Her English was barely discernable through her brogue, and yet it was English she spoke to everyone around her. She laughed with exaggerated expression often. It was sometimes a hideous screeching cackle as she tossed her head back and threw her hair around from side to side as if she were chained to the stool. She was a banshee.

"What is her story?" I asked a local to my left. He was a truck driver who ran fish from Dingle over the Conor Pass and onto Cork where it could be shipped to Spain. Sometimes he ran Dell Computer parts from to Holland to Ireland via ferry.

"What's her story?" he repeated to me. "Where does it begin and where does it end?"

We laughed and shrugged, but still I was curious about her. *An rud is annamh is iontach.* *

* - *What is strange is wonderful.*

She wore no wedding ring. She was difficult to make eye contact with, even though I sat right across the workbench. At last I bid her good evening. She was polite enough in her response and I reached for her hand, which she gave.

"I'm Michael."

"Hello, Michael."

"What's your name?" I asked.

"What's your name?" she asked me back.

"Michael."

"Well that's all you need to know then Michael."

I looked away and drank to the bottom of my porter.

"That cider will make you crazy, you know," I said, making a second pass at her.

"Why not?" she said.

"I know your name anyway. The truck driver told me what it is."

Her dark eyes looked at me.

"What is it, then?"

"Agnes."

She shook her head.

"Delores."

"No."

"Bernice."

"I am Mary. It is nice to meet you, Michael." She extended her hand, and I took the gesture to mean that she admired the way I sustained her previous smack down.

"Nice to meet you, too, Mary."

"Our children are at home with the minder. That's me husband there," she said with a tilt of her head.

I nodded and then looked over. He was Black Irish too, a Gaeltacht man. Tall and thin and pointy, with matted dark hair. His eyes were dark, too and some of his shaded teeth were absent. He had a heavy accent. He was in work clothes and he flashed a crazed wild smile most of the time.

This coupling was a stark reminder that I was in the far reaches County Kerry.

"Slan, Maire," I said.

"Slan go-foil."

I turned again to the truck driver. He was talking about Northern Ireland politics with an Australian and had not heard my exchange with Mary the banshee.

"It's a shame, but the English were so good at placing derelict Scots up there in the counties that it will be generations before a solution is found. Sometimes running a boatload of guns up is the only solution," he was saying to the Aussie. He was a big, broad proud fellow with white hair to his shoulders and a trimmed beard.

The Australian went to piss.

"I notice you're drinking pints of Budweiser."

"I know," he said. "I never thought this piss would take hold here, either. It has though. The young people like something different. I drink it because is it always the same. The taste never varies no matter where I drink it."

It turned out he had actually noticed my exchange with the banshee, and so the topic changed from politics and beer to the peril and glory of women. Before long, he was telling me how he once found himself stone broke in San Francisco. He had been on a six-month, self-guided ramble around the United States. All he had left was a Greyhound pass, so he hopped a three-day bus ride from the west coast to New York, where he'd planned to find a way to hustle a cheap flight home. The point of his story was that a Swedish girl gave him a hand-job in the back of the bus somewhere near Cleveland, but had to wrap his story up quicker than he would have liked when his lady came in through Dick Mack's front door. She was text messaging someone on a cellular phone with her right thumb but finished before she approached the truck driver.

"Hello, honey love," he said. He kissed her.

"How was your run today then?" she asked.

"Fucking ponderous, I'd say."

"You're always in such a hurry."

"I was fantasizing today about my breaks failing on the Conor Pass. I fantasize about whether I'd be able to steer her down that road with no breaks."

"Christ honey, perish the thought."

"I'd like to know," he said. "I'll never know, though, because even if it happened I'd have thirty vehicles on holiday in front of me."

"True, that."

"Have you been up over the mountain through the Conor Pass?" the truck driver asked me.

I told him I had.

He was talking close to me now.

"I know that I should be kind to the tourists because they spend money here and they are out looking at the scenery and the mountains and the beauty, but it also must be remembered that the Conor Pass road is a major passage to Tralee. When I'm in a hurry I've got to get my load through there. I cannot tell you how many times someone is puttering along the road, but when they see me coming in my truck, I can see the whites of their eyes."

"I won't tell you again to be careful," said the truck driver's wife, squeezing his hand.

They seemed like a suitable couple. They'd been together twelve years. Again, I noticed no wedding ring.

"Why don't I see many wedding rings in Ireland?" I asked her.

"People partner and live together rather than marry," she told me.

"They even have families together?"

"They do," she said. "Long, cold Dingle winters cause that, I'd say."

"I find that surprising since Ireland is so Catholic."

"That is how it stays Catholic," she said. She leaned in. "Without weddings there cannot be divorces."

The truck driver's attention drifted off.

"Divorce came to Ireland only in 1996 and only through the government. Before 1996 divorce in Ireland did not exist. The church still does not recognize divorce at all. A government divorce takes four years to obtain. You must wait four years."

"Four years?"

"Four years," she said. "No exceptions. How long must you wait to get a divorce in the America?"

She watched me look down into my empty pint glass.

After I left Dick Mack's I walked down the rest of Green Street, past Beginish and the photo shop and the chemist and the florist. At the bottom of the road I turned right and went two blocks further. I ducked in to John Benny's Pub. John Benny's, like seemingly everything in Dingle, is in the middle of a block. I leaned on the bar.

"Hiya, Shortie," I said to the tall blonde girl behind the bar.

She turned around and a smiled at me. "Crested Ten?"

"Right."

"You've come for the *Craic** have you?"

**Craic-Good times, conversation.*

I nodded.

She was anything but short. John Benny kept a close eye on her.

"I told you I was going to work at my brother's pub in Australia?" she asked while she poured the whiskey.

"You did. Going soon?"

"In two weeks. For five months. Longer if I can get the visa worked out."

She put the whiskey in front of me.

"And if not?"

"Back home to South Africa."

"Either way you won't miss this cold."

"No, I won't."

"Does John know yet?"

"No."

"I'll say nothing."

"Thank you, Michael."

"Good luck, Shortie."

She smiled.

I could see through the doorway to the other room that Peadar was among the musicians playing a traditional session. I reasoned that Peadar must have mended his feud with John Benny. The feud began when Peadar was playing a session one night in the pub but was made to pay for his pint. Benny had been playing the squeezebox with the musicians at the time, and thus was his excuse when Peadar confronted him after the session.

"You put a microphone in front of me and your man won't spare me a porter?"

"I cannot oversee everything when I'm playing a session, like."

"Bollix."

"Is drink your only motivation for playing, Peadar? For fuck's sake."

To end the argument, Benny poured Peadar a Guinness. Peadar accepted it, left it untouched on the bar, and walked out.

The group, along with Peadar, played a mighty session this night. The talking was kept to a minimum in the back room in which they performed. I'd had learned some of the melodies the traditional musicians played. Many of them were of a baleful nature. As such they still were calming. I sipped the Crested Ten while a woman stood and sang a traditional song alone while the musicians rested and listened to her. Only John Benny on his squeezebox gave her light chords to serve as a little backup. Her voice pierced the pub:

"Black is the color of my true love's hair
Her lips are like some roses fair
She's the sweetest smile and the gentlest hands.
I love the ground whereon she stands
I love my love - and well she knows
I love the grass whereon she goes.
But I know the day it never will come
When she and I will be as one."

I held on tightly to my little glass of whiskey and listened hard until she was finished. Both the liquid and those lyrics were tough medicine.

Most of the Irish ballads don't need vocals, for the individual instruments serve as the voices of the songs. And yet, the messages of these songs were very clear. They're kind of tunes that make one take a deep breath. My eyes remained glossed over and my heart slowed when the musicians resumed with the light but solemn whistle of *Innisheer*. My mind replayed, with nostalgia, what I'd done while I was writing earlier that afternoon.

"You're a picture of concentration today, Mr. Shiels." The young, English barman, in white shirt and dark tie, was passing through the lobby at Benner's Hotel. He was looking through his round spectacles for empty glasses amongst the antique easy chairs and mahogany coffee tables.

"Thank you, David. Don't let me take a drink until you see me turn off this laptop computer."

"Right then – at your insistence. But may I say, sir, that it's not at all like you."

"You may and you just did. It was very cheeky of you."

He smiled.

"You've taken good care of me, David. I'll finish the book in less than an hour and come into the bar. We'll drink Veuvre Cliquot."

"I'll organize the champagne."

"Thank you, David."

"Finish the book for today, you mean to say?"

"Finished for good."

"This is why the champagne, then. We are celebrating, Mr. Shiels?"

"In a manner of speaking, we are. I'd say it is finally finished. Today it is finished."

"Good on you then. The finish has been a long time in coming sir, hasn't it?"

"Longer than you know. And three months ago I told you not to call me 'sir' anymore, so knock it off, limey."

"Was it difficult to finish?"

"Aren't all endings difficult, David? And aren't all beginnings brilliant?"

"I shall keep that in mind, sir. When will it be published?"

"Six months, I suppose."

"Do you expect that she'll read it?"

"I should think that she would, yes."

"Do you expect that she'll like it?"

"That I cannot say. It doesn't matter. With each word I've written I've pushed her further and further away."

David picked up two teacups and spoons from the coffee

table near the leather loveseat. The loveseat was near the front window, which was framed by heavy yellow drapes. A crystal chandelier hung over the table. I sat in an easy chair in the corner next to the fireplace along the bookshelves. The old books gave the lobby warmth, but they were never taken from the shelves. English titles like *The Cloud Above the Green, In Field and Hedgerow, Kindred of the Dust,* and *Off With His Head* were relegated to serve as decorations. On one of the days I spent writing, I noticed a book on the shelf entitled *An Impossible Marriage* by Pamela Hansford Johnson, published – 1955. I never read it, but I kept it on the shelf near me each day that I wrote in the lobby at Benner's.

My computer sat in front of me on what seemed to be an old receptionist's desk. It served as an end table otherwise. The manager of Benner's, Muirean, didn't mind the curiosity of having me as "writer in-residence" in the hotel lobby, even though I stayed just west of town in room number five at the Tower View Inn, a guesthouse owned by Robbie and Mary Griffin.

"What will you do now?" David asked. "Now that it is finished."

I looked at him.

"I shall drink champagne."

Peadar and the boys finished playing *Innisheer*. I should not refer to them "the boys" because they were each older than I and there was one woman playing with them. Peadar waved from across John Benny's between songs. I lifted my glass to him. It was empty, except for the melting ice. Peadar swiveled back on his stool and the group began to play an up-tempo instrumental called *The King of the Fairies*, with the squeezebox leading. A large, ungainly woman, whom I suspected to be German, sprang to her feet and began to dance around in the middle of the floor. She was trying to mimic traditional Irish Step Dancing except her arms were flailing about.

I noticed John Benny watching from behind the bar.

"You have insurance?" I asked him.

"Not for that."

I slapped a five-Euro note on the bar and left. It was going to half-eleven and I didn't want to be drawn into hearing late night conversation or taken to the chip shop for grub.

Standing outside John Benny's Pub I breathed in fresh air. A brisk wind blew in from the harbor across the street. A tall ship was moored over there, and the mast flags were flapping. If I smoked cigarettes, I suppose I would have had one right then. As it was I listened to the muffled sound of voices and *The King of the Fairies* coming from inside the pub. It was dark and the Strand was empty.

I looked to my left down the street past the Betting Office in the general direction of O'Flaherty's Pub and the roundabout that leads either through Inch to Killarney or over the Conor Pass to Tralee. To the right I looked past the alley and up toward the Slea Head Drive roundabout. I'd need to walk back up to the top of town to get the Nissan Micra, which was parked in front of Geany's Pub. Some nights it was a long walk. Some nights it wasn't.

I looked again down the Strand and saw a heavy brown wooden door. The door was closed, but it was the door to James Flahive, and it was always closed. I'd never been inside, but a bald-headed Englishman once told me about the place and implored that I make it a point to go in sometime. I asked Peadar and the locals about it. They told me that the James Flahive Bar was permanently closed down. Looked like it tonight. But the Englishman told me that if you knocked on the door most nights after ten, Flahive would open the door.

I knocked.

I didn't expect the door to open, but I knocked again, and read the words painted on the window above the door:

Licensed to deal in wine, beer, spirits and tobacco for consumption on and off the premises seven days.

The only other indication that it was a pub at all were the script letters painted on the stone above the transom: James Flahive Bar.

"Oh me God it's you," the bald-headed Englishman said after he opened the door. "You finally took me advice, did'ya? Come in! Come in and meet James."

I shook the Englishman's hand and went inside. He closed the door behind us.

"I'm happy you are here tonight," I told the Englishman.

"Is this place what I described to you or what? It's a place where you say, 'What the fuck am I doing here?'"

James Flahive's Bar was much like Dick Mack's Pub but smaller and brighter. There were four stools along the bar and no other seating at all. Crates and boxes littered the floor at either end, and old pictures of Gregory Peck littered the walls. I noticed four cases of Club Orange soda in bottles piled on top of each other. The bar was no bigger than a living room, and there was a drain in the middle of the floor. Pulled heavy drapes foiled any window peeps. A plain looking fellow slept on a stool in the corner, his elbow propped on the countertop. There was draught Guinness, and there was the man-himself, sitting behind the counter.

"This is James Flahive," the Englishman said.

The old man didn't rise but I shook his hand, which was wide and smooth. He wore a gray jumper with an unbuttoned dress shirt underneath. I couldn't see his shoes. He must have been close on to eighty years-old.

"I'm Michael Patrick Shiels, sir. It is nice to meet you. Thank you for allowing me in."

"Failte. Failte. Welcome, Michael Patrick Shiels," he said in a grumble that was as gruff and low as a voice could be. "Where are you from?"

"Michigan, in the United States."

The Englishman laughed at me and the corners of Flahive's mouth rose a bit.

"Michigan, in the United States, he says," said the Englishman. "...as opposed to Michigan in Italy or Michigan, China, right, James? He's from Michigan in the U-S-of-A."

Flahive nodded and looked at me.

"There is a Georgia in Russia, you wanker," I said to the Englishman.

"Aye."

James Flahive didn't ask me if I wanted a drink, and I didn't ask him for one.

"It's a pity you didn't get here sooner," said the Englishman, buttoning up his denim jacket. "I was just telling James about the time I got completely pissed with me mates after a football match in Dublin. As a result I missed me flight home to London on Sunday morning."

"There are plenty of cheap flights," I said.

"Yes but when I left for the match on Friday, I didn't tell me wife the game was in Ireland. I didn't tell her I would be gone for the weekend. When I did finally get back she was gone. She'd left me," he said. "I was unlucky."

I looked over at James Flahive. He had been looking at me.

"I was unlucky, wasn't I, James?" the Englishman repeated. "I was unlucky."

James Flahive looked at him and smiled. His smile looked as if it caused some pain.

The Englishman told me another story about how he was once arrested for possession of marijuana. Since he'd had no other violations or citations on his record, he asked the officers if they might drive off, throw the bag of cannabis out the window and forget about the whole matter.

"The Bobbies told they might be more inclined to consider such an idea if I was willing to tell them who the supplier was. I thought about that for a minute. Then I agreed to tell them. 'Marijuana is a plant, you see. So as near as I can figure, God is the supplier.'"

"And?"

"And I was unlucky again."

He then took a drink of his beer.

"We've known each other a long time, my friend," James Flahive said to the Englishman.

"We have, James. We love each other don't we, James? We love each other."

James Flahive nodded and took his time rising from his seat.

"May I buy the American a drink before we go, James. Now that he's in such a rarefied establishment, we must welcome him to the club. Would you pour something for your man at this late hour, James?"

Flahive, standing, was looking at me again.

"A Crested Ten over ice, sir, if you wouldn't mind," I said.

The Englishman began poking through his handful of Euro coins. James Flahive began poking through his dusty whiskey bottles.

"Shiels is your name," Flahive asked, but not in the tone of a question. He then stopped looking at me and turned away to make the drink. He reached as high as he could to the top shelf and pulled down a bottle of not of Crested Ten, but of regular Jamieson. That would be fine. Then I heard the sound of ice being scooped from a plastic bowl into a glass.

"Goodnight, James," said the Englishman. "I've left the quid for his whiskey on the counter. I'll be seeing you tomorrow night…if you open, James."

Flahive waved the Englishman off with one hand while pouring the Jamieson with the other. The Englishman patted me on the back and then kicked the chair of his sleeping friend, who awoke with a start. James helped him up and they made for the door. The Englishman opened it just a crack, stuck his bald head out, and turned it both ways to look for the *Garda.**
Only when he saw no police did he make his way into the night, closing the door behind him.

* - *Police.*

My whiskey was in front of me. The gruff man-himself and I were alone now. He sat back down and looked at me.

"Chuirfeadh se cosa faoi chearca duit," he said.

"Sir?"

"The Englishman. He could talk legs under a chicken."

I smiled. "I've been trying to learn some of the Irish language."

"Where?"

"Geaney's Pub. Christina teaches me sometimes at night."

"Jaysus."

"I know. I never remember much the next day, but it makes for good Craic."

There were silent pauses in our conversation.

"Are you enjoying your holiday?"

"Yes. I've been to Dingle before."

"I thought you had," he said.

"I've never been in here, though. The locals told me you were closed down."

James Flahive didn't disagree.

"Do you have some connection to Dingle? You do, I'd say. I'd say you do."

"You could say that I do, Mr. Flahive. And I've sensed you were examining me for a reason."

"I didn't want to ask too much. I don't want to be forward," he said.

"It's alright. It's just that I once got married in St. Mary's Church…"

"Yes I know. I remember. The Canon was involved in that, was he not?"

"Father Padriag O'Fiannachta? Yes, Mr. Flahive. He married us. He was very good to us. It was two summers ago. August 25, 2001."

He nodded, and then said, "The wedding. T'was spoken of on the radio and written in *The Kerryman* newspaper. They called her a 'Runaway Bride.' I saw your faces in *The Kerryman*," he said. "It was during the regatta time, like."

"Yes, and on RTE radio and in *Kerry's Eye*, as well," I added. "And in the *Irish Independent*."

"I did hear it on the radio. On Marian Finucan's radio show. Everybody listens to that show. I didn't want to be too personal," Flahive said, not finishing his question.

"It's all right. Everyone in Dingle has been very kind to me. In a town of 2,000, everything is personal. That's why we chose Dingle in which to marry." I went on. "People stopped in the street and applauded us, Mr. Flahive, as we walked from the St. Mary's to Benner's after the ceremony for a little champagne reception. It was like an old-fashioned movie. They applauded us in the street. Dingle is a magical and romantic place."

All of a sudden I could hear myself talking too much so I went silent.

James Flahive drew a long breath and looked down. I took a drink of whiskey from the little glass. When I took a second gulp, he pottered about behind the counter. I looked around at the scattered photos on his walls.

"Listen," he said, stopping but not looking at me, "you don't worry about that at all. Don't worry about it at all. You don't worry about what happened after the wedding."

"Thank you, Mr. Flahive."

"Do you know why you shouldn't worry about it, Shiels?"

I remained quiet. He seemed intent.

"Because it happens all the time. Happens all the time."

"It does?"

"It does. It does. It happened in 1926."

"You're joking."

"No, 'tis no joke. A couple they were married. Married at the same church. The Benner's Hotel was not there at the time, but there was to be a gathering after the ceremony. T'was not to be a big reception but a party with drink. The Brideog went on to the party. But the husband, in a moment of madness, went down the street straightaway. He went down past the round-about to the old train station. Do you know where the petrol station is? Moran's Garage?"

I nodded.

"Well, that was the train station then. The husband boarded the first train to Tralee before anyone knew what had happened. He left the town and never made himself known in Dingle again," said James Flahive.

I wasn't sure what to say.

"I knew the woman," he resumed. "Her name was Mary. After that, she moved in with her sister. Mary lived out her days alone with her sister Nancy."

I took the last drink of my glass of whiskey.

"So you go on fine. You don't worry about that Shiels. It happens all the time."

"Every seventy five years or so, eh?"

"Ni haon maith a bheith ag caoineadh nuair a imionn an tsochraid."

"Sir?"

"There's no good in keening when the funeral has moved off."

5

Invite Yourself To Do It "Your Way"

WRITE YOUR OWN EULOGY

Lawyers are always prompting people to be certain they have a will drawn up...but have you ever considered writing your own eulogy? It seems we spend a lot of our lives worrying about what other people think and what they might be saying about us, so it would seem the idea of authoring your own eulogy would be appealing. After all, who better to tell everyone about you that you? And you'll have a captive audience! Do you want a preacher attaching some generic lines about your funeral being a celebration of your life, or would you rather have him read your reasons why it was a bash? It's your chance to tell everyone exactly what you want them to know about you. You might even choose to tell a few people off!

If you should happen to take the big dirt nap in the sky, your friends and relatives will greatly appreciate your note and find comfort in it. It will be a way for them to "hear from you" again and feel connected.

If nothing else, even if you don't allow it to be used at your funeral, the process and act of writing your eulogy can be very thought provoking. It forced you to review your life and take stock of where you are.

And there's something about actually writing it down that makes it seem real...and important...and permanent.

I gave it a shot...and here's what I came up with:

EULOGY OF MICHAEL PATRICK SHIELS
Written March 17, 2010

If you are reading this…my time has come. It may seem that maybe my time has come too soon, but, there's not much we can do about that, is there? It's a surprise we have to deal with now. Believe me, I tried to pack as much living as I could into the years I was given. Please try not to feel badly for me. I had lots of fun, visited lots of places, and met some very wonderful people, many of whom are sitting here today. Thanks for turning up. I always knew you'd come…and I always knew you cared. Some of you I haven't seen in awhile, but know that I certainly thought of you.

I am proud to say I got around in my lifetime. I visited more than thirty five countries. I guess I was always happiest when traveling, so…just think of my journey now as just another trip. And I didn't even have to cram into a coach class seat to fly this time!

Since I am often asked what my favorite destination was, I guess I should tell you that I always thought Paris was the most exciting place I'd ever been. I always felt very alive in the romantic "City of Light." Ernest Hemingway wrote that "Paris is a Moveable Feast." I loved Hemingway's writing, and visited Harry's New York Bar in Paris, where it is said he often sat and drank. I would say that Paris is sensory overload: a feast for the eyes, ears, taste, scents, and the occasional touch. If you go there, think of me haunting the outdoor cafes along the Champs Elysees, because I am sure to be sitting there examining the latest fashion trends and sipping Pouilly Fuisse. I also like the shady space under the Eiffel Tower because it seems so peaceful and playful.

Everyone knows, though, that I felt most comfortable in Ireland. Why did the air smell so fresh and scenery look so breathtaking during my nearly twenty visits there? I never could decide which sounded better: the Irish music or the Irish brogue. Jaysus I hope there is some Irish music playing at this funeral service, or at least at the wake!

Then again, I loved hot sand and warm ocean water on my feet. If heaven is one long beach walk, I won't mind that. Hell, I am sure, will have no shoreline and no waves on the horizon. And I doubt you can make a tee time in hell, though you may be forced to caddie for Bill Clinton.

My alter egos? I can admit them now. I liked, from time to time, thinking I was a suave and savvy as 007 James Bond. I also identified with the brooding but ominous Batman. Mainly, though, I'd name George Herbert Walker Bush, the forty first President of the United States, as my hero. He fought in the Second World War as a very young man and, as Ronald Reagan's vice-president, was loyal and appropriate. When he became president, he wasn't an ideologue and seemed very decent. He believed in the philosophy of "Peace Through Strength"...and yet allowed himself to cry from time to time. I met him once. And I came pretty close to writing a book with him.

I was a big fan of Joe's Stone Crab Restaurant in Miami Beach. Pardon the pun on this somber day, but if you want to experience a slice of heaven on earth, go there and order the Key Lime Pie. Or have it shipped to you through JoesStoneCrab.com I promise that is not "product placement" in this eulogy; the Key Lime idea just my last gift to you.

My son Harrison was a joy beyond anything I ever could have imagined. He made me laugh. He made me cry tears of happiness. He made me feel emotions I never knew I had. I am proud of him and excited for him. He is a handsome, cool dude. We played endless hours of Madden NFL video games on the XBox® and he almost always won. We also liked to play tennis, golf, swim, and "sack out." Most of all we liked to laugh.

Harrison, if you're listening to this, can I mention a few things?

Remember that Disney movie *The Lion King* we watched so many times? Watch it again and remember, "The great kings of the past are looking down on you." They're always there for you. And so am I. Because I live in you. You are part of me. Your ideas, your mannerisms, your experiences, are all part of me. So I am still there…in you. This means I am counting on you to do the right thing. Have fun. Trust yourself. Laugh a lot. Be smart. Remember everything I told you about women. And most importantly smile when you think of me. Do not, under any circumstances, be sad that I am gone. Get out the photos and look at the many great trips we took together: Disney World, the Windstar Cruise, Ireland, The Old Course at St. Andrews, the El Conquistador in Puerto Rico, New York City, The Grand Del Mar in San Diego, Chicago, Cedar Point, and the ski trips to Northern Michigan. I am in all of those places…and always with you.

On to others…

Christine believed in me more than I believed in myself, and always meant well for me…and tolerated my well-worn insecurities and shortcomings. You rescued me from a scrapheap of heartbreak and really propped me up. Impressive. Thank you from the bottom of my heart.

My Mother and Father really showed me how to have a great

time and work hard at the same time. I know they sacrificed for me. I had a great childhood.

As for everyone else, there are some things I will never forgive myself for. And some things I know I will never be forgiven for. I know I spent way too much time worrying about some silly things...and some silly people. But most of all, I tried.

I thank everyone who gave me the time of day, or was a fun acquaintance, or most especially a sincere friend. You made it all worthwhile.

Dean Martin was buried in a tuxedo...and I suppose I wouldn't mind the same snazzy duds. A bottle of Jameson won't last me long, so can I have a bottle of Veuve Clicquot champagne, too? And if there's a Cuban Monte Cristo cigar around, smoke it yourself. Let's not get crazy here!

I really had a fun time at "the party." Keep the party going for me, won't you?

Michael Patrick Shiels, father, friend, lover, author, writer, radio and television host, golfer, and...Batman.

I SHOT AN ARROW...AIMING HIGH

Where did it all start for me, this "invite yourself to the party" thinking?

I think it started in Second Grade.

Where will it all start for you?

What are your goals? Are you aiming high? Are your goals clearly defined? What are the odds your goals, your plans, or your aspirations will become reality?

Are you on target?

I firmly believe that an incident in Second Grade set my optimistic attitude for the rest of my life.

I became a believer when I was in the Second Grade.

What was the occurrence?

What was this happening that could be so powerful as to have a lifelong impact on the mind of a six-year-old?

It was simple.

And it happened on vacation.

My parents, Arthur and Gladys Shiels, and my aunts and uncles, each summer, would take us to Houghton Lake, Michigan for a week. Each family involved would rent a lakeside cottage in a small, six unit resort on the south shore. Since my brother and sister, Robert and Lori Shiels, and cousins Frank and Marybeth Tomasik, were of similar age, we had the run of the place: swimming or fishing off the end of the dock, rowing the boats around, nightly bonfires, and occasional trips to putt-putt golf, go-carting, or the souvenir shops.

One of our daytrips usually included a trip to Zubler's Indian Craft Shop, which had teepees and Native American displays and toys. One gray summer morning, we came back from Zubler's with wooden toy bows and arrows. The end of each arrow had a small rubber plunger on it. The kids involved, my siblings and cousins, organized a contest to see who could shoot their arrow the farthest. Each kid would take their turn shooting from the top of the hill overlooking the cottages and the lake.

I decided I would play a trick on the other kids, so while they lined up atop the hill, I hid down behind a tree midway down the hill. My plan was to surprise them by shooting my arrow across the target range when my oldest cousin took his turn shooting his down the range.

I readied my bow, aimed the arrow, pulled back the bow strong, and waited for my cousin's shot. When I heard the "twang" and saw his arrow shoot forward from his bow, I released my taught bow sting and felt my arrow slip skyward. I waited to hear their surprised reaction when my arrow flew crosswise in front of them, but their reaction turned out to be much bigger than I expected.

Why?

Because my arrow actually collided with his arrow and knocked it off course and down out of the sky!

What were the chances of that arrow being timed so perfectly and aimed so precisely that it would hit the other on in mid-flight and knock it down? The chances were so infinitesimal that I hadn't even considered trying it. (Ironically, that kind of precision was a fantasy of President Ronald Regan, who wanted to develop a "Star Wars Missile Defense System" to shield the United States from a Soviet attack!)

The point, if you'll pardon the pun, is that my arrow was not even intended to hit the other arrow and knock it down...but despite the odds and lack of effort or intent...*it did!*

Wow, I thought, standing frozen in my hillside spot by the tree for just a moment, that was something special. *That was an amazing moment! And it really happened to me!*

Perhaps the moral of the story is that the seemingly impossible can happen, even if by accident.

Perhaps the moral of the story is to ask myself: 'Why wasn't I originally aiming to actually hit the arrow? Why had my six year-old mind already chosen to eliminate that possibility from my mind? That was obviously a mistake because the subsequent evidence proved it was clearly possible.

Do we all aim too low?

Consider the widely-reported case of Bill Rasmussen, a simple television sports reporter in Springfield, Massachusetts. Upon being fired, he came up with the idea of starting his own cable television channel to air the Hartford Whalers hockey team and minor league sporting events in Connecticut. In the process of arranging for the nightly broadcasts, he discovered that buying blocks of satellite airtime for a few hours each night was more expensive that simply paying for a continuous twenty four-hour satellite feed. At that moment, Rasmussen's "arrow hit the other arrow," and he expanded his idea to create the twenty four-hour, nationwide sports network we now know as ESPN! Rasmussen's original idea was not even close to being the worldwide sports broadcasting monster ESPN has become.

In my case, as I look back on the Houghton Lake arrow incident, I know it propelled me to aim higher. It taught me, like Rasmussen, to look beyond the obvious. And more than anything, it allowed me to realize that the presumably impossible really can happen...

...especially if you *invite yourself to the party!*

Please E-mail to me specific examples of how you now have decided to invite yourself to the party at InviteYourself@aol.com

LaVergne, TN USA
16 November 2010
205047LV00002B/1/P